CORPOREAL GENEROSITY

SUNY SERIES IN GENDER THEORY

TINA CHANTER, EDITOR

CORPOREAL GENEROSITY

ON GIVING WITH NIETZSCHE, MERLEAU-PONTY, AND LEVINAS

ROSALYN DIPROSE

STATE UNIVERSITY OF NEW YORK PRESS

Published by
STATE UNIVERSITY OF NEW YORK PRESS,
ALBANY

© 2002 State University of New York

For information, address
State University of New York Press
90 State Street, Suite 700, Albany, NY 12207

Production, Laurie Searl
Marketing, Jennifer Giovani-Giovani

Library of Congress Cataloging-in-Publication Data

Diprose, Rosalyn.
  Corporeal generosity : on giving with Nietzsche, Merleau-Ponty, and
Levinas / Rosalyn Diprose.
    p. cm. — (SUNY series in gender theory)
  Includes index.
  ISBN 0-7914-5321-9 (alk. paper). — ISBN 0-7914-5322-7 (pbk. : alk. paper)
    1. Generosity. 2. Nietzsche, Friedrich Wilhelm, 1844–1900. 3. Merleau-Ponty,
Maurice, 1908–1961. 4. Levinas, Emmanuel. I. Title. II. Series.

BJ1533.G4 D49 2002
179'.9—dc21   2001049421

10 9 8 7 6 5 4 3 2 1

CONTENTS

VI   CORPOREAL GENEROSITY

ACKNOWLEDGMENTS

Some of the material in this book has been revised from the following original publications: "Nietzsche and the Pathos of Distance," in Paul Patton, ed., *Nietzsche, Feminism and Political Theory*, London: Routledge, 1993; "Giving Corporeality against the Law," in *Australian Feminist Studies* 11:24 (October 1996) (http://www.tandf.co.uk); "Performing Body-Identity," in *Writings on Dance*, 11–12 (summer 1994–1995); "Generosity: Between Love and Desire," in *Hypatia* 13:1 (1998), Indiana University Press; "Sexuality and the Clinical Encounter," in M. Shildrick and J. Price, eds., *Vital Signs: Feminist Reconfigurations of the Bio/logical Body*, Edinburgh: Edinburgh University Press, 1998; "What Is (Feminist) Philosophy?" in *Hypatia* 15:2 (2000), Indiana University Press. I thank the publishers and editors for permission to use revised versions of this material here.

The research and writing of chapters 4 and 5 were undertaken with the assistance of Australian Research Council Small Grants, chapter 4 while I was a Visiting Fellow in the Philosophy Department at Warwick University. The completion of the book was made possible with the assistance of a Humanities Research Program Writing Fellowship from the University of New South Wales (UNSW). I am grateful to these programs and to my own School of Philosophy at UNSW for granting me the time and space to undertake this work. In particular, I would like to thank Tina Chanter, the series editor, for her friendship, and her and Jane Bunker and Laurie Searl at State University of New York Press for their advice and support during the publication of this manuscript. The advice of State University of New York Press' anonymous readers has also been very helpful in the final revision of the manuscript.

This book has been written over a number of years and has undergone a number of revisions. During that time, my research has benefited from the inspiration, support, and guidance of a number of friends and colleagues, including Keith Ansell-Pearson, Barbara Baird, Christine Battersby, Jennifer Biddle, Constantin Boundas, Penelope Deutscher, Rachel Jones, Paul Komesaroff, Alphonso Lingis, Genevieve Lloyd, Kelly Oliver, Linnell Secomb, Cathryn Vasseleu, and Ewa Ziarek. Less visible but no less important has been the input of friends from outside of academia, those whose provocations grace the pages of this book. Good-humored debates with postgraduate students, especially Anne Gearside, Erika Kerruish, Matthew Paull, Thomas Martin, Karen Williams, and Sarah Rice, have often made me think again. For their ongoing intellectual generosity and friendship, I particularly want to thank Robyn Ferrell, Moira Gatens, Paul Patton, and Nikki Sullivan, who contributed to this book from beginning to end in ways beyond my ability to recount. Special thanks to my family, who continues to provide the inspiration for my writing, even though they may not recognize themselves in it. This work was always too late, though, to properly acknowledge the gift of friendship given me by Megan Fisher. It is in retrospect that I dedicate this book to her.

Introducing Generosity

GENEROSITY WOULD SEEM to be in short supply these days, the occasional acts of virtuous individuals notwithstanding. In the late 1990s we witnessed, throughout the Western world, a resurgence of conservatism in government and an intolerance of different ways of being in social and interpersonal relations. A graphic example of this, with which I am familiar, is the recent birth and rapid growth in Australia of "One Nation."[1] One Nation is, at the same time, the name of a political party and an expression of dissatisfaction with the status quo. The source of this dissatisfaction seems to be primarily economic, issuing as it does from people (primarily farmers, small business proprietors, and the elderly) who describe themselves as "ordinary, hard-working Australians" who have fallen on hard times through what they feel is neglect by successive governments to look out for their economic needs. There is also a personal element to this dissatisfaction. Government is not only accused of economic neglect, it is also accused of forgetting the contribution these people have made, and continue to make, to the well-being of Australian society. The charges of neglect and failure of recognition may well be valid, expressed as they are through a level of passion that is difficult to ignore. While the depth and breadth of that passion is disturbing enough, the remedy proffered by One Nation is of greater concern. While the slogan "One Nation" suggests aspirations for social unity through a kind of communal spirit, in reality it offers a program of social division and intolerance. As an antidote to the economic hardship and loss of status its supporters experience, One Nation targets groups that it claims have benefited too much from government policy, primarily welfare recipients, single mothers, Aboriginal Australians, and Asian immigrants. Through a "what about me" attitude, people who may at other times be generous would take from groups who could ill afford the loss. Such intolerance of difference and lack of generosity are not peculiar to Australian politics, nor to the present era. But that parsimony seems so endemic to the political rhetoric that supports economic rationalism, and a laissez-faire economy merits some attention, which, in turn, raises the question: Is there a connection between generosity and aspirations toward social justice?

The claim underlying the analyses in this book is that generosity is not only an individual virtue that contributes to human well-being, but that it is an openness to others that is fundamental to human existence, sociality, and social formation. Usually the former understanding of generosity, as a socially beneficial virtue, is said to exhaust its definition. Following Aristotle's discussion of magnanimity in Book IV of his *Nicomachean Ethics* (1975, hereafter referred to as NE), generosity is taken to be a habituated and cultivated character trait that guides a person toward giving to others beyond the call of duty. Provided that the person gives by "deliberate choice" (NE 1105a, 17–18), according to "right reason" (1138b, 18–21), that is, appropriately according to his or her means and the circumstances and without self-serving motives so that the act is neither wasteful or mean (1120a, 25–30), not only do the recipients benefit through an enhancement of their well-being, but so does the one who gives through the pleasure that this brings (1097b–1098a, 20, 1120a, 25–30). Without wishing to dismiss the value of generosity so understood, the emphasis on utility within contemporary social relations tends to reduce the gift to a calculable commodity (money or goods) and generosity to the logic of an exchange economy ("I will give you this in exchange for that"). The effect of this reduction is that, in the absence of agreement on how to measure the extent of the giver's means, the nature of the recipient's circumstances and the giver's motives, what seems generous to some, may, paradoxically, be parsimonious to others.

That generosity is difficult to distinguish from parsimony when understood in terms of an exchange economy where virtue is subject to calculation is no more apparent than in Tibor Machan's discussion of "Politics and Generosity" (1990). Machan argues that generosity, which he defines in keeping with Aristotle's model of virtue, can only flourish, or indeed can only be possible, within a libertarian political system as opposed to a welfare state. His point, put simply, is that "there cannot be any generosity involved in a polity in which one is forced to share one's wealth" (Machan 1990, 61). Giving through duty to people whose circumstances one does not know may be philanthropic or humanitarian but it is not generous, because generosity requires choice on the part of the giver and deliberation about the appropriateness of the circumstances. Machan effectively supports generosity as a "good trait" that makes us "better human beings" (63) in order to argue for the unequal distribution of wealth, or at least to argue against any systematic, state-directed sharing of commodities. This argument would be appealing to the supporters of One Nation, with whom I began, but it does seem decidedly mean. Generosity, in Machan's argument, would seem to run counter to social justice.

Machan is right to suggest that generosity as an individual, habituated character trait is impossible, by definition, in circumstances where one is obligated to give. And it should not be surprising if relying on individual magnanimity in a laissez-faire economy would not result in social equity given that, as Lester Hunt argues, generosity is not the same as justice (1975, 241–42). Justice is about fair outcomes and, in a social economy based on the exchange of commodities, ensuring a fair outcome requires calculating the value of what is given and assessing the benefit to the donor and the recipient. While Aristotle does evoke "the right reason" in his model of generosity (the generous person "will give to the right persons the right amounts at the right times" (NE, 1120a, 26)), and so seems to tie generosity to calculation and attention to outcomes, bringing about a fair outcome is not a central feature of generosity. To be generous an act "must be done *tou kalou heneka*, as Aristotle says [NE 1120a, 14], because of the [noble] value of the act itself, rather than for some other good it will bring us in return" (Hunt 1975, 235). What makes an act generous is not the value of the gift or the consequences of giving (in terms of either any benefit to the giver or to the recipient). Rather, as Robert Bernasconi suggests, generosity depends on the noble *proairesis* of the giver (1997, 267). *Proairesis* refers to the deliberate choice of a means toward an end (rather than "intention," as it often is translated) that places an act in the realm of morality. Or, as Aristotle defines it, *proairesis* is "a desire, guided by deliberation, for things which are within our power to bring about" (NE 1113a, 11). "[I]f one's *proairesis* is noble (*kalon*), then one seeks to give more and without measuring this more by reference to what has been received. In other words the gift . . . has the character of an excess (*hyperbole*) such that it cannot be measured by any calculation of its value" (Bernasconi 1997, 267). Noble "desire," without calculation or expectation of return, is the basis of generosity; a fair outcome that can be measured, is necessary for justice, and neither can be reduced to the other.

If generosity is not reducible to justice and, indeed, if we take Machan's line of argument, if generosity would only flourish in a polity not intent on achieving social and economic equity, then why might it matter? Answering this question requires moving away from the model of generosity understood simply as an individual character trait that inclines one to give to others as a result of choice guided by deliberation. The problem with this understanding of generosity is that it assumes that the individual is already constituted, prior to the act of giving, as a reflexive, self-present self separate from others. Machan, for example, not only assumes this but insists that individual sovereignty and the right of private property are basic rights that must be in place before generosity is possible (1990, 65). Giving, according to Machan, is exercised *subsequent* to individual sovereignty and property ownership as part of the means for establishing communal relations of contract and exchange (65, 68). Paradoxically, perhaps, Machan, in his discussion of the conditions under which generosity is possible, assumes the very conditions he is arguing for: a libertarian polity guaranteeing individual property rights and individual freedom of choice to give to others. Yet these are the conditions that are least likely to produce generous dispositions and are most likely to foster a "what about me" attitude and the kind of calculation of benefit that, as Bernasconi suggests, giving exceeds.

The idea of generosity offered in this book challenges the individualism apparent in Machan's account as well as the economy of contract and exchange that he insists is not only the basis of social relations but is characteristic of generosity itself. Generosity, on the contrary, is not reducible to an economy of exchange between sovereign individuals. Rather, it is an openness to others that not only precedes and establishes communal relations but constitutes the self as open to otherness. Primordially, generosity is not the expenditure of one's possessions but the dispossession of oneself, the being-given to others that undercuts any self-contained ego, that undercuts self-possession. Moreover, generosity, so understood, happens at a prereflective level, at the level of corporeality and sensibility, and so eschews the calculation characteristic of an economy of exchange. Generosity is being given to others without deliberation in a field of intercorporeality, a being given that constitutes the self as affective and being affected, that constitutes social relations and that which is given in relation. On the model developed in this book, generosity is not one virtue among others but the primordial condition of personal, interpersonal, and communal existence. And while understanding generosity as a prereflective corporeal openness to otherness may not guarantee social justice, it is a necessary move in that direction.

This idea of generosity, underlying and developed in the analyses here, has a history informed by my reading of Jacques Derrida on identity, difference, and the gift. While Marcel Mauss' *The Gift* (1967) is credited for initiating the idea that giving, rather than commodity transactions, establishes communal relations and the social identities of the parties concerned, it is, as Alan Schrift suggests, Derrida's discussions of the impossibility of the gift that have prompted much of the current interest in the topic (Schrift 1997, 1).[2] The paradox I pointed to in Machan's discussion of generosity, that the conditions he assumes are necessary for generosity to be possible are the conditions that may make it impossible, is not peculiar to his account. This paradox, according to Derrida, is the aporia of the gift.

Derrida, in a way I discuss in more detail elsewhere, criticizes Mauss' idea that giving establishes reciprocal relations of obligation (Diprose 1994, ch. 4). Mauss (1967) finds that beneath the artifice of free and equal contracts between self-present sovereign individuals lies a social economy based on the gift. Insofar as a gift is of the order of a "potlatch" (to nourish or consume), its circulation determines the social rank and identity of a society's members. It bestows prestige on the one who receives it and, more important, a moral obligation toward the giver, which cannot be repaid in ways other than by maintaining a social bond (Mauss 1967, 6). The power of such gifts to constitute a social bond lies in their spiritual status: transfer of a possession can only establish a social relationship between persons if that possession carries the significance of being part of the personhood of the giver (10). While social contract theorists also assume that part of one's personal property is exchanged through contract (with the state in exchange for protection or with another in exchange for financial reward), according to Mauss, if the gift has the power to establish a social relation it is because it remains part of the personhood of the giver, so that its circulation is one that seeks a return to the place of its birth (19). So, contrary to Machan's model of social economy, a social relation is not constituted by the exchange of commodities deemed separate from the self but through the gift of part of oneself to another. The identity of the giver and the recipient is not given in isolation prior to the giving of the gift. As what is given is in essence part of the substance of the giver and, as the social identity and status of the recipient is enhanced by the gift, then, contrary to the logic of identity in Machan's model of social exchange, what is constituted through the gift is the social identity of each in relation to the other. Finally, contrary to the contract model of social exchange, where the giver pledges obedience to the state with this gift in exchange for its protection, the debtor in this relation is not the giver but the recipient. The gift constitutes the social identity of the parties and an enduring social bond that obligates the recipient to the donor.

While departing to some extent from Machan's model of social relations that supports his idea of generosity, Mauss does treat the gift as a commodity, separable from its donor through an act of will and returned through a bond of obligation. Insofar as he does this, Mauss, according to Derrida, remains caught within the logic of exchange and contract (Derrida 1992, 24). Within this logic, which is also Machan's logic, the gift and giving are impossible. Generosity is impossible because, under the logic of contract and exchange, the gift is recognized as a gift (it functions as a commodity) and, once recognized, the gift bestows a debt on the recipient and is annulled through obligation, gratitude, or some other form of return (12–14). Contrary to Machan's thesis, that only in a polity of sovereign property owners is generosity possible, Derrida's analysis suggests that it is precisely this economy of contract and exchange between self-present individuals that makes generosity impossible. The gift is only possible if it goes unrecognized, if it is not commodified, if it is forgotten by the donor and donee so that presence (the gift as (a) present and the presence of both the donor and the donee) is deferred (23–24).

This aporia of the gift would not matter much if it was not for the way Derrida, following Heidegger, ties the gift to the gift-event of Being: Being gives itself in the present on the condition that it is not (a) present (Derrida 1992, 20, 27). In deference to this qualification I read Derrida's account of the gift as a version of his account of the constitution of self-identity and difference: like *différance*, generosity describes the operation that both constitutes identity and difference and resists the full presence of meaning, identity, and Being so that the self is dispersed into the other. Derrida defines *différance* as

> the systematic play of differences, of the traces of differences, of the *spacing* by means of which elements are related to each other. This spacing is the simultaneously active and passive . . . production of the intervals without which the "full" terms would not signify, would not function. (Derrida 1981, 27)

Self-identity, a manner of being, cannot be constituted without a production of an interval or a difference between the self and the other. No self-present identity, no relation to Being, is generated without this relation to the other. However, as identity is produced through the other, the "full" terms so constituted cannot simply refer to or signify themselves. While this production of intervals constitutes an identity as present by separating the present from what it is not (from its other), the

> interval that constitutes it as present must, by the same token, divide the present in and of itself, thereby also dividing, along with the present, everything that is thought on the basis of the present, that is, in our metaphysical language, every being, and singularly substance or the subject. (Derrida, 1982, 13)

As one's identity and social value are produced through a differentiation between the self and the other then the identity of the self is dispersed into the other. *Différance*, like giving-itself, describes an operation that both constitutes identity and difference and resists and disorganizes the totalization or full presence of meaning, identity, or Being. It is the operation of *différance* that insists on the gift: the ultimate dispersal of all identity within the event of its constitution. Giving is that which puts the circle of exchange in motion and that which exceeds and disrupts it (Derrida 1992, 30). And this impossible structure of the gift is such that if self-present identity is claimed in being given to the other, a debt to the other is incurred.

Only in invisible silence does generosity do its work of personal and social formation, and then only by maintaining an openness to others that is its condition. Only on the condition that a sovereign subject is neither the agent nor product of generosity does it do its formative work. Moreover, the movement of generosity is such that, if self-present identity (individual sovereignty) is claimed, something has been taken from the other without acknowledgment of the accompanying debt to the other incurred. Understanding generosity in terms of Derrida's analysis of the impossibility of the gift helps locate the parsimony endorsed by other accounts such as Machan's. Machan's claim that individual sovereignty and property ownership come before generosity overlooks the possibility that in claiming freedom and property as one's own, something has already been taken from others. The generosity of the individual property owner who gives his or her acquisitions, which is the only generosity that Machan recognizes, is built on the generosity of others that Machan would rather forget. The same theft and forgetting uphold the platform of One Nation. In staking their claim that their gifts need greater recognition by devaluing or forgetting the gifts of others they consider less worthy, the supporters of One Nation would build the value of their own gifts through the theft of others.

In suggesting that generosity is infected with a selective forgetting, I have already added to Derrida's analyses of the impossibility of the gift, at least by insisting on a different emphasis. By tying the gift to its radical forgetting and its operation to the deferral of self-present identity, Derrida's account may help expose the individualism and parsimony of Machan's and One Nation's positions, but it also invites interpretations of his work that are no more concerned with social justice than Machan or One Nation seem to be. Critiques of individualism and its metaphysics of presence can and have lead to (postmodern) claims, although not by Derrida, of the death of individual sovereignty in favor of the dispersal of identity and meaning. Emphasizing the way that the gift does its work only by being forgotten and then through the dispersal of presence overlooks how, in practice, the generosity and the gifts of some (property owners, men, wage earners, whites) tend to be recognized and remembered more often than the generosity and gifts of others (the landless, women, the unemployed, indigenous peoples, and immigrants). It is in the systematic, asymmetrical forgetting of the gift, where only the generosity of the privileged is memorialized, that social inequities and injustice are based. In attending to the connection between generosity and social justice, which is the aim of all the analyses in this book, it is necessary to shift the emphasis away from, while keeping in mind the aporia of the gift to consider how, as Bourdieu puts it, "the *disposition* of the *habitus*, which is generosity [. . .] tends, without explicit and express intention, toward the conservation and increase of symbolic capital," with the effect of maintaining relations of domination and dependence (Bourdieu 1997, 233, 239). Or, as I would rather put it, it is necessary to address the question of the systematic but asymmetrical forgetting of the gift that allows the generosity of the forgotten and the parsimony of the memorialized to constitute hierarchical relations of domination within economies of contract and exchange. The analyses in this book therefore borrow from Derrida's account of the impossibility of the gift in his critique of presence, while attending more centrally to the asymmetrical distribution of the effects of its operation.

Besides this shift of emphasis toward questions of social justice, the second way my analysis of generosity moves beyond Derrida's early work on the aporia of the gift is in its emphasis on the corporeal dimension of giving. Attending to the corporeal dimension of generosity matters for three reasons. First, if generosity can only do its work if it goes unrecognized, then it is not governed by conscious intention, deliberation, or reflection, at least not primordially. Generosity operates at the level of sensibility (carnal perception and affectivity). The openness to otherness that characterizes generosity is, I will argue, carnal and affective, and the production of identity and difference that results is a material production. Second, the asymmetrical forgetting of generosity at the foundation of social injustice depends on the asymmetrical evaluation of different bodies. Some bodies accrue value, identity, and recognition through accumulating the gifts of others and at their expense. Hence, not only is generosity most effective at a carnal level, rather than as a practice directed by thought or will, but the injustice that inflects its operation is governed by the way social norms and values determine which bodies are recognized as possessing property that can be given and which bodies are devoid of property and so can only benefit from the generosity of others, and which bodies are worthy of gifts and which are not. Third, this social discrimination and normalization operates through bodies and impacts on bodies. Judgments that would efface or devalue differences arise just as much within the affective and transformative dimension of intercorporeality as any generous welcoming and production of difference. Accounting for the corporeal dimension of generosity allows the possibility of better locating the operation of social injustice as well as the openness to others that would enhance its overcoming.

One predominant form in which the systematic asymmetrical forgetting of the gift takes place is in the social constitution of sexual difference, and this is the focus of the analyses provided in chapters 1 and 2. As Schrift points out, the question of gender in relation to social exchange has been the other development, besides Derrida's account of the aporia of the gift, "that has brought the problematic of the gift to the center of critical attention" in recent times (1997, 2). In his own analyses of generosity, Schrift highlights the work of Hélène Cixous (with Nietzsche) in articulating the relation between generosity and sexual difference. According to Schrift, Cixous differentiates between "masculine" economies of contract and exchange based on the possession of property and "feminine" economies where giving is truly generous, occurring "without expectation of return" (Schrift 1997, 11). As giving must exceed any expectation of return in order to do its work of personal and intersubjective formation, a "feminine" economy, according to Cixous, promotes the "establishing of relationships" whereas, because men fear the openness to the other that generosity brings, they "wish to annul that openness by returning the gift as quickly as possible" (Cixous 1981, 48). While applauding aspects of Cixous' analysis, Schrift remains uneasy with the distinction between "masculine" and "feminine" upon which it relies. I share this concern and do not hold to this division between the "masculine" and "feminine" insofar as it might create the impression that women are essentially more generous than men. But what Cixous' analysis points to that is consistent with those I provide in the opening chapters is not just the productive dimensions of generosity but that in an economy such as ours, where property and value accrue toward men, women's generosity in the constitution of intersubjective relations is likely to be disregarded at their expense. It is this emphasis, on the injustice arising from forgetting the gifts of women while memorializing those of men in an economy of contract and exchange, that guides my analyses of the gift and sexual difference, rather than any claim that the economy of the gift is "feminine."

While the injustice arising from forgetting the gifts of women is highlighted in chapters 1 and 2, the other aim of these chapters and of chapter 3 is to begin to develop a picture of the operation of generosity by elaborating the giving of corporeality to and through the bodies of others as a model of the social constitution of identity and difference. While this ontology is developed initially by addressing the constitution of sexed identity and difference, the analysis is broadened, in chapters 1 and 3, to consider the constitution of identity and difference in general terms. In the process of building this model, attention is given to the way an ontology, based on the idea of giving corporeality, shifts our understanding of the nature of social discrimination and injustice. Injustice, as I have suggested, is located in the way that normalizing social discourses, in commodifying the gift, forget or devalue the generosity of women and others. This is illustrated most graphically in chapter 2 through an analysis of the contemporary moral and legal discourses that govern the buying and selling of sexed body "property." The ontology of the gift is also developed by contrasting it to the contract model of social relations (chapter 2) and to proposals for an aesthetics of self as a means of redressing social discrimination and normalization (chapter 3).

The philosophers used for developing this ontology are primarily Nietzsche (chapter 1) and Merleau-Ponty (chapters 2 and 3), with some reference to the work of Derrida, Foucault, and Butler. Nietzsche's philosophy has been interpreted, notably by Schrift (1994), as promoting a social economy based on generosity rather than revenge, where self-overcoming involves the noble gift-giving virtue, and intersubjective relations are no longer creditor-debtor relations; an economy where "gifts can be given without expectation of return, and debts can be forgiven without penalty or shame" (Schrift 1994, 35). However, it is not so much in this promise of an economy based on generosity as a virtue that I find Nietzsche philosophy useful but in the ontology underlying it. Self-overcoming, I argue in chapter 1, is a process of production of self in relation to others that involves the generation of distance (or division) within the self and distance (or difference) between self and others. While self-overcoming appears to be an individual enterprise based on an abundance and a generosity of the noble self, Nietzsche's model of the self as a corporeal cultural artifact normalized through moral evaluation (as a mode of "will to power") and his understanding of the self-other relation as a creditor-debtor relation point to how self-overcoming takes place through the other's proximity and within a social milieu. The production of distance (difference) is therefore an intercorporeal event governed by will to power as interpretation. While the event involves giving by the "noble" self, it also relies on the other's generosity (particularly a woman giving of herself), a generosity that is denied, to the other's detriment. It is in this subliminal account of the constitution of identity and difference through intersubjectivity that I find a giving at work, a giving exploited and effaced by claims that generosity belongs to one kind of virtuous individual.

While Nietzsche's ideas of the self as a body, self-overcoming, and will to power point to an understanding of the production of identity and difference in terms of giving corporeality, it is with Merleau-Ponty's philosophy that this understanding comes to fruition. Merleau-Ponty rarely speaks of generosity or gift giving and is not concerned with virtues. However, his thesis that perception, agency, and subjectivity in general take place as a body opened to the bodies of others lends itself to an account of corporeal generosity that is my aim to develop. Also, his suggestion that personal corporeal styles undergo "sedimentation" through a social history of encounters with other bodies is useful for accounting for the limits of generosity and for locating parsimony in interpersonal relations. Hence, Merleau-Ponty's understanding of human existence in terms of intercorporeality begins to figure centrally in the analysis from chapter 2 on. Nietzsche's philosophy, however, is not abandoned. The individualism apparent in his philosophy gets some further critical attention in chapter 3 and, more positively, his account of the relation between truth, language, and cultural and self-formation is borrowed and developed in an analysis of generosity and cultural difference in chapter 8.

After developing an ontology in terms of giving corporeality in the first part of this book, the chapters in the second part focus on the affective dimension of interpersonal relations by positing and elaborating the claim that affectivity arises through and inspires the generosity of intercorporeal existence. Both erotic life (chapter 4) and affects in general (chapters 5 and 6) are framed in terms of arising within giving corporeality through the other's body, a generosity that gives up any assumed integrity to the self but that also transforms existence. While delineating affectivity in terms of corporeal generosity, two further concerns regarding social justice are addressed: the conditions under which erotic relations could be productive and those under which they may involve parsimony and a violation of being (chapter 4), and how social ideas and norms condition affective life (chapter 5). The conclusions are laid out and illustrated in more concrete terms through an analysis of the clinical encounter (chapter 6), taken as paradigmatic of a carnal encounter between strangers. Here the proposed relation between affectivity and corporeal generosity is used to account for the affectivity experienced in the medical examination and for how discrimination and social normalization of bodies operate at an intercorporeal, prereflective level, beyond the terms of the "normal" body of medical discourse. Interpretations of Merleau-Ponty's philosophy (both his earlier work on "body-intentionality" and his more mature model of perception and intercorporeality) provide the basis for these analyses in conjunction with aspects of the work of Sartre, Beauvoir, Butler, and Foucault.

The chapters in the third part of this book focus on theorizing the relation between corporeal generosity and the formation of community. This is done by developing the suggestion, raised in Part II, that the generosity of intercorporeal existence is such that our relation to existing ideas that govern social relations and social constitution of the body is ambiguous and open. Here the focus is on examining, through critical engagement with Levinas' work, how, given this ambiguity and in the interests of attaining social justice, ideas and the community they govern may be transformed through the generosity of intercorporeality. The thesis developed is that existing ideas and the sociality they support are opened to new paths of thinking and modes of living through a generous response provoked by the other's alterity. This generosity involves a dispossession of self and is born of an affective, corporeal relation to alterity that generates rather than closes off sexual, cultural, and stylistic differences. The thesis is elaborated through an account of the generosity of critical thinking (characterized by feminist thinking) that transforms existing ideas (chapter 7), an examination of what might consist in a generous response to cultural difference manifest in the expression of ideas that contests those that support one's own culture (chapter 8), and a general account of the relation between generosity and community formation that draws together the relevant points from previous chapters (chapter 9). What emerges is an understanding of community formation and social relations that, by the idea of corporeal generosity, bases community formation on the production and transformation of differences rather than on assumptions of commonness or on ideals of One Nation.

The philosophy of Levinas, rather than of Merleau-Ponty, is drawn on extensively throughout the analyses in Part III. Levinas, more explicitly than either Nietzsche or Merleau-Ponty, describes subjectivity in terms of generosity as I understand it. His work lends itself to a philosophy of the gift, insofar as he bases a sociality that does not absorb difference on giving to the other without expectation of return. Subjectivity, for Levinas, is the passivity of exposure to another, a giving of oneself without choice, a movement toward another arising from a disturbance of the self provoked by the other's alterity. Moreover, this being-given to another is sensibility, being affected, and this carnal offering to another is inspired by alterity. This carnal generosity is also a being-put-into-question that makes me responsible for the other that moves me. And so with this understanding of generosity provoked by alterity, Levinas puts ethics, as "other-directed" sensibility, at the foundation of social existence.

While integral to the idea of corporeal generosity that I expand upon in Part III, there is a limitation with Levinas' account of subjectivity and alterity. He tends to locate this generosity of subjectivity, opened by and to another, prior to and as a precondition of both ontology and politics, and not the other way around. For Levinas, a politics of conscious, volitional acts effects an ontological closure to the other, who would otherwise be welcomed in the passive being-given to the other that characterizes the ethical relation. While suggesting that, whatever is said and done, I cannot help but be opened to and responsible for another is important for restoring generosity, intercorporeality, and difference to their central place at the foundation of human existence and social relations, it also implies that what I do or say, the nature of social relations of domination, and how I am constituted within them make no difference to the response to alterity that I "am." In order to maintain a focus on the connection between generosity and social justice, it is necessary to contest this tendency in Levinas' work to render questions of social justice and ontology secondary to ethics (understood as radical generosity). I do this in the analyses in Part III, particularly in chapter 9, by suggesting, through reconsideration of Levinas' critiques of Merleau-Ponty's ontology of intersubjectivity, that politics and ontology are inseparable from ethics and by retaining relevant aspects of the work of Nietzsche and Merleau-Ponty for this purpose. While this revision of Levinas' ethics implies, in keeping with the aporetic structure of the gift, that unconditional generosity is impossible, this impossibility is not a license for either political passivity or institutionalized parsimony. On the contrary, locating generosity within an ontology of corporeal intersubjectivity that is not reducible to either volitional acts or an affectivity that exceeds them grounds a passionate politics that aims for a justice that is not yet here.

The picture of corporeal generosity built in the pages that follow is developed and examined from three general perspectives: in ontological terms, as the realm of the social constitution of identity and difference; as the domain of affectivity, inseparable from but not reducible to social norms; and as the means of community (trans)formation. The structure of this book is such that it also traces the evolution of an idea. The first two chapters draw on papers written around the publication of *The Bodies of Women* (Diprose 1994) and highlight the ontology of giving corporeality, a theme present in germinal form in that book but undeveloped there. The chapters that follow not only develop the idea of corporeal generosity further but also mark a shift in emphasis beyond exclusive attention to the issue of sexual difference to consideration of the production and effacement of other differences. There is also a shift through the book in the philosophical framework used for elaborating the idea of corporeal generosity from the work of Nietzsche and Derrida to Merleau-Ponty and then Levinas, a theoretical development designed to be cumulative rather than substitutive. The critical engagement with the work of these philosophers, and the subsequent revision necessary to imagine a politically sensitive notion of generosity, is mediated throughout by the work of feminist philosophers including, and most directly, Beauvoir, Butler, and Gatens. Aside from providing interpretations of these and other philosophers in developing the concept of corporeal generosity, the analysis maintains a focus on the theme of social justice by framing the development of the concept of corporeal generosity in terms of particular social issues and political problems concerning sexual difference, sexuality, and cultural difference. This development of the idea of corporeal generosity, then, is at the same time an exploration of the role of intercorporeal relations in the social production, maintenance, or effacement of differences with the aim of promoting ways to foster social relations that generate rather than close off sexual, cultural, and stylistic differences.

PART I

GIVING IDENTITY AND DIFFERENCE

blank 18

ONE

NIETZSCHE AND THE
PATHOS OF DISTANCE

JEANETTE WINTERSON, in her novel *Sexing the Cherry*, describes the city of Jordan's dreams. A city

> whose inhabitants are so cunning that to escape the insistence of creditors they knock down their houses in a single night and rebuild them elsewhere. So the number of buildings in the city is always constant but they are never in the same place from one day to the next.
>
> For close families, and most people in the city are close families, this presents no problem, and it is more usual than not for the escapees to find their pursuers waiting for them on the new site of their choice.
>
> As a subterfuge, then, it has little to recommend it, but as a game it is a most fulfilling pastime and accounts for the extraordinary longevity of the men and women who live there. We were all nomads once, and crossed the deserts and the seas on tracks that could not be detected, but were clear to those who knew the way. Since settling down and rooting like trees, but without the ability to make use of the wind to scatter our seed, we have found only infection and discontent.

In the city the inhabitants have reconciled two discordant desires: to remain in one place and to leave it behind forever. (Winterson 1989, 42–43)

This is a postmodern city. It is built on the recognition that one's place within a political and social space rests on unstable foundations. Places can change. This instability arises from the complex creditor/debtor relations that characterize subjectivity: the self only gains a place in the world through the other's proximity, making self-present autonomy, freedom from debt to one's creditor, difficult, if not impossible. The best that one can hope for is a reconciliation of the desire for stability, for proximity to oneself (and hence to one's creditor), and the desire for change, distance, difference.

Winterson's city encapsulates Nietzsche's philosophy of self—a philosophy that sits uneasily between two streams of thought in Anglophone philosophy. On the one side is social contract theory and liberal individualism which, in the name of stability and sameness, assumes that society consists of relations of contract and exchange between free and equal, autonomous, and self-present individuals. On the other side is the declaration that self-mastery and self-identity are dead, along with the ideal of uniform social relations that these notions of self support. Rather than a society consisting of unified individuals governed by a common good, this alternative position variously posits a self dispersed into a multiplicity of differences, and it promotes a distant respect for difference (not othering the other, letting the other be) over universal values or a common good that is said to be both invalid and oppressive.

Nietzsche's aesthetics of self has more in common with this latter position than it does with the self-presence underscoring the contract model of social relations. However, the reading of his philosophy that I offer below cautions against simple declarations of the death of self-presence that assume the ability to promote change and difference by declaring the dispersal of identity and by distancing oneself from others. My aim is to explore Nietzsche's contributions to an understanding of the social production of identity and difference (including sexual difference) as the "problematic of the constitution of place" in relation to others in terms of a giving of oneself to and through the other.

There are at least two aspects of Nietzsche's philosophy that I will highlight that warn against the form of postmodernism mentioned. The first is his analysis of the self as a corporeal cultural artifact, which suggests that any change in self involves a material production rather than a change of mind (or a simple declaration that the self is dispersed). Second, while Nietzsche's project for self-overcoming reads at times like an escape from others, there is much to suggest that the other, through her generosity, is deeply implicated in this process of self-formation. His philosophy of the body, his understanding of the self/other relation as a debtor/creditor relation, and his concept of will to power (understood in ontological terms) all draw on a concept of distance as a process of production of a division within the self and difference between the self and others. This is a distancing that is infused with proximity, a production of identity and difference through the other's generosity, so that denial of the trace of the other in the self's overcoming, whether through respect or arrogance, incurs an unacknowledged debt to them. This understanding of the operation of distance in Nietzsche's philosophy has important consequences for rethinking sexual difference within the context of a postmodern aesthetics of self.

THE BODY AND ONE'S PLACE IN THE WORLD

For Nietzsche, the problematic of the constitution of place is a question of the social constitution of a body. In *Thus Spoke Zarathustra,* he claims that "body I am entirely, and nothing else; and soul is only a word for something about the body" (1978, 34). In contrast to the assumptions that the self's identity can be reduced to consciousness, and that the mind directs the body, Nietzsche claims that the body is what compares and creates, and that thought and the ego are its instruments. This body, however, is not an asocial fact. Like any "thing," a body is the sum of its effects insofar as those effects are united by a concept (1967, 296). The "body is only a social structure composed of many souls" (1973, 31), where "soul" refers to a corporeal multiplicity or a "social structure of the drives and emotions" (25). So, for Nietzsche, one's place in the world is built through the concepts that govern the social world and sculpt the body—a body that is a "unity as an organization" and therefore a "work of art" (1967, 419).

How the corporeal self is constituted as a social structure of drives and emotions is first a question of how the body is unified through social concepts. Second, and related to this process of unification, is the question of how thought and the ego are instruments of the body. The body is the locus of pleasure and pain (which are always already interpretations), and thought arises from and is a reflection on pleasure and pain (a point I develop further in chapter 7). To quote Nietzsche:

> The self says to the ego, "Feel pain here!" Then the ego suffers and thinks how it might suffer no more—and that is why it is *made* to think.
>
> The self says to the ego, "Feel pleasure here!" Then the ego is pleased and thinks how it might often be pleased again—and that is why it is *made* to think. (1978, 35)

Thought, then, is about the projection of bodily experience into the future; the conscious thinking subject is an effect of temporalizing the body.

The target for much of Nietzsche's critical attention is the manner in which experience is unified and the body is temporalized in the social relations of modernity. Here the embodied self is constituted by social concepts and norms that discourage difference, inconsistency, nonconformity, and change. His account in the second essay of *On the Genealogy of Morals* begins with the idea that the unification of any body relies on the operation of memory and forgetting. "Forgetting" is the incorporation of bodily affects before they become conscious and a making way for new sensations by allowing one to "have done" with the old (1969, 58). But while this not-remembering is necessary for the constitution of any self as present, the making of the modern moral subject, the individual who is responsible for his or her acts enough to enter social contracts, requires a faculty that opposes forgetting—memory.

Nietzsche describes how the social and moral discourses of modernity constitute a particular kind of memory, a memory that unifies a selection of activities, events, experiences, and effects so that they belong to one person (1969, 58). This memory makes the self constant and apparently unchanging through time by projecting the same body into the future. The operation of memory and forgetting unifies experience in another sense—it makes different experiences the same. What is remembered is not just an experience but a socially prescribed mode of interpreting that experience. As Nietzsche explains in *Twilight of the Idols* (1968, 50–53), effects and events are incorporated by interpretation using prevailing moral norms and the concept of cause. Unpleasant feelings are said to be caused by actions considered undesirable. Pleasant feelings are said to arise from good or successful actions (52). Hence, "everything of which we become conscious is arranged, simplified, schematized, interpreted through and through . . . pleasure and displeasure are subsequent and derivative phenomena" (Nietzsche 1967, 263–64).[1] So even forgetting as having done with an event involves first, dividing effects into those that are written into the body and those that are not. Second, events which are incorporated and upon which one reflects are divided into a cause and an effect, where the effect is pleasure or displeasure and the cause is interpreted according to social moral norms. Then, when encountering a new event or effect, the memory "calls up earlier states of a similar kind and the causal interpretations which have grown out of them" (Nietzsche 1968, 51). New experiences are subsumed under habitual interpretations, making every experience a fabrication (Nietzsche 1973, 97).

The individual is not the author of this dutiful memory—it is created through what Nietzsche calls the "mnemotechnics of pain" (1969, 61): techniques of punishment that carry social norms and moral values. "Body I am entirely," insofar as my conscience, sense of responsibility, and uniformity, is created by an ordering of sensations and by projection of the body into the future through a social disciplinary system. This ensures not only that my experiences are consistent over time but, as we are subjected to the same moral values, we will have "our experience in common" (Nietzsche 1973, 186). Forgetting in conjunction with a selective memory becomes a social instrument of repression against the dangers of inconsistency and nonconformity. A society that favors consistency and conformity discourages us to leave our place behind.

Contrary to social contract theory and liberal individualism, Nietzsche proposes that the individual is a culturally specific corporeal artifact whose existence is a product of the exclusion of other possibilities for one's embodied place in the world. But this account leaves Nietzsche with a problem shared also by those who find the assumption of self-presence and ideals of universal values oppressive: how can change be effected given that the self is the result of a socially informed material process of production? How can different possibilities for existence be opened, how can one leave one's place behind, without assuming the possibility of stepping outside of either one's present body or one's social context? It is Nietzsche's concept of a distance within the self that addresses this apparent impasse.

DISTANCE AND SELF-OVERCOMING

The body that conforms to a uniform mode of subjection is one that acts out a social role imposed upon it.[2] In contrast to this actor, Nietzsche, in *The Gay Science*, privileges a process of self-fabrication with the artistic ability to stage, watch, and overcome the self according to a self-given plan (1974, 132–33). He draws on two features of art and the artist to characterize self-overcoming (163–64). The first is the suggestion that the self, like any artifact, is an interpretation, a perspective, or a mask. Second, the relation between artists and their art illustrates the point that creating beyond the present self requires that we view ourselves from a distance in an image outside of ourselves. Leaving behind the influence of social concepts that restrict our place in the world requires treating one's corporeality as a work of art.

The distinction that Nietzsche makes between the self as artist and the image or spectacle of the self staged beyond the present body could imply a unique, extra-social invention. But at a less ambitious level it suggests that one is never identical with oneself. Nietzsche sometimes refers to this difference within the self as the "pathos of distance,"

that longing for an ever increasing widening of distance within the soul itself, the formation of ever higher, rarer, more remote, tenser, more comprehensive states, in short precisely the elevation of the type "man," the continual "self-overcoming of man," to take a moral formula in a supra-moral sense. (1973, 173)

What Nietzsche is suggesting here is that the ability to move beyond oneself hinges on a distance within the soul (where the soul is something about the body). A distance or difference within the self, between the present self and an image of self toward which I aspire, is necessary for transformation of the corporeal self. We should not confuse the artist and his work, says Nietzsche, "as if [the artist] were what he is able to represent, conceive, and express. The fact is that if he were it, he would not represent, conceive, and express it" (Nietzsche 1969, 101). The self as a work of art is never the same as the self that creates it, not because the self as artist is the true or essential self in contrast to a false, unique, extra-social image projected, rather, the image the artistic self creates is a moment beyond the present self that creates it. The difference, or distance, between the two is a precondition to self-formation and transformation.

In *Thus Spoke Zarathustra*, Nietzsche accounts for this distance within the self in terms of a process of self-temporalization of the body that subverts the notion of linear time assumed in normalizing social structures. Unlike the "last man," who views himself as the essential, unchangeable endpoint of his history (Nietzsche 1978, 202), the overman views himself as a moment. He risks his present self or, as Nietzsche puts it, "goes under" (14–15). But unlike the "higher man," who, in a manner not unlike the "postmodern" self, affirms the future by negating the past and skipping over existence, thereby changing nothing (286-95), the overman risks himself by "willing backwards": "To redeem those who lived in the past and to recreate all 'it was' into 'thus I willed it'—that alone I should call redemption" (139). Moving beyond the present self is not a matter of declaring oneself born again by simply reaching for a new part to play: it requires working on oneself. The overman then is the self that is a moment that temporalizes itself by recreating its past as a way of projecting itself into the future. This self-temporalization produces a distance or difference within the self.

The idea that the corporeal self is reproduced differently as it is temporalized through the production of a distance within the self would seem to be at odds with Nietzsche's doctrine of eternal recurrence. Problems arise if we accept eternal recurrence as either a cosmological hypothesis, where the world repeats itself infinitely (Nietzsche 1967, 521), or a psychological doctrine, where self-affirmation involves the desire for the self to recur eternally the same (Nietzsche 1978, 322). However, as David Wood (1988) has demonstrated, interpreting the doctrine of eternal recurrence exclusively in either of these ways is ultimately untenable.[3]

Nietzsche's presentation of the doctrine in "The Vision and the Riddle" in *Thus Spoke Zarathustra* (1978, 85–87) suggests another interpretation. Here, eternal recurrence is presented in terms of a further revaluation of linear time that suggests that there is always difference in repetition. Here, Zarathustra, on a "bridge across becoming," recounts his vision of climbing a mountain while carrying on his back his "archenemy, the spirit of gravity." Zarathustra is attempting to climb toward the future, but the spirit of gravity, of which man suffers if he cannot go beyond himself, threatens to drag him back toward himself. "You threw yourself up high," says gravity to Zarathustra, "but every stone must fall . . . the stone will fall back on yourself" (156).

The spirit of gravity is suggesting a notion of return that is cyclic: you cannot escape what you are; you will always return to yourself the same. While Zarathustra affirms this notion of repetition of self ("was that life? well then! once more"), he goes on to reinterpret it. He points to a gateway called "the moment," claiming that from this moment a path leads backward to eternity and another contradictory path leads forward to eternity: the future contradicts the past, and both the future and the past lead out from the present moment. Zarathustra then goes on to suggest that all that leads backward from the moment, all that has been, has been before, as has this moment. And because all things are knotted together, then this moment draws after it all that is to come. Therefore, he asks, must not all of us have been at this moment before, and must we not eternally return?

What Nietzsche seems to be suggesting is a return of self involving a temporality where the self does not seek to escape the past (linear time) nor simply to repeat it (cyclic). By describing time as emerging out of the moment, Nietzsche is suggesting, in keeping with his notion of self-overcoming, that one temporalizes oneself. The self recreates the past (or what one has been) at every moment as it projects itself toward a future. The future is also created out of the present. The contingent future, governed by others, is made one's own through the present, where the present is a reconstitution of the past. And by making the present moment its own, the self also distances itself from a necessary past and future.

At the same time, according to Nietzsche, each moment eternally recurs and contains every other moment that constitutes the temporalized self. As Zarathustra suggests, there is no outside the moment that is the present self: "how should there be an outside-myself? There is no outside" (217). This is not to say that the self is transcendental or unchanging. On the contrary, to recreate the past, or one's "it was," by making it "thus I willed it" is to give birth to the self anew. But while the self is different at every moment, these different moments are not self-contained. There is no outside the self in the sense that the moment, which is the present self, contains traces of its relation to a past and future that are different. The structure of the moment is one where the self exceeds its present self rather than one where the self is self-present and self-identical. Man is "an imperfect tense" (Nietzsche 1983, 61): his past is never complete in relation to his present.

The distancing effected by making the moment one's own is not a state of mind: it "creates a higher body" (Nietzsche 1978, 70)—the overman "begets and bears" (Nietzsche 1973, 113) a future corporeal self that is beyond and different from himself. The pathos of distance within the self, generated by making the moment one's own, allows the self to remain in one place while leaving it behind forever. But this is not a simple rejection of one's embodied place in the world. Nietzsche's formulation of a distance within the self reopens what is denied by social discourses which, in assuming an unchanging subject over time, assume that "what is does not become" (Nietzsche 1968, 35). This assumption of sameness is an "escape from sense-deception, from becoming, from history" (ibid.). The history that conformity disavows is the process of incorporating new experiences and shedding the old, reconciling conflicting impulses, the ongoing process of corporeal self-fabrication, according to concepts that one has inherited and cultivated (Nietzsche 1973, 96–104; 1974, 269–71).

DISTANCE AND THE CREDITOR/DEBTOR RELATION

While Nietzsche's understanding of creative self-fabrication allows a reconciliation of the discordant desires in Winterson's dream, it remains an uneasy formulation with respect to justice and the other. Nietzsche often speaks as if the distance within the self effected by making the moment one's own is generated by the self alone; in Nietzsche's work, self-overcoming is often presented as an autonomous, self-contained project. Yet in *Untimely Meditations* ("Schopenhauer as Educator"), for example, Nietzsche suggests that rather than finding ourselves within ourselves, we are more likely to find ourselves outside of ourselves, that is, in our effects, in "everything [that] bears witness to what we are, our friendships and our enmities, our glance and the clasp of our hand, our memory and that which we do not remember, our books and our handwriting," in the objects we love (Nietzsche 1983, 129). In other words, the self is not just divided between the remembered and the forgotten, the future and the past, but between the self and the other. There is something about our relation to others that mediates the place we occupy within social relations. Hence, contrary to some postmodern formulations of a dispersed self who does not "other" others, creative self-fabrication, changing places, implicates others in some sense. The distance necessary to self-overcoming is given in proximity to others.

Nietzsche's genealogies of justice and punishment typically reveal the ways others are involved in the constitution of one's place in the world.

These genealogies contain a tension between understanding the self/other relation in terms of a contract between creditor and debtor and understanding it in terms of a gift of being. The most fundamental social relation is, Nietzsche claims, the creditor/debtor relation, where "one person first measured himself against another" (1969, 70). Inflicting pain on another was "originally" a way of recovering a debt rather than creating the memory necessary for conformity. And this involved evaluating different parts of the body to ensure that the pain inflicted was equivalent to the debt owed (62–65). Under such a system, evaluation is of the body and operates by mutual agreement. Debts can be repaid through the body via a contractual arrangement between creditor and debtor. If the relation between self and other can be said to involve a contract, this contract is written in blood, and the status of the creditor is built from the flesh of the debtor.

But what is the nature of this debt that is supposedly repaid through corporeal measurement? As determining values, establishing and exchanging equivalences is the most fundamental social arrangement, it is not just a question of commodity exchange. A precondition to such exchange of gifts and commodities is evaluation of one's own body in relation to another, a process of evaluation that is constitutive of one's place in the world. While Nietzsche sometimes speaks as if there is an original difference between debtor and creditor, the self only becomes different, a distinct entity, by distancing itself from others. This distancing itself is a mode of production involving measurement and will to power, whereby identity and difference are given.

The relation between self and other is governed by will to power: by language as an expression of power, by the use of concepts to measure, interpret, and draw distinctions. According to Nietzsche, if we eliminate concepts that we impose, such as number, thing, activity, and motion, then

> no things remain but only dynamic quanta, in relation of tension to all other dynamic quanta: their essence lies in their relation to all other quanta, in their "effect" upon the same. The will to power not a being, not a becoming, but a *pathos*—the most elemental fact from which a becoming and effecting first emerge. (1967, 339)

To say that will to power is pathos refers us to the distinction between ethos and pathos that Nietzsche evokes elsewhere (1974, 252). Ethos is usually understood as a way of life, of one's habits and character, whereas pathos is the condition of transient affectivity. While we think of our way of life as a given and an enduring ethos, our life, Nietzsche argues, is really pathos, a dynamic process of changing affective experience. Will to power is pathos: it is the movement by which experience is constituted and entities come into being so that they are in relation and can be affected and can affect.[4]

Will to power as interpretation operates within intersubjective relations where, as Nietzsche claims in reference to love, "our pleasure in ourselves tries to maintain itself by again and again changing something new into ourselves" (1974, 88). Measuring the other is a way of enhancing our own form, capacities, and effects. But again, neither the self nor the other (whether the other is another person or a "thing") exists in essence apart from this relation, that is, apart from "the effect it produces and that which it resists" (Nietzsche 1967, 337). In other words, individuals, and the differences between them, are not given in themselves. They are an effect of

> creation and imposition of forms . . . [within] a ruling structure which *lives,* in which parts and functions are delimited and co-ordinated, in which nothing whatever finds a place that has not been first assigned a "meaning" in relation to a whole. (1969, 86–87)

Will to power is this process of the constitution of identity and place, of delimiting one from another, through the assignment of "meaning" to effects and their interrelations. So any difference between parties to a contract is an effect of will to power as productive interpretation by which entities are constituted in relation. This distance/difference between self and other is predicated upon measurement: the credit of identity and difference is extracted in proximity to the other in a process where debts may be incurred.

Justice, for Nietzsche, is the constitution of identity and difference without debt. In an exchange economy, justice would be reciprocal exchange, exchange without loss or without a debt being incurred by either party. One way Nietzsche puts this idea of justice within an exchange economy is, as Schrift points out (1994, 34), in terms of giving with an expectation of equivalent return:

> Justice (fairness) originates among approximately *equal powers.* . . .
> [T]he initial character of justice is *barter.* Each satisfies the other

in that each gets what he values more than the other. Each man gives the other what he wants, to keep henceforth, and receives in turn that which he wishes. Thus, justice is requital and exchange on the assumption of approximately equal positions of strength. For this reason, revenge belongs initially to the realm of justice: it is an exchange. Likewise gratitude. (Nietzsche 1984, 64)

That giving would be reciprocated in equal measure, without debt or loss, and so that justice could be achieved, assumes the parties involved are already of "approximately equal power" (1969, 70; 1984, 64). At one level, "approximately equal power" means that both parties have the power to enforce their own evaluations. But in the context of Nietzsche's understanding of will to power as production of identity through measurement, "approximately equal power" also means a balance in the distribution of productive power. The possibility of justice, that mutual understanding necessary for return of gifts and equitable exchange without loss or debt, assumes that the selves involved are already constituted by the same mode of evaluation. That is, justice in an exchange economy assumes that will to power as interpretation operates uniformly to produce all bodies as the same. As Nietzsche puts it in *Beyond Good and Evil*:

> To refrain from mutual injury, mutual violence, mutual exploitation, to equate one's own will with that of another: this may in a certain rough sense become good manners between individuals if the conditions for it are present (namely if their strength and value standards are in fact similar and they both belong to *one* body). (1973, 174)

Belonging to one social body, within which it is possible to settle one's debt to the other, to give without loss, and to refrain from taking from the other, assumes a shared mode of evaluation by which the corporeal self is constituted.

But the possibility of such mutual understanding is at best limited in Nietzsche's model of self-fabrication. A social body may share a language, a mode of interpretation and evaluation, and a mode of self-creation. But self-evaluation occurs in relation to another, and there is always a disjunction between how one evaluates oneself and how one is evaluated by another.

Interpretation of the other is a translation that as a "form of conquest" (Nietzsche 1974, 137) reduces the tempo of the other's style (Nietzsche 1973, 41). The style projected becomes overlaid by other masks constituted through misunderstanding. The constitution of identity is dissimulation where one's absolute identity is deferred:

> Every profound spirit needs a mask: more, around every profound spirit a mask is continually growing thanks to the constantly false, that is to say *shallow* interpretation of every word he speaks, every step he takes, every sign of life he gives. (1973, 51)[5]

Further, while one's identity is a self-fabrication of the body using concepts that one inherits, there is always a disjunction between the social concepts we share and how each person embodies them:

> Ultimately, the individual derives the value of his acts from himself; because he has to interpret in a quite individual way even the words he has inherited. His interpretation of a formula at least is personal, even if he does not create a formula: as an interpreter he is still creative. (1967, 403)

What Nietzsche exposes in his genealogy of justice and the creditor/debtor relation is that justice, giving with expectation of equivalent return and hence the exchange of equivalences, already assumes sameness. And second, insofar as the parties involved are only at best approximately the same, then evaluation involves some subtraction from the other to the benefit of the self. Social exchange does not begin with a contract between independent individuals (1969, 86). It is always a matter of will to power as self-constitution, and insofar as this exchange is "successful" or "just," it assumes and promotes sameness. Yet in assuming that the other is the same, one reduces the other to the self, one takes from the other, and "deliberately and recklessly brush[es] the dust off the wings off the butterfly that is called moment" (Nietzsche 1974, 137), that contradictory moment that is the site of self-overcoming and the production of difference.

Despite indications that one's identity and place in the world can never be reduced to another's, the discourses of modernity assume sameness and encourage the desire to stay in one place. Law (which embodies notions of just and unjust) reflects a community's customs in the sense of a mode of evaluation and interpretation (Nietzsche 1969, 71–76; 1984, 219). While some law may be necessary to preserve a style of life against difference and transgression, Nietzsche objects to laws (moral or secular) that impose absolute values equally upon all. In this, the notion of justice changes from one that explicitly assumes sameness to one that attempts to achieve sameness of outcome through the production of a corporeal memory, discussed above. Yet what is good for one another is "a question of who he is and who the other is" (a question of identity as measurement) and, as this question cannot be answered (identity is dissimulation), then, "what is right for one cannot by any means be right for another" (Nietzsche 1973, 132, 139). The change in the meaning of justice to equal rights for all is, therefore, the beginning of injustice. "For, to *me* justice speaks thus: 'Men are not equal' " (Nietzsche 1978, 101). " 'Equal rights' could all too easily change into equality of wrongdoing," because it legislates against anything rare, against self-overcoming, against the ability to be different and the need for independence (Nietzsche 1973, 125; 1978, 101). "Equality" legislates against the possibility of the production of distance necessary for changing places.

Relating Nietzsche's notion of will to power as the productive measurement involved in self-constitution to his claim that equality is only possible if equality is already actual suggests that democratic institutions only achieve equality of outcome, and then only approximately, through taking from, negating, or expelling difference. A community, for example, that maintains itself by uniform laws and expects conformity from its members "stands to its members in the same vital basic relation, that of creditor to debtor" (Nietzsche 1969, 71). This is a society that assumes a contract with its members where, in exchange for giving protection, the community expects its members to conform to its laws in return. An expression of nonconformity is taken as a hostile act, a refusal to return the gift. A debt is incurred by the lawbreaker and the "community, the disappointed creditor, will get what repayment it can" through punishment or expulsion (ibid.). This expectation of the return of the gift and the negation of difference involved is not only true of the constitution and maintenance of a uniform community but also of the individual who inhabits it. The democratic, "selfless" individual constitutes its place in the world by negating the value of the other's difference:

Slave morality says No to what is "outside," what is "different," what is "not itself"; and *this* No is its creative deed. This inversion of the value positing eye—this *need* to direct one's view outward instead of back to oneself—is the essence of *ressentiment*; in order to exist, slave morality always needs a hostile external world; it needs, physiologically speaking, external stimuli in order to act at all—its action is fundamentally reaction. (Nietzsche 1969, 36–37)

The democratic, consistent self who can make promises and so enter into contracts is produced and maintained through the operation of will to power as evaluation, by exploitation and appropriation, and through the imposition of a particular form and through the exclusion of others.

Even that social body of equal and harmonious forces, where one can safely assume the return of gifts in the interests of justice, exists as such by marking itself off from an "outside" to which it is hostile:

Even that body within which, as it was previously assumed, individuals treat one another as equals—this happens in every healthy aristocracy—must, if it is a living and not a decaying body, itself do all that to other bodies which the individuals within it refrain from doing to one another: it will have to be will to power incarnate, it will want to grow, expand, draw to itself, gain ascendancy—not out of any morality or immorality, but because it *lives,* and because life *is* will to power. (Nietzsche 1973, 175)

In the context of the reading of will to power that I have provided, what Nietzsche is suggesting here is that even within the pretense of equality, whether within a "healthy" aristocracy or a nihilistic democracy, the self, or the complex of selves rendered equal, maintains itself by marginalizing others deemed inappropriate to the system. Prior to the mutual exchange of gifts that characterizes justice within an exchange economy, something has already been taken from or given by the other in the constitution of the "difference" between them.

Nietzsche insists that the "overman" is not guilty of this parsimony that misappropriates the other. Self-overcoming, he claims, is not built upon the assumption of sameness or the negation of the other's difference but upon a mode of self-affirmation that seeks the other after the event, that "seeks its opposite only so as to affirm itself more gratefully and triumphantly" (Nietzsche 1969, 37). Self-overcoming and the overcoming of justice based on the expectation of the return of gifts belong to those communities and individuals who, as Schrift suggests, have the power to forgive transgressions of their laws and values, who have been delivered from revenge (1994, 34–35). Schrift also suggests that Nietzsche, through his ideas of the "overman" and the overcoming of justice based on the creditor/debtor relation, points to an economy based on generosity. "In this economy, gifts can be given without expectation of return, and debts can be forgiven without penalty or shame" (Schrift 1994, 35). Translating this suggestion into ontological terms of the production of identity and difference through will to power, if there is a difference between a generous and a parsimonious relation to the other, it is that creative self-fabrication, rather than negating the other's difference by reducing the other to the self, constitutes a distance, as difference, between self and other. This ability to create distance, to bestow value and meaning, through abundance of power rather than revenge against difference, requires the "gift-giving virtue," or more correctly, it involves the self giving itself without expectation of return (Nietzsche 1978, 74–77).

However, while the self that overcomes itself may not expect or acknowledge a return for the difference it generates, it gets a return through the other anyway. Despite Nietzsche's occasional claims to the contrary, the self cannot give itself without the giving of an other. The pathos of distance within the self, necessary for self-overcoming, is, as with democratic normalization, predicated upon the production of a distance or difference between self and other. Nietzsche admits as much in the same passage describing the pathos of distance within the self, referred to at the beginning of the previous section on self-overcoming:

> Without the *pathos of distance* such as develops from the incarnate differences in classes, from the ruling caste's constant looking out and looking down on subjects and instruments and from its equally constant exercise of obedience and command, its holding down and holding at a distance, that other, more mysterious pathos could not have developed either, that longing for an ever increasing widening of distance within the soul itself. (1973, 173)

So the distance within the soul, within that social structure of drives and emotions that is the self and by which the self transforms itself, is generated through the production of another distance. The eternal return to self involved in making the moment one's own is a return through and from the other. That the overman, in applauding his own generosity, forgets this passage through the other and the giving of the other involved may absolve the other of any debt, but it is a forgetting allowed only by the other's generosity, by the other's capacity to forgive and forget debts, a generosity denied in the self-overcoming that memorializes itself by claiming the moment as its own alone.

This other distancing, necessary to leave one's designated place behind, has its productive effects and so requires further consideration. It is a production of distance that applies not only to relations between classes (as the quote above points to) but also to relations between the sexes. It is to the operation of distance between the sexes, its effects on women, and the possibility of women's artistry that I will now turn.

WOMAN AND ACTION AT A DISTANCE

Just as will to power as measurement is involved in the constitution of any self separate from another, Nietzsche suggests that men create an image of woman in order to shore up something about themselves (1974, 126). In particular, the democratic man who conforms to an unchanging image of himself requires a certain construction of the other to affirm and maintain the appearance of self-consistency and autonomy. This reactive, parsimonious approach to the other does not have to be explicitly denigrating. A man can maintain himself by constructing an ideal and essential image of woman that is simply complementary to himself yet designed for his consumption. This image still serves to affirm the self as unchanging: it silences the noise of other possibilities, the "noise" of the "forgotten." As Nietzsche puts it in *The Gay Science*:

> When a man stands in the midst of his own noise, in the midst of his own surf of plans and projects, then he is apt also to see quiet, magical beings gliding past him and to long for their happiness and seclusion: *women*. He almost thinks his better self dwells there among the women. (1974, 124)

The truth of woman, the eternal feminine, promises to affirm an unchanging self. But as identity is constituted in relation, the self that posits itself as autonomous and transcendental is not complete without incorporation or negation of what is other: man's desire is to possess this image of woman that he has constituted in relation to himself.[6]

To those who seek possession, Nietzsche issues a warning:

[Man thinks] that in these quiet regions even the loudest surf turns into deathly quiet, and life itself is a dream about life. Yet! Yet! Noble enthusiast, even on the most beautiful sailboat there is noise, and unfortunately much small and petty noise. The most magical and powerful effect of woman is, in philosophical language, action at a distance, *actio in distans*; but this requires first of all and above all—*distance*. (1974, 124)

Possessing the image of woman as other to the self does not bring the omnipotence or self-completion promised. If woman was the complementary image man constructs, possessing this image would bring a kind of death to the self. It would efface the distance within the self necessary for self-overcoming.

While conformity relies on constituting and possessing an image of woman, under the pretense of autonomy, self-overcoming relies on maintaining a distance from this image. Leaving one's place behind requires sexual difference: a "noble" mode of valuation, a self giving itself, a spontaneous mode of self-affirmation "seeks its opposite only so as to affirm itself more gratefully and triumphantly" (Nietzsche 1969, 37). But in distancing himself from woman, the generous, creative man still incurs a debt to her. In the definition of active self-evaluation just given, Nietzsche implies an original distance between self and other. Yet as I have argued, he also acknowledges that even in creative self-fabrication the "pathos of distance" involved is located at "the origin of language itself as an expression of power" where the "noble" spirit names itself, gives itself identity and value "in contradistinction to all the low, low-minded, common, and plebian" (1969, 26). The distancing/differencing effected by will to power in self-overcoming materially constitutes woman as other to the aesthetic self. While the key to self-overcoming lies in maintaining this distance from the image of woman so constituted, something remains to be said about its effect on women.

Nietzsche not only claims that the creative man must distance himself from the image of woman he necessarily constitutes, he also claims that "woman forms herself according to this image" (1974, 126). This suggests that women are only artistic insofar as they are actors of a role imposed upon them. For women to be artistic in the proper sense would require the ability to overcome oneself according to one's own plan. This requires distance within the self between the present self and the concept or image toward which one aspires which, in turn, is predicated upon a distance between self and other.

In the extract given above from *The Gay Science,* there are two modes of self-constitution apparently open to women in relation to men: proximity, resulting from possession by a man, and action at a distance. The first, from a woman's perspective, requires her unconditional submission to the concept of unfathomable depth that man has of her. In obeying man in this way, women think, according to Nietzsche, that they will find "depth for their surface" (Nietzsche 1978, 67). But in submitting to men's needs, women reduce the distance between themselves and the other and hence the distance within themselves necessary for self-overcoming. Nor do they find depth for their surface. Like the actor, they reflect forms not their own, merely repeating themselves according to an image provided by others.

Submission results in the constitution of woman's bodily self as a calcified image of shame, calcified because submission collapses the difference between her appearance (surface effects of will to power which, to recall an earlier point, is the pathos "from which becoming and effecting first emerge") and the concept of unfathomable depth that man has of her (Nietzsche 1974, 125). Such a woman is the concept, the truth of woman, fetishized. Submission brings shame in two senses. It involves being sexually possessed by a man, and connected to this is the shame involved in the revelation through submission that woman is not the profound, unfathomable depth, the mysterious eternally feminine, which man's desire seeks. In submitting to man's desire, in giving up everything that she could be, woman's shame is constituted in revealing herself as surface (which is all there is to existence). The shame deals a double blow when, having accepted her gift, man loses interest. Again, to quote Nietzsche:

There are noble women who are afflicted with a certain poverty of spirit, and they know no better way to *express* their deepest

devotion than to offer their virtue and shame. They know nothing higher. Often this present is accepted without establishing as
profound an obligation as the donors had assumed. A very
melancholy story! (1974, 125)

The second mode of self-constitution that Nietzsche attributes to
women is action at a distance. From a woman's point of view, this involves
maintaining one's virtue where virtue means both distance from man's desire
as well as maintaining one's difference (the image of her that man's desire
constitutes). This woman maintains the appearance of being unfathomable
depth over the shame of being a surface effect of will to power. Or, as
Nietzsche puts it:

[O]ld women are more skeptical in their most secret heart of
hearts than any man: they consider the superficiality of existence
its essence, and all virtue and profundity is to them merely a veil
over this "truth," a very welcome veil over a pudendum—in
other words, a matter of decency and shame, and no more than
that. (1974, 125)

Action at a distance requires that woman maintain the profound image of
difference that man has of her. Woman's virtue, her gift-giving virtue, is to
not reveal this image as fraudulent, not to expose how man's desire, and so
his self-overcoming, is dependent on this image. But the sexual "difference"
so constituted is in accordance with a concept given by man. It is in man's
interest, rather than woman's, that this distance, as antithetical "difference," is
maintained.

Action at a distance, in "philosophical language" (as Nietzsche stresses),
does not bring autonomy. Action at a distance is defined philosophically (in
the language of Newtonian physics) as the idea that one body can affect
another without any intervening mechanical link between them. The bodies
are separated by empty space, yet when one moves so does the other.
Woman is still moved by man's desire: a kind of mimicry is implied where
woman is changeable, only to the extent that man's interpretations move her.
This "action at a distance" does not distance woman from the other, nor
does it allow the distance within herself necessary for her self-overcoming.
In fact, the mimicry implied in woman's virtue of living up to the image

that man has of her is similar to Dionysian experience described by Nietzsche in the *Twilight of the Idols*. Here,

> the entire emotional system is alerted and intensified: so that it discharges all its powers of representation, imitation, transfigura- tion, transmutation, every kind of mimicry and play-acting, con- jointly. The essential thing remains the facility of metamorphosis, the incapacity *not* to react (in a similar way to certain types of hysteric, who also assume *any* role at the slightest instigation). . . . [The Dionysian individual] enters into every skin, into every emotion; he is continually transforming himself. (Nietzsche 1968, 73)

This kind of changeability is creative, and Nietzsche explicitly ties it to a feminine disposition of dissatisfaction (1974, 98–99) and histrionics (317). But it is only a precondition to change. To be productive, the immediacy of mimicry must be offset by the distancing within the self necessary to stage and overcome the self. This distancing is the effect of the Apollinian world of images and language, that is, will to power as interpretation, where the self is constituted as separate from another. But, as I have argued, what woman becomes through this action at a distance is in accordance with a concept provided by man. So neither in submission to the democratic man nor at a distance from the artist do women embody the kind of aesthetics of self enjoyed by Nietzsche's "overman." Contrary to the assumptions of some postmodern aesthetics, it would seem that man's desire to create him- self anew is satisfied only if woman remains in one place forever. Self- overcoming relies on woman giving herself on man's terms, a giving denied by any claims that self-overcoming is an autonomous project and a giving from which she does not benefit.

Nietzsche is not insensitive to the difficulties faced by woman as the object of man's desire. The imperative placed on women by men is to hold together a contradictory image of both virtue and shame, distance and submission, depth and surface. He claims that the comedy of love (1974, 125–26) and the impossibility of harmonious relations between the sexes (1969, 267) are based on the contradictory nature of man's self-constitution: the requirement of both distance and proximity in relation to the other. He also suggests that woman's skepticism, about her role in relation to man, and in the assumption of an essential self, is founded on the impossibility of being the contradictory double image of virtue and shame that man requires. On the effect on women of this requirement, Nietzsche observes:

> Thus the psychic knot has been tied that may have no equal. Even the compassionate curiosity of the wisest student of humanity is inadequate for guessing how this or that woman manages to accommodate herself to this solution of the riddle, and to the riddle of a solution, and what dreadful, far-reaching suspicions must stir in her poor unhinged soul—and how the ultimate philosophy and skepsis of woman casts anchor at this point!
>
> Afterward, the same deep silence as before. Often a silence directed at herself, too. She closes her eyes to herself. (1974, 128)

OTHER PLACES FOR WOMEN

Woman's solution to the riddle of a femininity constructed by man is to "close her eyes to herself." This closing is an opening in its suggestion of other possibilities for self-formation aside from conforming to an impossible image of the feminine posited by men. Man's dependence upon women conforming to an image of the feminine, as well as other possibilities for women, is suggested by Nietzsche in the following passage:

> Would a woman be able to hold us (or, as they say, "enthrall" us) if we did not consider it quite possible that under certain circumstances she could wield a dagger (any kind of dagger) *against* *us?* Or against herself—which in certain cases would be a crueler revenge. (1974, 126)

As man's self-overcoming depends upon woman's conforming (whether in submission or at a distance) to an image of her that man has constituted for himself, then if woman does not conform to this image, she effectively wields a dagger against his notion of self. That woman can wield the dagger suggests the possibility of nonconformity, the possibility of artistry, the possibility of being-given that opens possibilities for her own existence.

Several modes of revenge are open to women, several ways of distancing themselves from the concept "woman" and recreating the self differently.

One possibility that Nietzsche mentions, in the context of woman closing her eyes to herself, is that she can find "atonement" for her honor through bearing children (1978, 66; 1969, 267; 1974, 128–29). However, as Alison Ainley suggests, Nietzsche tends to place a lower value on pregnancy in women than he does on the "spiritual" pregnancy of the overman (1988a).[7] A second mode of revenge is feminism of equality, but as my discussion above indicates, Nietzsche does not approve of this option: "equality" amounts to turning women into men and is therefore not a distancing at all.[8]

The possibility of woman's creativity comes uneasily from Nietzsche's uncertainty about distance. In submission or at a distance, woman is not what she promises to be or what man thinks she is ("even on the most beautiful sailboat there is a noise"). The metaphor of noise suggests that women exceed the concept "woman" that man posits. That women may change places rests on what Nietzsche means by noise, and this calls for a further reassessment of the notion of "distance" in his philosophy.

Jacques Derrida suggests, in his reading of Nietzsche, that perhaps woman is distance itself (1979, 49). Perhaps, but this needs qualification. Woman, operating at a distance, is the complementary image or the difference that man posits in constituting himself as present. But the "empty space" between them is effected by will to power as interpretation by which borders are established, bodies constituted, and identity and difference given. Distancing, will to power as the measurement of woman, is the difference that precedes, exceeds, and constitutes the distance within the self and between man and his "other" woman. Given the necessity of this other distancing, woman cannot be possessed—she exceeds the difference or distance over which man reaches for her or, more exactly, for himself. In proximity, or when possessed, woman will be noisy—there will be excess information. A woman is more than the concept that man has of her. Her truth or identity, and therefore his, is deferred and sexual difference, as distancing, is always already maintained.

If the truth of woman is to work for man, he must turn away from her—he cannot live with this concept, but he cannot live without it. But not only does the creative man turn away from the truth of woman that he has constituted, so does the creative woman ("she closes her eyes to herself"). Nietzsche says of truth as a woman: "Certainly she has not let herself be won" (1973, 13). Women do not become this essential image, even in submission. As Nietzsche puts it:

Reflect on the whole history of women: do they not *have* to be
first of all and above all else actresses? Listen to the physicians
who have hypnotized women; finally, love them—let yourself be
"hypnotized by them"! What is always the end result? That they
"put on something" even when they take off everything.
    Woman is so artistic. (1974, 317)

Even when forming herself by submitting to the concept of "woman" that
man projects, woman is acting as something other to both this concept and
to herself.[9]

So woman's artistry lies in her power of dissimulation, and her power
of dissimulation is based on the idea that, as absolute identity is always
deferred, the uncovering of the veil that is the surface of woman reveals not
the truth of woman nor therefore man's self-presence but further dissimulation. This "putting on something" even when they take off everything is
not necessarily a deliberate resistance to subjection. It is a feature of intersubjective evaluation: "Around every profound spirit a mask is continually
growing thanks to the constantly false . . . interpretations" (Nietzsche 1973,
51). Man's evaluation of woman, whether active or reactive, creates the mask
that is woman's socially inscribed difference in relation to him. But the
distancing and giving involved in the constitution of woman's difference in
relation to man ensure that the distance between them cannot be effaced—
something will always be "put on," which maintains a distance or difference.
Men may assume that they can capture the dangerous plaything they need
to discover the child in themselves (to create themselves anew), but the old
woman's advice to these men is: "You are going to women? Do not forget
the whip" (Nietzsche 1978, 67).

It is one thing to conclude that "woman" is distance (or distancing)
and, therefore, that women do not coincide with either the surface as fetish
or with the truth of woman beneath. It is another to suggest that the
concept of woman that man forms for himself has no effect on women.
Derrida, for example, following Nietzsche, appears to risk this conclusion:

That which will not be pinned down by truth is, in truth—
feminine. This should not, however, be mistaken for a woman's
femininity, for female sexuality, or for any other essentializing
fetishes which might tantalize the dogmatic philosopher, the

impotent artist, or the inexperienced seducer who has not yet escaped his foolish hopes for capture. (Derrida 1979, 55)

and,

Because a "woman" takes so little interest in truth, because in fact she barely even believes in it, the truth as regards her, does not concern her in the least. It rather is the "man" who has decided to believe that this discourse on woman or truth might possibly be of any concern to her. (Derrida 1979, 63)

It is necessary to qualify Derrida's distinction between the "feminine" and an "essentializing fetish." Women may not coincide with either, but the distance/difference between female sexuality (the surface that is a woman at any particular moment) and the feminine (the undecidable concept of woman) is what constitutes women—at least insofar as women are artistic. Even in "overcoming" themselves, women rely on concepts that they have inherited, whether or not they may interpret these differently from men or differently from each other. Women are not outside nor completely inside the feminine as the truth of woman. But the truth of woman, as elusive and as changeable as it is, is a name, and as the opening discussion of the social constitution and normalization of the corporeal self suggests, "what things are called . . . gradually grows to be part of a thing and turns into its very body" (Nietzsche 1974, 121–22). Even if what things "are" can never be decided, concepts of "woman" have their material effects in the constitution of the "social structure of drives and emotions" that is a woman. Woman may not believe in man's discourse on her but, given the constitutive effects of this discourse on woman's difference, to imply, however carefully, that it does not concern her at all is a little hasty.

Nietzsche's understanding of the "pathos of distance" not only exposes that normative discourses assume a male subject but also that they rely on constructing woman in a certain way. Man creates an image of woman as other in order to secure his corporeal identity. At a distance, woman's "difference" is complementary and promises to affirm man's self-presence; in proximity, her "sameness" heralds the death of the self. There is no exchange between man and his creditor, woman. Rather, woman's "gift" to man is his (impossible) self-certainty; the "return" for her investment is a contradictory corporeality—suspended between virtue and shame. Insofar as women fulfill this impossible role as man's other, they uneasily embody these contradictory concepts without a place of their own. But, as I have argued, the operation of will to power is such that the corporeal self that is a woman also remains open to possibilities aside from those that position her under man. The embodied meaning of "woman" is dispersed beyond virtue and shame, beyond the riddle of femininity that Nietzsche tends to uphold.

If there is a limitation in Nietzsche's approach to the problematic of the constitution of place, it is in the suggestion, apparent at times in his work, that an aesthetics of self can avoid incurring a debt to the other. This assumption is amplified in some postmodern claims that we can simply declare an end to self-identity and its attendant commodification and negation of the giving of others. To deny that an aesthetics of self involves the other is merely a disavowal of the giving of distance and, hence, of difference, involved in the constitution of one's embodied place in the world. As I have argued, Nietzsche's idea of the "pathos of distance" suggests the impossibility of such an uncontaminating space. Further, that action at a distance, in its simplest formulation, still relies on keeping woman in her place is testimony to the dangers lurking in any claims to the possibility of leaving one's place behind forever.

Two

GIVING SEXED CORPOREALITY
BEFORE THE LAW

THE ANALYSIS in chapter 1 of Nietzsche's idea of the production of distance in the social constitution of identity and difference, particularly sexual difference, points to a domain of giving, a kind of generosity not subject to deliberation and choice by an individual and overlooked and forgotten by normative discourses that frame social relations in terms of commodity exchange. This is not to suggest that corporeal generosity lies outside of the normative production of identity and difference. The evaluation of bodies involved in this production is an operation of power that not only mediates the creditor/debtor relation but constitutes it by determining the value and identity of what is exchanged as well as the value and identity of the parties to the transaction. The productive generosity that is not subject to deliberation, choice, or "consent" does not lie outside of this normative operation of power but precedes and exceeds its terms.

That there is a generosity that conditions and disrupts the normative discourses that govern social exchange is made apparent in the following analysis of contemporary moral and legal discourses that mediate the buying, selling, and donation of sexed "body-property." Here a nonvolitional giving of corporeality is considered in terms of a critique of these discourses, a critique not only of how they constitute sexed identity and difference to the disadvantage of women but particularly how they determine consent and coercion in relations between the sexes. Merleau-Ponty's account of the intercorporeal basis of identity provides a way of elaborating the giving that precedes and exceeds the terms of these discourses. Also his idea that corporeal styles of being undergo a process of "sedimentation" in their social constitution suggests a way to understand coercion and parsimony in relations between the sexes beyond the usual terms.

The practice of transferring cells, fluids, and organs from one body to another, via some kind of storage facility, is considered one of the wonders of modern medicine. But what also provokes wonder are the legal and moral questions evoked by this practice. Questions such as: Who owns the cell line produced from someone's pancreas or the zygote held in storage after its genetic parents become estranged? What moral status does the zygote itself have? Who has ultimate claim over the fetus in a surrogacy arrangement? Does a sperm donor have any claim to, or responsibility for, the product of his ejaculation? Should the product of that event have the same rights to know his or her genetic origin as an adopted child? Should a person be permitted to sell his or her blood or kidney to the highest bidder? And so on.

Such questions, and the legislative responses to them, share a problematic assumption: that the corporeal substances at issue are someone's property. In keeping with an economy based on social contract theory and liberal individualism, it is taken for granted that the human body is owned by the particular self to which it is attached, as is that part of "nature" transformed by the body's labor.[1] Accompanying this is the assumption of natural freedom and autonomy: the equal right of individuals to be free from interference, and the right to do with one's body what one will, providing that this does not harm others.[2] The property status of the human body and this idea of freedom as autonomous self-government lead to something of a paradox in social relations. On the one hand, insofar as the body is considered part of the person, the idea of freedom renders the human body inalienable. Possession of this body by another would at best commodify the person; at worst, it would reduce the person to a slave. On the other hand, insofar as the body is considered a person's property, the right to do with it what one will should allow its alienation within an exchange economy. It is given to the law to resolve this paradox. In an exchange economy, the law's raison d'être is to protect this property from unwelcome possession, right down to the smallest cell, and to ensure that the disposal of it, and the access of others to it, is just.

Two alternatives have emerged in moral and legal discourses that aim at determining to what extent and under what conditions body property can be justly alienated: either the transfer of body property is allowed under the terms of a contract, in which case money can exchange hands, or it is only allowed in terms of a gift. I argue that neither alternative guarantees justice, particularly when the body involved is sexed. Justice is only possible if the giving of corporeality is understood beyond these terms of relations between self-present, autonomous property owners. Yet, as I will suggest, such an understanding challenges the very foundation of the law and its assumption of personal property rights.

Underlying the battle between contract and gift as paradigms for the biomedical alienation of body tissue is, as I have suggested, a paradox: the desire to avoid commodification of the person (which, it is said, would negate his or her "natural" freedom) warns against the exchange of body property, while the desire to preserve the individual's autonomy as sovereignty over his or her body (the right to use the body as he or she will) works to endorse such an exchange. This paradox seems to be resolved by giving legal status to the transfer of body tissue to another in terms of a contract, providing that the contract is understood to be governing the provision of a service. Under the conditions of a service contract, it is assumed that my autonomy is preserved if I have *consented* to relinquish, to another, the control I am said to have over my body. And commodification of my person is apparently avoided: the corporeality being transferred is viewed as the product of work done (in the service of transforming "nature" through the body's labor) rather than part of the personal substance of the worker. Hence, under a service contract, I can receive payment for the *service* (rather than for part of my personhood), and I do not incur any personal loss in the transaction.

Or so the story goes. On the basis of this model of contract, it is possible to sell my blood in some democracies and my organs in others. But not all bodies or body products are given the same moral weight within this schema. While there has been a lucrative and apparently unproblematic trade in some body products for centuries, such as hair for the production of wigs, and while the sale of blood and organs does occasionally pose legal and practical difficulties for some,[3] the exchange of sexed body property under a service contract, for procreative purposes or for pleasure, has proven to be particularly and consistently controversial. The surrogacy contract, for example, generates far more bad press than the sale of hair. Examining why this might be the case exposes some problematic assumptions at the heart of the service contract.

The notorious case of Baby M (in New Jersey in 1987) illustrates the difficulties. The case involved a contract between "intending" parents, Elizabeth and William Stern, and a "surrogate,"[4] Mary-Beth Whitehead. In exchange for a fee, Whitehead agreed to carry a fetus to term and to relinquish the child to the Sterns after birth. However, Whitehead struck a blow against the foundation of contract by breaking her promise to give up the child. Also up for challenge, at least potentially, in the legal battle for Baby M that followed was the property status of the human body and the products of its labor, the individuation of persons and the corporeality said to pass between them, and the assumed linearity of corporeal exchange.

Even if we grant that cells and tissues are owned by someone and can be alienated in terms of a service, who provided the service for whom in this case was, to say the least, ambiguous. A child was given a world by a body, blood was transmitted to and enhanced a zygote, a gamete was transferred from William Stern to Whitehead, her gamete enveloped his, and so on. Determining a singular outcome and its proper owner in such a process of production is frustrated by the indeterminate constitution and multiplication of cells, the formation, transformation, and crossing of borders, and the fluidity of identity and difference. However, the surrogacy agreement, like all service contracts, effectively constitutes the uniform, intentional, linear transmission, through objective time and space, of a corporeal unit originating in one atomized, static individual and arriving in another. And the presiding judge in the case of Baby M removed any further ambiguity by ruling in favor of the Sterns. He argued, among other things, that this was a service contract between the genetic father and Whitehead, a contract that she, as the provider of the service, was obliged to honor. In effect, this determination commodifies the surrogate's body by reducing it to a storage facility, and it secures the genetic father as the origin and destination of procreative property.[5]

The surrogacy contract, upheld by this and similar judgments, has been widely condemned as unjust, particularly by defenders of women's rights. There have been two common arguments posed against it. First, it is said that the surrogacy contract extends patriarchal control over women's reproductive bodies because the surrogate loses control of her body for the duration of the contract (Dodds and Jones 1989, 7)[6] and because upholding the contract amounts to the extension of paternity rights (Pateman 1988, 217). Second, it is argued that the surrogacy contract is unjust because a woman's decision to enter into it is not autonomous. This criticism is based on the claim that a decision is only autonomous if the person making it is fully informed of its consequences for her future well-being and an "intending surrogate" cannot know in advance what traumas her decision may bring (in giving up the child, for example).[7] This objection implies that the intending surrogate is subject to some kind of coercion, even if she actively seeks the arrangement. The types of "coercion" cited include the undue influence of economic need upon the intending surrogate's decision and the social imperative to procreate.

Without denying the importance of these objections, one immediate problem with them is that they are, for the most part, just as applicable to other service contracts but are raised as if they are not.[8] Am I, for example, any more in control of my body than the surrogate, given that I am not allowed to smoke or drink alcohol at work? Is economic need a form of "coercion" peculiar to surrogacy, or does it also inform decisions to enter into other work contracts? If the social imperative to procreate compromises the autonomy of an intending surrogate, can this also be said of all women involved in procreation? Despite the wider applicability of these objections, their use against the surrogacy contract is rarely accompanied by arguments against other work or service contracts (such as those for selling blood) and never directed against procreation in general. In raising these problems I am not endorsing the service contract as a model for the alienation of body property. I am suggesting that these objections to the surrogacy contract fail to locate why such contracts may be unjust. Indeed, by relying on the model of autonomy as control over one's body property and by restricting the charges to some sexually specific contracts, these kinds of arguments risk reinforcing a tradition that excludes women from social exchange on the basis of the sex of their bodies.

I suggest that the injustice of the surrogacy contract lies neither in an extension of patriarchal control over women's reproductive bodies nor in its failure to uphold women's autonomy understood in terms of informed consent. If the law fails women in the surrogacy contract, it is for the same reason it fails in all service contracts: it is based on a contradiction. As I have argued, while the law exists to preserve autonomy and freedom (the independent self-government of personal property) within social exchange, social exchange rests on the negation, by "consent" of the same autonomy and freedom, as they are understood within this paradigm. Based on this model of social relations, the feminist demand for justice is impossible: I can only be fully autonomous and free if I keep my body to myself (an ideal that warns against social relations), and my consent to lend my body to others (a practice necessary for social relations) can only be fully informed (and therefore autonomous) if I have already lived through that experience. The injustice of surrogacy and other service contracts can be located not in the law's failure to guarantee these impossible conditions but, as I will go on to argue, in the law's determination of embodied identity and difference both through and apart from the biomedical alienation of body property.

This determination by the law proceeds by the partitioning of bodies. As I have indicated in the discussion of the case of Baby M, in determining who transfers what to whom, the service contract reduces the ambiguity of body intersubjectivity by atomizing and commodifying corporeality. In doing so, it also determines the identity of the corporeal units constituted (the "buyer," the "seller," and the "item" exchanged) and their position within social exchange. Second, the law, in determining which forms of corporeal exchange can be governed by contract and which cannot, effectively determines simultaneously which bodies so constituted accrue property and value and which do not. In both of these ways, the law constitutes identity and difference and distributes property according to norms about what is proper to bodies. And here I evoke a familiar theme: when dealing with sexual difference, the norm around which corporeal property is distributed is male. Either the law treats sexed bodies as if they are identical in their difference and, as in the case of Baby M, upholds a contract which, while apparently sexually neutral, deems the male body to be the origin and destination of procreative property, or in determinations intended to redress this injustice, women's bodies are considered other to what is the proper subject of social exchange, and they are excluded accordingly.

It is also here, within the determination of sexed identity and difference, that the law determines consent and coercion. In partitioning bodies, the law also designates what is proper to each, so that the attendant accumulation of property by the body said to be its proper owner seems to occur by the consent of the other; the subtraction of property from that which is said to be its proper place is held to occur by coercion. So, for example, if the law allows women to enter the procreative market, and if the law assumes that procreative property belongs to men, then its arrival at this destination appears to be with the consent of women. Under similar conditions, the law has had difficulty recognizing rape: "no" cannot mean "no" if it is assumed that what is extracted by men from the sexed bodies of women is destined for its proper place. What is at stake in these encounters between the sexes is not so much a woman's control over her body or her informed consent. Prior to such considerations is the legal determination of sexed identity and difference, whereby men accrue property and therefore identity through an almost invisible theft of the corporeality of women.

This kind of determination of sexed identity and difference is no less apparent when women are excluded from social exchange, but rather than building consent into the terms of the contract, the coercion of women becomes the grounds for their exclusion. For example, those who oppose sex-specific contracts only, on the grounds that within them women lose control of their bodies, often justify singling out these contracts from other service arrangements by the claim that the relation between a woman and the body tissue involved is more intimate and less separable from her personhood than that implicated in other service contracts. Carole Pateman, for example, singles out both the surrogacy and prostitution contracts for criticism on these grounds. The surrogacy contract is wrong, she says, because it illegitimately separates the fetus from the surrogate's selfhood (Pateman 1988, 215).[9] The prostitution contract is wrong, says Pateman, because a woman is involved in the sex act more directly than "the involvement of the self in other occupations" (207). So while some would allow the alienation of women's body property for exchange on the market, Pateman, among others, would prevent the way this property gravitates toward men by arguing that it belongs to the personhood of women. For Pateman, the consequence of legally endorsing economic contracts involving such personal corporeality is the commodification of the woman herself and her subsequent reduction to an object of exchange between men.

The immediate problem with arguing that the fetus or the sex act are inseparable from a woman's personhood is that it leaves little room for claiming, as Pateman would like, that surrendering a child for adoption is less wrong than surrogacy, or that a woman is less commodified in sex for pleasure than she is in sex for profit. A possible way to avoid this kind of difficulty is to suggest that insofar as a corporeal substance is thought to belong to someone's personhood and yet is alienable in theory, it should only be alienable in practice as a gift. While I will entertain this line of thought for awhile, I want to suggest that the gift, so understood, is no less problematic than contract in its determination of sexed identity and difference.

This paradigm of the gift for the transfer of body property is favored in Australia over contract for its apparent legal, practical, and ethical advantages. An apparent legal advantage is that in giving away (rather than selling or exchanging) an organ, a body product or part, the original "owner" cannot be held legally responsible for the quality of the product, nor for any consequences after it reaches its destination. So, for example, under relevant legislation in Australia (the Artificial Conception Acts [New South Wales, Western Australia, Australian Capital Territory], the Status of Children Acts [Victoria, Queenland, Tasmania, Northern Territory], or the Family Relationships Act [South Australia]), donors of gametes used in various reproductive technologies have no legal rights or responsibilities in relation to any children resulting from such arrangements (although this lack of responsibility also is true of the service contract, depending on where one is positioned within it). An apparent practical advantage of the gift as a model for governing the alienation of body tissue is that it reduces the temptation to give too much of one's body away, to the detriment of one's physical well-being. On the basis of such considerations, it is illegal in Australia to sell one's blood and organs, although one is encouraged to give them away. An assumed moral advantage is that allowing the gift rather than the sale of body products seems to minimize the commodification of the body and hence the potential dehumanization of social exchange.

On the basis of these perceived advantages, the gift is the model used currently in Australia for legislation in relation to surrogacy insofar as it is allowed at all. In terms of the Surrogacy Contract Act 1993 (Tasmania) (the only legislation I know of in Australia that allows surrogacy in any form), private, "voluntary" surrogacy is permitted, while commercial surrogacy contracts are not. One real advantage of this legislation, beside the apparent ones mentioned, is that it allows the surrogate to change her mind about giving up the child (as no contract can govern the arrangement, the surrogate cannot be held to her promise). While the legislation seems reasonable, given the objections to the surrogacy contract, it is, upon closer scrutiny, merely the reverse side of contract and hence does not guarantee justice. The reasons for recommending prohibiting a surrogacy contract, while allowing private surrogacy, retain all of the assumptions of atomized individualism upon which contract theory is based: upholding the right of an intending surrogate to "use and control her body as she sees fit", while avoiding doing harm to the surrogate by "the breaking of the mother/child bond which develops *in utero*" (NBCC 1990, 27–28).

If the law says no to the surrogacy contract and yes to the gift while remaining faithful to the concept of autonomous self-present identity, then, as in Marcel Mauss' (1967) paradigm of the gift, discussed in the Introduction, a problematic determination of womanhood has been made. The contract is negated either on the grounds that another contract has been formed with a child *in utero* (in the case of the Tasmanian legislation) or on the grounds that the fetus is proper to a woman's personhood and hence inalienable (to take part of Pateman's argument). If giving a child to another is disallowed on the basis that this involves breaking a maternal contract, deemed different to the surrogacy contract only in being more essential, then the "surrogate," while no longer legally culpable for breaking her word to the "intending" parents, would be morally culpable for keeping it. Or, to follow part of Pateman's line of reasoning, if "surrogacy," or the giving of sexual pleasure, is criminalized on the grounds that maternity, or something called "female sexuality," is assumed to be proper to the woman's personhood, then we may circumvent the tendency for procreative or sexed property to accrue toward men, at least temporarily. But while the giving by women of this property is no longer conceivable in terms of automatic consent, it starts to look like surrender under duress. The assumption that giving what is said to be proper to women must involve coercion accounts for the widespread opposition, among feminist theorists, even to "noncommercial, voluntary" surrogacy. Similarly, arguing that sexuality or the sex act is inseparable from a woman's personhood risks reducing all heterosexual sex to rape (or it at least implies that explicit consent should be given for every sexual encounter).[10] And, in a context where some sexed body property attracts value,[11] to rule that women can only give away what is deemed proper to them amounts to allowing a man's body to accrue value without responsibility but not a woman's. When the gift is understood to be the other side of contract, the determination of sexed identity and difference is no less problematic: a woman is free only if she gives nothing of herself away, and a norm of male body property is both produced and maintained by holding that women's body property lacks currency within social exchange.

If, however, we grant that identity and difference are produced *through* the giving of corporeality rather than before it then an altogether different picture of justice in the flesh emerges. Based on Merleau-Ponty's model of the constitution of embodied identity, for example, the emergence of a body I can call our my occurs not prior to but through the "alienation" of corporeality (Merleau-Ponty, 1964a).[12] In this scheme of things, the distinction between self and other is neither original nor final. Prereflective "recognition" that one's body is an object for the other constitutes a difference between the two. But this bodily distinction from the other cannot be absolute. Through prereflective perception that, as a body, I am perceived by another, a system of indistinction is established between my body as I live it, my body as the other sees it, and the other's body as I perceive it. This tripartite system is one of "syncretic sociability": that is, the self is produced, maintained, and transformed through the socially mediated intercorporeal "transfer" of movements and gestures and body bits and pieces. Just as through the look and the touch of the other's body I feel my difference, it is from the same body that I borrow my habits and hence my identity without either body being reducible to the other or to itself.

This brief account of intercorporeal existence raises a number of points against the idea of autonomous self-presence underlying the way in which the giving and selling of body property are usually conceived. First, insofar as I am a self, the giving of corporeality is already in operation. While the self is constituted through the building of a partition between one body and another, it is also by this differentiation that my corporeality is given to, and takes place in, the world of the other's body as it lives from and with me. It is not the case that I first exist in control of my body then decide to give my body away. Rather, it is because my body is given to others and vice versa that I exist as a social being. Hence, corporeal identity is never singular, always ambiguous, neither simply subject nor object. Second, it is through this ambiguity of bodily existence that new possibilities for existing are open to me. Whether learning a new skill or inheriting someone else's kidney, my possibilities are borrowed from the bodies of others, always with an incalculable remainder. Hence, my "freedom" to act in becoming what I am is compromised rather than guaranteed by keeping my body to myself. Finally, as the "alienation" of corporeality grounds rather than follows after the constitution of self, then the difference between consent and coercion is at best indeterminate. For the most part, I do not choose, and so neither consent to, nor are coerced into, the process of corporeal generosity that makes me what I am. For the most part giving corporeality happens without any thought at all.

On the other hand, while freedom is the capacity to remain open to the bodies of others, my freedom to give and receive corporeality in becoming what I am is not absolute. Bodies, as they are lived, are socially constituted, built from an intertwining with others who are already social beings. So while my "freedom" is not limited, in the first instance, by others taking over control of my body, it is limited by "the lessening of the *tolerance* allowed by the bodily and institutional data of our lives," as Merleau-Ponty puts it (1962, 454). That is, my tolerance to embodied projects, and hence what I tend to do and become, is limited by the style of my embodied existence. This style, one's capacities and characteristic gestures, is subject to "sedimentation" in the operation of giving. That is, through habit and in accordance with the institutional setting in which my corporeal identity is constituted, I develop a pattern of existence that leans toward certain practices and that cannot tolerate others. So the ethics of giving blood, gametes, sexual pleasure, or children to another is not decided on the basis of whether these gifts are alienable, unconditionally and universally, and therefore whether giving them puts one's freedom at risk. Rather, our freedom to give in any of these ways is limited by the habits and capacities we have developed as well as those of the bodies with whom we dwell, limits guided by the social significance of the corporeality in question. More generally, insofar as we tend toward sex-specific projects, any consent or coercion involved is grounded most fundamentally in the social constitution, through the law in all of its forms, of differences between sexed bodies.

There is another way to put this "on the one hand"/"on the other hand." On the one hand, giving corporeality is not the province of a singular sexed subject but the realm of an ambiguous relation to the world of the other, the open possibilities inherent in dwelling-with, the realm of indeterminate sexual difference. And if the gift opens possibilities for existence, then its operation rests on not determining anything about who gives what to whom ahead of or during an encounter. Or, as Derrida would have it, for there to be the gift it must go unrecognized and radically forgotten because, if the "donor" or "donee," in his or her assumed self-presence, recognizes the gift as separate from him or her then either a debt will be incurred (and the gift is no longer a gift as such) or the gift will be annulled by some form of return (Derrida 1992, 12–14). Insofar as the law (and I include within this the feminist opposition to surrogacy and prostitution discussed earlier, what Moira Gatens has called "justice feminism")[13] commodifies sex-specific gifts and determines their point of departure, arrival, and return in ways already discussed, it also determines sexed identity and difference in such a way that women seem incapable of giving anything except that which already belongs to someone else or that which must be extracted by force. It is through these kinds of determinations that injustice is done: the gift of an incalculable sexual difference is effaced, and woman is constituted as the second sex.

On the other hand, while injustice is perpetuated through the law's determination of who gives what to whom in its constitution of sexed identity and difference, it would be a mistake to assume that justice can be restored through lawlessness, through forgetting the gift entirely, if by this we mean that other possibilities for existence would emerge from the free play of the gift after suspension of the law's determinations.[14] While Merleau-Ponty, for example, sometimes implies otherwise, the ambiguity of body interlacing, that is the domain of generosity, is not temporally prior to or separate from the process of socio-legal determination that would reduce ambiguity and so close off possibilities for existence. Giving corporeality is opened through the same law that governs the commodification and determination of sexed bodies. (To take the simplest of examples, the legal determinations in the case of Baby M raised as many questions about who gave what to whom as they answered.) Further, nothing much would change if the law were suddenly suspended, because the determination of sexed identity and difference is not confined to explicit laws; it proceeds through those bodies that the law constitutes. It is not that the law should be suspended nor, therefore, that the determination of the gift should be forgotten. Rather, what should be remembered is that the giving that is more often than not forgotten by the law is woman's, and the gifts that the law more often than not remembers are man's.

The possibility of justice then rests with the law's ability to remember this giving of women's corporeality without naming or determining the lived body that "is" a woman. This is not the same as giving women equality with men before the law. Such a stroke of the pen does not remedy the unjust determination of sexed identity and difference under discussion. The injustice needing remedy is that which Drucilla Cornell, following Lyotard, defines as "damage accompanied by the loss of the means to prove the damage" (1991, 110). That is, in a sociality where autonomous identity is assumed and woman is defined as other to the proper subject of social exchange, womanhood is damaged in the constitution of sexed identity and difference. In such a culture "scarred by gender hierarchy," as Cornell puts it, a theory of justice that seeks sexual neutrality ignores the damage done to women in the production of this scar and doubles the injustice by insisting that this damage be translated into the terms of a system that does not recognize it (Cornell 1991, 110, 114). (The rulings over Baby M and the difficulty in proving rape are cases in point.) Rather than equality alone, justice requires the interrogation of this system of injustice, a questioning that opens up the operation of generosity, that irreducible production of possibilities for existence inherent in body intersubjectivity. Or, as Derrida puts it, justice is not a matter of neutralizing differences but, rather, it requires us "constantly to maintain an interrogation of the origin, ground and limits of our conceptual, theoretical, or normative apparatus surrounding justice" (1990, 955).

So where does this leave the law on surrogacy, rape, prostitution, in-vitro fertilization, or any other form of "alienation" of sexed corporeality, medically assisted or not? It leaves the law with the task of remembering that women already give corporeality to the world in the mode of dwelling-with that constitutes them as sexed beings in relation to others. Some women "give" children to themselves, to others, and to the world (simul-taneously). The difference between this and "surrogacy" is in a name by which a woman, rather than some other representative of the law, would attempt to determine the gift and its (interim) destination. Some women "give" sexual pleasure to themselves, to men, and to other women. The difference between this and prostitution is that in prostitution the gift is recognized in terms of an explicit value that the law would rather efface. This is not to suggest that the "surrogate" or the "prostitute" is above the law in the embodied living of her projects. Rather, it is to suggest that there is nothing essentially immoral about "surrogacy" or prostitution that would not also be immoral about procreation or sexual relations in general. And, in legislating against these particular forms of giving, while allowing the practices upon which they are based, the law serves only to uphold its own authority in the determination of womanhood. It does not serve women or justice.

While some women give and are already given through sex for pleasure and through procreation, it would be unjust to force the gift in either of these ways. The surrogacy contract is unjust for forcing the gift, as is rape. And this is not because maternity or something called female sexuality is proper to woman's body and therefore inalienable in any essential sense. Rather, forcing a woman to give corporeality through sex or children is unjust, first, because it denies the generosity of women while memorializing that of men. Second, giving involves a metamorphosis, a structuring of a particular situation through incorporation and corporeal reconstitution, the possibility of which is dependent upon the tolerance to it allowed by the lived bodies involved. A woman can say no to giving because her body, which is her indeterminate self, cannot tolerate the gift; her characteristic pattern of existence is not open to the project in question. (And, as the possibility of saying no and meaning it assumes nothing about a proper body, there is no implication that an explicit yes must precede the gift. Yes is implied in the giving itself.)

What is being questioned in these suggestions is the authority we invest in the law (assumed, incorrectly, to lie outside us) to determine the origin and destination of gifts and, hence, sexed identity and difference. The direction of the debates and legislation surrounding the medical alienation of corporeality makes the question more urgent only because of what it exposes about this authority. It seems that while we can consider giving a zygote in a test tube the status of a person and have no problem attaching value to a male gamete, we still render the gifts of women selfless. Some women disappear, as the invisible becomes real in the interests of someone else's autonomy.

THREE

PERFORMING BODY-IDENTITY
THROUGH THE OTHER

IN CONTRAST TO the ideas of atomized identity and body property that uphold the contract model of social relations criticized in chapter 2, perhaps life is a dance. Perhaps identity is a performance, the choreography of which is captured in the following passage from Nietzsche's *Thus Spoke Zarathustra,* entitled "The Other's Dancing Song":

> Into your eyes I looked recently, O life; I saw gold blinking in your night-eye; my heart stopped in delight; a golden boat I saw blinking on nocturnal waters, a golden rocking-boat, sinking, drinking, and winking again. At my foot, frantic to dance, you cast a glance, a laughing, questioning, melting rocking-glance; . . . and my foot was already rocking with dancing frenzy.
>
> My heels twitched, then my toes hearkened to understand you, and rose; for the dancer has his ear in his toes.
>
> I leaped toward you, but you fled back from my leap, and the tongue of your fleeting, flying hair licked me in its sweep.
>
> Away from you I leaped, and from your serpents' ire; and already you stood there, half turned, your eyes full of desire.

With crooked glances you teach me—crooked ways; on
crooked ways my foot learns treachery.
I fear you near, I love you far; your flight lures me, your
seeking cures me: I suffer, but what would I not gladly suffer for
you. . . .
I dance after you, I follow wherever your traces linger.
Where are you? Give me your hand. Or only one finger. . . .
I am weary of always being your sheepish shepherd. You
witch, if *I* have so far sung to you, now you shall cry.
Keeping time with my whip, you shall dance and cry! Or
have I forgotten the whip? Not I. (Nietzsche 1978, 224–26)

My concern in this chapter is with the performance of identity, the ability
to transform the self through action, or the concept of having one's ear in
one's toes, as Nietzsche would have it. This idea of performativity and the
self-transformation it effects is offered by Nietzsche and others as an alternative to the model of self that grounds the social contract. While a promising alternative, the idea that the self is performative raises concerns with
the limitations to this ability to perform oneself differently.

The quote from Nietzsche suggests that the self is transformed and
transported through the toes, through the body. This is consistent with his
idea of self-overcoming, discussed in detail in chapter 1—the idea that the
self is corporeal and open to transformation, is reproduced differently, through
the production of distance within the self. This idea is relevant to the issue
of social justice insofar as Nietzsche proposes self-overcoming as a way of
opening the embodied self to possibilities of existence beyond those normalized through moral systems of evaluation and punishment. But the quote
above also raises the question of the role of the other in the performance
of self. Why, for example, are Nietzsche's (or Zarathustra's) toes hearkened
to understand "life"; is the other necessary to prompt him to dance? This
description of the dance of life suggests that identity is not performed or
transformed through oneself but is given through the field of the other. But
if this is the case, if the transformation of identity relies on the other's
generosity, why then would Zarathustra (representative of creative self-
performance) need to whip the other into submission in order to complete
the dance? Does creative performance, which transforms the self beyond
normalized categories, subject the other no less than the consistency of self

demanded by contracts? In addressing these questions I will first elaborate on what I mean by performing body-identity, pointing to the significance of the idea and integrating Nietzsche's approach to the subject with that of contemporary thinkers such as Michel Foucault and Judith Butler. While my primary concern is with the neglect of the role of the other in the performativity of self, and with the subsequent lack of consideration of the limits to performativity, the idea is important for how it suggests that the performance artist may have something to say to the sociality that lies beyond the stage.

By performing body-identity I mean that the self does not have an identity except through action. The deed, act, or performance is the self actualized. And as action implicates the body, then the self's identity is performed through the body. Self-identity is equivalent to body perfor-mance. The idea that the self is constituted in the act is at least as old as Hegel, but it is an idea that has not received much positive attention in the democracies of modernity. This is because our morality and politics depend on another idea: that the self's identity is located in consciousness, and this self-reflexive consciousness comes before, causes, and remains unchanged within the act. The idea that the thinking self or the will causes the body to act in this way or that makes the self responsible for the act. That I can be held accountable for my acts is the rock upon which morality and the law are built. The idea that the thinking self is given before and remains unchanged through the act and indeed through sequential actions is the rock upon which the social contract is built. If it cannot be said that the self remains unchanged through a series of actions, then promises cannot be made, contracts cannot be signed, no one could be taken at his or her word and, according to this view of things, social relations would have no basis. So to say that the self's identity is performed and reconstituted within the act is no trivial claim; it challenges the very foundation of the moral, social, and political relations of modernity. But why issue such a challenge?

To those who make this claim, to those who claim that the self is constituted in the act rather than before it, this other self of contract theory is a fiction—a handy fiction that makes us equally responsible, accountable, calculable, and consistent through time. In short, it makes us dull. Human beings suffer from "gravity," as Nietzsche puts it (Nietzsche 1974, 343). Under the weight of this view of the self, we are drawn back to whom we think we are, we cling to our vocations and take ourselves too seriously. To illustrate what he thinks is our fate under the burden of this gravity, Nietzsche uses the parable of the tightrope walker who falls to his death when a jester jumps over him (Nietzsche 1978, 19-23). The tightrope walker dies from his vocation in the wake of the fool who surpasses him. If we do not lighten up, remain open to change, and become flexible we will perish. For Nietzsche, at least, the model of the self that makes us accountable for past acts and consistent over time is itself responsible for the nihilism of modernity.

Clearly we have not perished, nor has the moral, social, and political system supported by this model of identity. However, as the analysis of the surrogacy contract in chapter 2 illustrates, much injustice has been done in the name of this model of self-identity. This model not only legislates against change in one self over time but also against difference between selves or, rather, against transgression of borders of identity and difference. It supports homophobia, sexism, racism, ageism, and a variety of other "isms" and phobias. How so? The law, moral and secular, is universal and normalizing in treating us as if we are or should be the same. Or rather, in maintaining our institutional structures, the law divides us into different categories and regulates our behavior according to what is expected for our proper place. We are treated well if we have the same identity as that privileged within these structures. And the law operates with the model of self-identity just outlined: it assumes that the self is behind and the cause of actions and, on this basis, the body that acts is reduced to a passive material object that we push or cart around. The body is thought to signify or represent the self that lies behind the action. If I cannot live up to the expectations of law, if I am a body that is different to that assumed by the law, then I will be punished or disadvantaged on one of two grounds: on the grounds that the self has been taken over by the body and is no longer in control of and the cause of its actions, or on the grounds that the self is still the author of its actions but is itself faulty. So to live up to the law, to reap the benefits of the self privileged under the law, I have two options: to change my mind or change my body.

We used to think that to get a better deal under the law, all we had to do was change our minds; change our attitudes, our desires and beliefs, our psychic identities to match that desired under the law. But to "pass" you must have the proper body, the body that signifies the identity desired by the law. If you are poor do not steal; if you are black, you would do better to pass as white; if a woman, you would do better to pass as a man; if you have a few wrinkles, get rid of them; if you are in a wheelchair, get up and walk.

That I would need to change my body to live up to the "normal" identities assumed by social and political institutions suggests, contrary to the model of identity based on self-present consciousness, that identity has something to do with body performance. That is, self-identity is not behind and the cause of the body's actions but an effect of the body's performance. Identity is an effect of body performance in two senses: we attribute an identity, personality, or set of thoughts and attitudes to another on the basis of her or his actions. Second, insofar as a body acts consistently over time and according to a category or an identity proper to this body, this is an effect not of the doer behind the deed but of disciplinary production by the law. Let me expand on this second point. According to Nietzsche, Foucault, Butler, and others, body identity is constituted through a repetition of acts, through habit formation. Under the guidance of the law and its regulatory moral and disciplinary mechanisms, bodies are trained to repeat what are considered good acts and to discard the undesirable. The law is an artist in naturalizing its categories of identity, in performing them through bodies.

One effect of this disciplinary production of identity is, as I said, consistent performance. As Nietzsche puts it:

[People] confound themselves with their role; they become victims of their own "good performance"; they themselves have forgotten how much accidents, moods, and caprice disposed of them when the question of their "vocation" was decided—and how many other roles they might perhaps have been *able* to play; for now it is too late. Considered more deeply the role has actually *become* character; and art, nature. (Nietzsche 1974, 302)

Besides consistency, the other effect of the law's performance of body identity is the artifice of difference. We are trained to perform different body identities according to that required by the place we occupy within the social structure.

As Judith Butler suggests, insofar as men are privileged in our culture and the family is central to the reproduction of our social institutions, then the disciplinary production of gender difference takes center stage in the law's performance of body identity (Butler 1990, 128-41). Our vocation in this respect is decided on the basis of our genitals or perhaps a strand of DNA. Around a fold of the skin is built a mask of habits, desires, and gestures considered proper to that body. Insofar as disciplinary mechanisms are successful in reproducing female body identity, this will manifest in a woman's desire for men and motherhood and in the way she talks, walks, stands, and even, as Iris Marion Young argues, in how she throws (Young 1990). Femininity is a performance that, while a cultural production, takes on the appearance of nature through both the habit of it all and the fiction that this performance is caused by a self, soul, or psyche said to lie behind it (Butler 1990, 136).

Besides inconsistency, one thing the law cannot tolerate is ambiguity in identity, transgression of its categories of identity and difference. Transgression occurs when the body performance does not match the identity expected of or assigned to that body. Because it performs femininity across a male body, male to female transvestism is such a transgression and transsexualism more so.[1] Also transgressive is same-sex desire, the hermaphrodite, the muscle-bound East German woman athlete (or, more recently, the Chinese woman swimmer), and Madonna dressed as a man, gyrating over a submissive Asian woman.[2] The law spares no money, time, or energy in its effort to eliminate these ambiguities and transgressions. The Anglican Archbishop of Adelaide insists that Madonna's concert be banned, the *Women's Weekly* is outraged, and the International Olympic Committee wheels out its chromosome and drug tests. While these are obvious arms of the law, even the most politically correct of us are equally guilty of policing identity. Because the law performs identity through us, through our bodies, it does not need to show its hand. It needs only these bodies for its work to be done. So the sign goes up outside of a lesbian bar: "Women only; Lesbians only; Women-born women only; genetic female dykes only; no boys over the age of twelve" (quoted in Zita 1992, 122).[3] Or, in *The Crying Game,* Fergus, despite his best intentions, love, and pacifism, throws up at the first sight of Dil's naked male body. And even I am shocked at Madonna's dance, not because dressed as a man she seduces another woman but because the other woman is Asian.

We attempt to keep body-identity in its place, not just because the categories of difference uphold our social institutions but because, and in virtue of this, any ambiguity in the other's difference threatens the security of our own identity. It is the other's laughter, the other's questioning that prompts Zarathustra's dance. And only if the other is brought to heel, made to cry, and forced to keep time with the whip can Zarathustra rest in peace. Ambiguity and transgression of categories of body identity are threatening because they expose identity as art, not nature. If I cannot be sure of another's performance, if identity is not natural, then I cannot be sure of my own. Here I can offer a diagnosis of my response to Madonna's performance: my discomfort at watching the Oriental other submit to the time of the whip reveals my preference for the exotic other remaining untouchable, a preference equally reductive of the other's identity as the demand that she be the same and no less a foundation for my own (Western) self-image. We avert our eyes or efface that which confounds the assumption that identity and difference are natural and that everything, including ourselves, is in its proper place. And not only does the law work through us to keep the other in place, we also work on ourselves. The surgeon does not force the trans-sexual to match her genitals with her body performance. The transsexual presents herself willingly to the surgeon's knife.

Perhaps none of this would matter if everything ended happily in its proper place. But as Nietzsche suggests, we confound ourselves with our "good performance." There is no more of a secure place for the transsexual after the operation then there was before. This lack of security is also true in Foucault's case of Herculine Barbin, the nineteenth-century French hermaph-rodite, whose ambiguity was denied not by matching genitals with perfor-mance but by matching performance with what science determined was the sex of the genitals (Foucault 1980b).[4] Despite the ambiguity of Barbin's geni-tals, it was decided shortly after birth that Barbin was more a girl than a boy. She was raised as a girl, educated in a convent school for girls, and performed her femininity as well as any female could. However, at age twenty (in what amounted to a serious failure of performance), she took a woman lover. After confessing this to her doctor and priest, it was decided on legal and moral grounds that Barbin was in fact a man. With this she was required by law to dress as a man and to exercise the political rights and economic privileges enjoyed by men at the time. After a period of living in anger, misery, and isolation, Barbin killed herself. Of course there are many more far less dra-matic instances of the misery that the policing of identity causes. We may not die of boredom, but we will confound ourselves and suffer from our perfor-mance for, to a certain extent, none of us can live up to the law.

So how do we deal with the law's performance of body-identity and the marginalization of difference and ambiguity it effects? By the same means—performance. Some would say that the injustices resulting from policing identity can only be redressed through a particular kind of performance; a flexible, self-affirming, lighthearted performance. To quote Nietzsche again:

> Precisely because we are at bottom grave and serious human beings—really, more weights than human beings—nothing does us as much good as a *fool's cap*; we need it in relation to ourselves—we need all exuberant, floating, dancing, mocking, childish and blissful art lest we lose the *freedom above things* that our ideal demands of us. (Nietzsche 1974, 164)

To turn nature back into art, we need to give ourselves style against the law. Or, as Foucault puts it, we need to create ourselves as works of art without reference to the disciplinary moral code (Foucault 1984, 346). Rather than securing our own identity by saying no to the other's ambiguity, we must practice an "aesthetics of existence" on ourselves or "overcome" ourselves, as Nietzsche would put it.

The importance of the idea that identity is a body performance and that this is how the law of identity and difference is naturalized cannot be overstated. However, I question the extent of the creativity implied in an aesthetics of existence in our ability to reperform identity against the law. How we formulate the limits to our creativity depends upon where we think the ability to dance comes from. If we think that identity is performed through the body without conscious intervention, if it is a material production, then we cannot recreate ourselves by changing our mind. Neither Nietzsche or Foucault can take this path, given that for them there is no consciousness separate from, and the cause of, the body's actions. While Foucault's aesthetics of existence may not depend on a presocial mind, it does seem to depend, as Butler points out, upon the existence of a multiplicity of bodily pleasures that have somehow escaped the law's determinations (Butler 1990, 96–97). It is on the basis of using these pleasures that, according to Foucault, one can build up a stylistic performance. But he provides no account of how this bodily multiplicity managed to escape social production in the first place. Indeed, the very idea runs against his earlier work on disciplinary power, which implies that no body escapes the work of the law.[5]

Butler provides her own account of the origin and possibility of stylistic performance. She suggests that we can subvert strict categories of identity and so add style to our existence, because the production of identity by the law is itself unstable. Using gender identity as her focus, Butler argues that because identity is actualized as it is performed, rather than being caused by an inner essence identity is open to disruption. It is open to disruption because it is constituted through a repetition of acts; a repetition of public acts with socially established meanings and a repetition of these imitations by ourselves over time. Identity is parody or imitation without an authentic original. And, Butler suggests, there is always difference in repetition, that is, the repeated act is always slightly different from the prior instance of its performance because of the different social context in which it is performed. This disjunction between the meaning of repeated acts means that one's identity is always open to change. To quote Butler:

> Gender ought not to be construed as a stable identity or locus of agency from which various acts follow; rather, gender is an identity tenuously constituted in time, instituted in an exterior space through a *stylized repetition of acts*. . . . The possibilities of gender transformation are to be found precisely in the arbitrary relation between such acts, in the possibility of a failure to re-peat, a de-formity or a parodic repetition that exposes the phantasmatic effect of abiding identity as a politically tenuous construction. (Butler 1990, 140–41)

Butler instances drag as a kind of parody that, through a disjunction between anatomical sex, gender identity, and gender performance, exposes gender identity as a tenuous construction. But she also thinks the mundane can be disruptive. For her, style or political resistance to the policing of correct identity comes from the disjunctions inherent in body performance (dis-junctions between the body and performance and between repeated acts), not, as Foucault would seem to have it, from a multiplicity of body pleasures that have somehow escaped the normalizing social code.

While I think Butler's is an interesting thesis that overcomes some of the problems of a Foucauldian aesthetics of self, it has itself suffered from parody. Under the weight of individualism and identity politics her critical intervention into disciplinary production of body-identity has tended to be reduced to a superficial pluralism. Jacquelyn Zita, for example, in her essay "Male Lesbians and the Postmodernist Body," chastises those she labels "postmodernists," such as Butler, for trivializing identity politics by advocating replacing two sexed identities with many ways of inhabiting a body (Zita 1992). In light of Butler's kind of thesis, says Zita, the self-titled "male lesbian," who is ostracized by the lesbian community for obvious reasons, would no longer have to claim that his male body signifies a female and hence a lesbian identity; "he could become a 'lesbian-identified-non-lesbian-hating-male' who loves his own body and acknowledges his heterosexual privilege" (123). Or, to avoid the hostility a female lesbian could attract because she has sex with a man to conceive a child, she could claim her identity as a female-lesbian-gay-male-loving mother.

While I think this is a misreading of Butler's particular analysis of performing gender, hers is an account that lends itself to such reductions. The reason is that, for the most part, there are only two terms in Butler's account: the performing body and the law. And as the performing body in its singularity disrupts its own identity through repetition, then it can be said to be open to becoming anything at all. With this, there would be, as Zita suggests, as many identities as there are bodies, and each identity would be limited only by the acts it could invent or by the different contexts it could find. However, that performance could be so free is itself suspect, and even if it were so free, there is nothing to stop another sign going up on the door: "only female-lesbian-gay-male-loving mothers allowed." And there is nothing to stop the law from tearing it down. Body performance would be no more open to ambiguity and therefore no less oppressive in this proliferation of the law's categories from two groups to many single bodies.

There is a third term forgotten in this haste to liberate ourselves from the law. Identity is ambiguous and open to change, not just because of a deformity inherent in repetition over time but also because body performance is never singular. And body performance is never singular, because between the body and the law is the other. I have already suggested, along with Nietzsche, that it is the other who prompts the dance. I also want to argue that, as we dance with the other, identity is not only ambiguous and open to change, but it is limited in its potential.

For Merleau-Ponty, as mentioned in chapter 2, and in a way that I will elaborate on in more detail here, body-identity is never individual: it is fundamentally intersubjective, based on the nonvolitional generosity of intercorporeality and fashioned with reference to the social and familial situation. Further, it is because the body is constituted in relation to others that it is ambiguous, opened to the world and to others, and so can act at all. Insofar as any body claims absolute self-identity by assuming an absolute interval between that body and the body of the other, this generosity is suppressed in favor of rigid identity and the condemnation of transgression of singular identity that this entails. In "The Child's Relations with Others," Merleau-Ponty argues, alongside Lacan's model of the "mirror stage," that the self does not carry, in isolation from others, a distinction between the inside and outside of itself, between the objective body, as it is seen and touched by others, and the phenomenal body as it is lived, feels, sees, and touches (Merleau-Ponty 1964a). The distinction between self and other is based on a difference between the experience of one's own body and the body of the other. This experience arises through the condition that one's body is an object for another and therefore distinct from the other. However, the distinction from the other cannot be absolute. Through a perceived objectification of one's body by another, a system of indistinction is established between my own body as it feels to me, its visual or objectified image, and the body of the other. Insofar as the child identifies with its image of the other's image of itself, it cannot easily distinguish between what it lives, what the other lives, and what it perceives the other is doing. This tripartite system is one of "syncretic sociability": the transfer of socially coded movements and gestures between dispersed bodies.

So my body-identity, while based on perception by and therefore a distinction from others, arises through the organization of the body given to and by the corporeality of others. And this constitution of the body subject through the other occurs not by conscious intervention but by mimesis and "transitivism": by identification with other bodies and by the imitation and projection of gestures. While this indistinction between self and other is reduced by saying "I," by taking up one point of view as the subject of language, the structure of language is such that each person, while being an "I" for herself or himself, is also a "you" for others (Merleau-Ponty 1964a, 151). The self is a lived body ambiguously caught between subject and object, inhabiting the world of the other's body even with a lived distance between the two. It is because bodies are opened onto others, rather than being distinct, that we can act, be affected, have an identity, and remain open to change without conscious direction. The generosity of intercorporeal existence is not governed by choice but is where agency, perception, affectivity and, combining all of these, identity, are born. Hence, we cry at the movies, even though we sit apart from the action. And we turn into our partners, and even our dogs, just by dwelling with them.

There are two points to be made in light of this account of performing body-identity against tendencies in Nietzsche's, Foucault's, and Butler's accounts. First, while my identity is constituted through a stylized repetition of acts, I do not build this body alone: I only have an identity because as a body I am given to, and take place in, the world of the other's body. I act because, as Nietzsche puts it, "my toes hearkened to understand you," and my toes hearkened to understand you because it is through you that my body identity is constituted. It is because my body is always already given to the world and to the other that the relation between my body, the other, and the world is ambiguous and hence open to possibilities.

This corporeal opening toward the other and the world has two sides. I structure the situation by the (prereflective) projection of my body onto the world. Through movement, I incorporate objects and others within the situation and resolve it according to the project at hand. I drive a car in this way; not by consciously calculating the distance between my body, the car, and the gateway but by the prereflective projection of my body (the gestures of which have been built up through mimesis and repetition) onto the world, making it part of my body spatiality. By incorporating the car and breathing in I might just make it through. I would also perform drag this way, not by simply donning the garb of a foreign body and playing on the difference between that performance and the sex of my body but by implicitly incorporating that foreign body, its gestures, movements, and habits, into my performance.

The other side of the story is that my body identity is transformed in this performance through the world of the other, and not simply because of a deformity of meaning inherent in repetition. As performance involves an opening of the body onto the world of the other, it polarizes and gathers together the body; its senses and extremities are unified, and certain aspects are privileged depending on the task being carried out. Method actors will be familiar with this reconstitution of the body through the other. By the imitation and repetition of the gestures of a character, I almost become that character in the way I walk, talk, and stand. And depending on the commitment to the performance and the duration of the play or filming, it can take some time to undo the changes that performance has effected. Robert De Niro's performance in the film *Awakenings* is exemplary of this phenomenon.

He played the part of Leonard, a patient suffering from a catatonic form of parkinsonism. His performance carried so much depth and detail that Oliver Sacks, the neurophysiologist who supervised the filming and who the film was about, was concerned that De Niro would contract the disease. Sacks noted later:

> I knew how deeply he might identify with the characters he portrayed, but I had to wonder now how *neurologically* deep he might go—whether he might actually, in his acting, *become* Parkinsonian, or at least somehow duplicate the neurological state of the patient. Does acting like this, I wondered, actually alter the nervous system. (Sacks 1991, 383)

That performance could go so deep to effect a body transformation may explain what puzzled a journalist for the *Sunday Times* (London) recently (October 12, 1995): why leads in love stories (from Burton and Taylor to Firth and Ehle) so often really fall in love.

To summarize the first point: as bodies are constituted and live as an interworld of potentiality given to and opened onto others, we have no means of "knowing" or becoming a body other than through a familiar dwelling-with others in the world. This point, that transformation of identity is effected through the other, is not necessarily lost on Butler, but it does tend to be submerged under her emphasis on the arbitrary relation between acts of a singular body in time. And it is a point lost on some of her critics and disciples, who pin their hopes for freedom from the policing of identity on the metamorphosis of a body living in splendid isolation. But, in claiming a singular body-identity, I not only deny the corporeal generosity of intersubjective existence, effectively stealing from the other and effacing the ambiguity of her or his difference in ways already discussed, I also cut off my own potentialities for existence. For, as Irigaray puts it, "One does not move without the other" (Irigaray 1981).

The second point to be made about this account of body performance is that what I can become is limited, not so much by the acts I can invent but, prior to this, by the social history of my carnal intertwining with others. As I argued in chapter 2, there is a limit to the generosity by which bodies are given to each other in the opening of possibilities for carnal existence. As our potentialities for existence are opened through the bodies of others who are already social beings, the conducts that constitute our identity and hence our modes of being will vary depending on with whom we associate and under what social rules. The law is not a disembodied phenomenon performing identity directly on bodies; it works through the cultural other with whom we dwell. So our "freedom" to become what we will is limited by "the lessening of the *tolerance* allowed by the bodily and institutional data of our lives" (Merleau-Ponty 1962, 454). Second and related to this, as identity is constituted through a repetition of acts, our style of existence then is subject to what Merleau-Ponty calls "sedimentation": we develop a bodily "attitude towards the world [that], when it has received frequent confirmation, acquires a certain favored status for us" (441). So, De Niro may have become parkinsonian after *Awakenings*, and Firth and Ehle may have stayed in love after *Pride and Prejudice*, except for the absence of a corporeal history that would favor that development and the lack of sufficient sustained commitment to their new performance. Again, the point about "sedimentation" of corporeal styles is not lost on Butler (1990, 140). However, in her account, habitual ways of being seem too easily disrupted through a disjunction between repeated acts. What I am suggesting is that habit is only overcome, and new possibilities opened, in any substantial way through another's body and then only through an acquired familiarity. Or, as Merleau-Ponty puts it, "As long as we are alive, our situation is open, which implies both that it calls up specially favored modes of resolution, and also that it is powerless to bring one into being by itself" (1962, 442).

While no body engaged in a project simply repeats identity, no body is free to create itself and its world anew. To claim otherwise, to imply that I can become whatever I want in my singularity, is to risk repeating the moralism of liberal individualism which, in denying the ambiguity of identity and its dispersal in the other, makes me fully accountable for what I am, on the grounds that I could have acted otherwise. If I could have acted otherwise, then I could have lived up to the singular, unambiguous identity assigned me under the law. Suggesting the possibility of freedom in a singular identity further entrenches the law, the law that cannot tolerate the dance. "Keeping time with my whip, you shall dance and cry! Or have I forgotten the whip? Not I!" (Nietzsche 1978, 226).

PART II

GENEROSITY AND THE POLITICS OF AFFECTIVITY

blank 74

FOUR

EROTIC GENEROSITY
AND ITS LIMITS

THE ANALYSIS SO FAR has posited corporeal generosity as the nonvolitional, intercorporeal production of identity and difference that precedes and exceeds both contractual relations between individuals and the practices of self-transformation figured in some postmodern aesthetics of self. All production of identity and difference is not only social and corporeal but also passes through the bodies of others, and parsimony and social injustice rest on memorializing the generosity of some while forgetting the giving of others.

This chapter begins the task of examining the affective dimension of interpersonal relations. The understanding of affectivity to be developed grounds affects in the generosity of intercorporeal existence. Rather than being an aspect of personal existence that occasionally disrupts the integrity of the self for better or for worse, affecting and being affected will be viewed as the basis of the production and transformation of the corporeal self through others. So understood, affectivity is also the domain of politics. If the corporeal generosity that accounts for the production and transformation of the self is grounded in affect rather than conscious reflection, then so is parsimony and hence prejudice, discrimination, domination, and submission. So in accounting for the generous basis of affectivity, I will also attend to its politics.

This analysis of the generosity and politics of affectivity begins with the extreme case: erotics and sexual relations. It is usually within the realm of eroticism and sexuality that affectivity is viewed as that which either puts the self most at risk or that which might secure the self's liberation from social constraints. However, both views are based on the same individualism that haunts the contract model of social relations, criticized in Part I. In the context of this model, sexual desire is viewed as an exceptional affect that destabilizes an otherwise self-controlled, self-contained self, and protection of this self is secured, it is assumed, if desire is accompanied by love understood as a relation of mutual exchange between equals. It is against this model of desire and love that my account of erotic generosity will be posed.

Radical feminism, for example, is concerned with the harm that sex seems to pose to women's physical, psychical, and social well-being through their sexual objectification and subordination within patriarchy. Protection from harm can be secured, it is said, through the promotion of more egalitarian love relations and through erecting a legislative barrier against practices, such as pornography, that eroticize the domination and subordination of women. Concern about the sexual objectification of women is, of course, as old as feminism itself. What is relatively new is an anxiety among radical feminists about the way some women, and worse some women who call themselves feminists, valorize the objectification of women in the name of women's sexual liberation. This anxiety is well documented in the 1990 anthology *The Sexual Liberals and the Attack on Feminism* (Leidholdt and Raymond 1990). Here, Catharine Mackinnon, for example, equates the opposition to her own anti-pornography campaign by groups such as FACT (Feminist Anti-Censorship Task Force) with the death of feminism as she knows it (Mackinnon 1990, 9). Such groups, she argues, in thinking that sexual liberation can be achieved for women by appropriating rather than opposing the "visual violation" of women, fail to recognize that "misogyny is sexual, and that sexuality, socially organized, is deeply misogynist" (13).

Sheila Jeffreys, in the same book, defends her ideal of safe sex by mounting a similar argument, not just against feminist defense of pornography but also against practices such as lesbian sadomasochism and butch femme role playing, which she says eroticize domination and submission (Jeffreys 1990, 25, 133). Unlike Mackinnon, Jeffreys does not think all socially organized sexuality is deeply misogynist, but she does suggest that insofar as women derive pleasure from sexual practices that rely on a power imbalance, this marks the degree to which they have internalized their oppression (133). So "keeping women and children safe" (25) is not just a matter of erecting a protective barrier through legislation but also requires working toward a more egalitarian sexuality in lesbian as well as heterosexual relations. This can be achieved, she says, by women exorcising from themselves any negative sexual feelings (those associated with submissiveness in sex) (26) in favor of positive sexual feelings (134), although the origin of these remains unclear. Wendy Stock is also concerned with eradicating any power imbalance from sexual relations without abandoning sex altogether. Her formula for safe sex involves therapeutic measures which, by helping a woman "experience and believe in her own body integrity," would bring her sexual pleasure under her control rather than her partner's and so would achieve a "sexuality based *not* on a submission/domination dynamic but on mutual exchange between equals" (Stock 1990, 152–53).

It is not my intention to repeat the well-rehearsed arguments that radical feminism tends to rely on a simplistic model of power and an essentialist model of male sexuality as inherently aggressive and women's sexuality as universally positive.[1] In any case, the positions just outlined add a complication to the radical feminism of the 1970s. Safe sex for women, if it can be achieved at all, not only seems to require protection from men but also from other women and even from themselves. But perhaps more problematic is that these radical feminist ideals of safety and mutual exchange are shared by the new liberation discourses that they are designed to oppose. Berkeley Kaite (1987), for example, in supporting pornography as a means of transgressing restrictive categories of gender identity, relies on the surprising claim that pornography involves a mutual exchange of looks between the consumer and the pornographic model. While more sensitive to the relation between sex and power, Chantal Nadeau (1995), in a critical appropriation of Gilles Deleuze's analysis of masochism, bases her qualified support for lesbian sadomasochism on the claim that it involves a contract that gives women freedom and control over their sexuality. Rather than assuming that sexual liberation for women can be achieved by appropriating the images of women's sexual subordination and without dismissing the labor of feminism in exposing and opposing sexual violence against women, as some of the new sexual liberation discourses (such as Kaite's) tend to, I want to take advantage of that labor to question the current discourse of safe sex in both its liberationary and prohibitive forms. I want to question the ideals of self-control and a mutual exchange between equals apparent in both ideals of safe sex, while still accounting for the feminist concern that sex can be violent and a violation of being.

There are at least two aspects of the modified radical feminist position that I find disturbing. First, insofar as it is *anti-sex* (Mackinnon) and/or posits a genuine love against a sexual desire contaminated by patriarchal representations, it is thoroughly entrenched in an anti-sex tradition that begins with Western philosophy itself. Plato, as it is well known, based his epistemology on privileging spiritual love over physical desire, and a similar valorization of love over sex can be found in the tradition of egalitarian political philosophies from the eighteenth century until today. This tradition is anti-sex insofar as it is anti-body, promoting a politics of immunization, through egalitarian love and friendship, against the threat that the body seems to pose to freedom and autonomy. But, as I will go on to argue with reference to Sartre, despite their talk of freedom and autonomy, these anti-sex discourses are no less anti-women than the sexual libertarianism set up against them. Second, insofar as radical feminism proposes the possibility of *safe sex*, through self-control and body-integrity and/or by erecting a barrier between women and others, it lacks generosity—not a generosity that would ignore sexual violence or endorse women giving themselves to others at any cost, but a generosity foreshadowed in Beauvoir's anti-individualism, although remaining underdeveloped in her work. This is a generosity of mind and body, of love and desire that undermines those distinctions and that, by assuming the ambiguity of existence, views the erotic encounter as one means of extending one's own existence through others without entrapment.[2]

I begin with Sartre because, perhaps surprisingly, his philosophy of love, desire, and freedom in *Being and Nothingness* (1989) shares all of the sentiments of the radical feminism that I have outlined.[3] It therefore allows me not only to indicate the extent to which the contemporary discourses of safe sex repeat an older logic but also to point to what may be problematic about that logic and its privileging of love over sex. More positively, the revision of Sartre's ontology by others in the existential phenomenological tradition, Beauvoir and Merleau-Ponty in particular, provides a way through some of these difficulties by positing an understanding of the affectivity of sexual relations in terms of the generosity of intercorporeal existence.

Sartre's discussion of love and sexual desire is framed by his concern with the maintenance of individual freedom. Freedom refers to the human capacity to constitute existence through practical consciousness, or the for-itself. Through our conscious embodied projects, we not only constitute existence outside of us by introducing form, meaning, and our purposes to being-in-itself, but we also transcend what we are (our being-in-itself) toward future possibilities. This freedom of self-realization is possible because there is no essence grounding our existence. But absolute freedom is impossible: we can only choose to be; we cannot be the foundation of our own existence.

If, in considering the relation between freedom and sexuality, we focus on Sartre's comments about holes and the slimy toward the end of *Being and Nothingness* (Sartre 1989, 600–15), as has often been the case in feminist scholarship,[4] we will encounter the kind of misogyny about which Mackinnon is concerned. Sartre equates "slime" (that which threatens to engulf the for-itself) with feminine passivity, and he likens "holes" (that which appeals to our freedom to fill up existence) with the "obscenity of the feminine sex" (613). For Sartre, it would seem, women's sexed bodies both ground and threaten man's freedom. However, if we take these comments in the context of Sartre's earlier, more considered discussion of the body and sexual desire, we find something less misogynist and more consistent with the ideals of radical feminism. There we find that sexual relations are a problem for Sartre, insofar as they compromise the freedom of both the self and the other, whatever their sex. It is also on the basis of this concern for freedom that Sartre condemns both sadism and masochism and that love shines through as the most likely means by which the freedom of both the self and the other can be preserved within concrete relations. However, this privileging of love is supported by an ontology that, while not blatantly anti-women, is somewhat misanthropic, an ontology where the freedom of the for-itself seeks protection from the apparent danger of both the freedom of others and the weight of one's own body. It is in this ontology, which is both individualist and anti-body, that a logic of safe sex is grounded.

Sartre's ontology is not obviously individualist, in that while the self is for-itself, it is also always for-others: others have the freedom to make of us what they will. However, our being-for-others is exclusively in the mode of objectification: "my being-as-object is the only possible relation between me and the Other" (Sartre 1989, 365). While I cannot know nor therefore capture the other's view of me, the other's look nevertheless has the affect of transforming my project from being-for-itself to being-for-itself through the eyes of the other. My freedom is alienated in concrete encounters with others, and this claim, combined with the assumption that interpersonal relations are based on objectification, implies an original separation between two objectifying consciousnesses. So while Sartre is not individualist insofar as he claims, by occasional qualification, that it is not the case that I first exist then move toward the other (1989, 363, for example), he is individualist in the sense that all concrete relations with others are hostile relations of objectification between centers of an impossible freedom. It is within this conflict between competing looks that desire and love arise.

Desire—and by desire Sartre means sexual desire—belongs to one of two general modes of response to the alienation of my freedom in the other's look. Through desire I defend myself from the other's freedom by objectifying the other in return (Sartre 1989, 363). This desire is of a body for a body. And just as Sartre is not obviously individualist, he is not obviously anti-body. Indeed, he devotes a significant proportion of *Being and Nothingness* to rescuing the body from its secondary status and givenness in Cartesian dualism and biological determinism (303–60). In his general discussion of the body for-itself and for-others, Sartre establishes a model of the body as a socially situated structure variously lived by oneself and variously perceived by others depending on the situation and the project at hand. This has positive consequences for Sartre's model of sexual desire, to a point. It allows him to claim that sexuality is an ontological rather than a biological question (384). This means, first, that sexual desire is not determined by the body's facticity (383): it does not originate in an instinct, a sex organ, or an aim set by the sex of the body. Rather, desire is an embodied project of a body in situation. Hence, my desire does not depend on any essential masculine or feminine aim but on how I live my embodied projects. Second, sexuality is an ontological rather than a biological question in the sense that sexual desire does not arise in a single body that seeks the satisfaction of pleasure for its own sake (384), but by being a body-for-others. I have already said that desire arises in the wake of the other's objectification of me. The point here is that if desire is my response, what I desire is a body, and I desire a particular body not because of its facticity (its sex, or what it wears, for example). Rather I desire a particular body as a body in situation where its significance for me is given by its attitude toward the world (386) (which would include objectification of me) and by my interpretation of that attitude. For Sartre, I have no sexuality outside of this ontological structure of a lived body-for-itself-for-others. In this way, he gives the body its due in desire without resorting to a biological determinism that would either privilege heterosexuality or destine men to sexual domination and women to sexual submission.

However, in the end, Sartre's model of sexual desire does betray an anti-body logic: we find that what is wrong with desire is that it is *too* embodied. While desire may begin as a body-in-situation, for another body-in-situation it also begins and ends in trouble. According to Sartre, in desire, and unlike in any other project, consciousness is "troubled," "clogged," or overtaken by one's body, and the for-itself, and hence one's freedom, is compromised (Sartre 1989, 387–89). The motive of desire is, as I have said, to protect one's freedom by possessing the freedom of the other. Desire attempts to do this by reducing the other's body, by the "caress," from a body-in-situation to "flesh" (390–91). The caress strips the other's body of its situation, its meaning, its projects, its future (in short, its social dimension and its freedom). And the other's body is reduced to flesh, not just for me but, more important, for the other. If I am to possess the other's freedom and so protect my own, what matters is that, as the result of my caress, the other lives his or her body as flesh, as inert matter that he or she no longer transcends toward possibilities. The problem with all of this is that, according to Sartre, in the process of eliminating the other's freedom, I sacrifice my own. I can only compel the other to feel the passivity of his or her fleshness if I imply my own, if my caress also incarnates my own consciousness, reduces me to flesh and deadens my possibilities (390, 395).

Sartre's purpose in describing desire is to show how it fails as a project of the for-itself to be its own foundation. But, as this failure, for Sartre, is inherent in all concrete relations with others, it is not my interest here. What is interesting, and problematic, about Sartre's view of desire is that in its consummation in the sexual encounter, it fails to achieve anything at all. Desire paralyzes, and we are left with mere flesh enjoying flesh, a state of the human body that Sartre, in his discussion of the body-for-others in general, reserves for the corpse (Sartre 1989, 344). In comparison to any other body state, including hunger, desire is deadly: all freedom is lost in favor of a double submissiveness and passivity. And it is not the case that Sartre would prefer that one freedom remain alive in the face of the other's

sexual submissiveness. Such a situation would be either sadistic or masochistic. Sadism is the attempt to possess the other as flesh without returning
the favor (399).[5] And Sartre is contemptuous of sadism for its violence, its
nonreciprocity, and the sadist's self-delusion in assuming a freedom that in
reality is enslaved. Masochism is where I give up my freedom entirely,
allowing the other to make me exist as flesh (377–79). For Sartre, masochism
is the ultimate vice: it is a kind of submission saturated with guilt for the
way the masochist consents to his or her absolute alienation in the other,
allows the other to dominate, is fascinated by his or her own objectness for
others, and loves his or her failure even to achieve these limited aims.

   While sadism and masochism are embodied projects that should be
avoided for the domination and submission they promote, desire, because it
is too embodied, is not a project at all. Sartre may have personal grounds for
this belief, but he has no ontological grounds. Within the context of his
general account of the body-for-itself-for-others, the only grounds for assuming that sexual desire is any more embodied or any less open to possibilities than any other project directed toward the world of others would
be if Sartre himself privileged a kind of disembodied consciousness. And this
would appear to be the case. Despite all of his work in arguing that the body
is always lived as a body in situation open to possibilities, his reservations
about desire rest on assuming first, that to the extent that desire is a project
directed toward the other's body and one's own body becoming flesh, this
is not a project of self-realization that opens possibilities, and second, that the
freedom of every other project depends on a body that, while a center of
reference for my project, is only a contingency that consciousness transcends.
Or, as Sartre puts it:

> In desire the body, instead of being only the contingency which
> the For-itself flees toward possibilities which are peculiar to it,
> becomes at the same time the most immediate possible of the
> For-itself. Desire is not only desire of the Other's body; it is—
> within the unity of a single act—the non-thetically lived project
> of being swallowed up in the body. Thus the final state of sexual
> desire can be swooning. (Sartre 1989, 389)

Insofar as Sartre is anti-sex, this rests on assuming that the body is inherently
passive and the locus of submission, and that freedom is won only if I avoid

the other's touch so that my own body stays in the background as that which consciousness transcends.

This fear of one's own body and the proximity of the other's body is doubled by Sartre's privileging of love over desire. Love belongs to a second mode of response to one's alienation in the other's look. While desire seeks to protect the self by negating the other's freedom, love accepts the other's freedom but attempts to take it over (Sartre 1989, 364). In love, therefore, I do not objectify the other but turn myself into an object for the other's fascination. Not a fleshy object that would absorb the other's body but a center of freedom that would absorb the other's subjectivity in tact. So, as the other's object, I must be freely chosen: as it is the other's freedom I am after, this must be preserved (367). And while I am the other's object, I am not just any object among others. I demand to be the privileged occasion of the other's love, that toward which *all* the other's transcending, meaning-giving activity is ultimately directed (367–68).

While love fails to assimilate the other in this way, for reasons that I do not have the space to pursue, it does not necessarily fail to preserve freedom per se, if the other, in discovering the freedom inherent in my demand to be loved, demands to be loved by me in return (Sartre 1989, 374). In this mutual demand to be loved, each gives himself or herself to the other (and hence alienates his or her freedom), but only in order to found the other's existence (376). Hence, the meaning-giving activity, the freedom and the otherness of each, is preserved. This, for Sartre, is the basis of the joy of love (371): one's own existence is given meaning and value by the other, while his or her otherness and mine are spared. However, indicative of Sartre's anti-body logic, this mutual love of two subjectivities is only possible if the other, in demanding to be loved in return, presents herself or himself as a subject rather than a body-object (374–75). As there must be nothing in the demand to be loved that invites possession, the body (which by definition invites possession as flesh) must not become an explicit theme. Sartre privileges a kind of disembodied love, because, while just as in desire both subjects fail to become their own foundation, in love "at least each one has succeeded in escaping the danger of the Other's freedom" by experiencing the other in their subjectivity (376).

With Sartre's ontology, we would seem to have all of the ingredients for a radical feminism and its ideal of safety in erotic relations. We have condemnation of both domination and submission in relations with others, a distaste for the sexual encounter, insofar as this implies passivity, possession and a loss of freedom, and a valorization of love as a reciprocal relation in which freedom is preserved. But all of this is at the cost of appreciating the subtleties and complexities of our erotic life and of our relations with others in general. Sartre (and one suspects, radical feminism) begins from the problematic assumption that relations with others are based on objectification and that, through our objectification of others and ourselves, either the body reigns as flesh, in which case domination or submission follows, or consciousness puts its body and that of others at a distance, and freedoms are preserved. But this love, and its freedom, is fraudulent, however egalitarian it may appear. And not just because it is based on a dubious individualism and mind/body dualism but because, to the extent that Sartre's model of sexual desire can be considered misogynist, insofar as he associates the passivity of flesh with the female body and women's sexuality, his model of love is also misogynist. Any egalitarian project based on accepting the tradition that associates the body with passivity, submission, and femininity and that seeks to distance itself from this body and its associations entrenches rather than challenges those assumptions. And, as Simone de Beauvoir's analysis of love suggests, an ideal of love that follows this logic in the interests of promoting women's freedom does not even succeed in its aim of protecting women from domination.

While never confronting Sartre directly and while not without contradiction, Beauvoir challenges the individualism of his ontology, its anti-body logic, and the ideal of protection that it implies. First, however, her most obvious departure from Sartre's existentialism, as others have elaborated on in detail, is the way in which she adds consideration of women's social and economic situation to her analyses of relations between the sexes. And this is no less true of her accounts of love and desire. But in contrast to a radical feminist position that includes the same considerations, it turns out that, for Beauvoir, love, far from being a woman's answer to her problems, may in fact be her undoing.

In *The Second Sex* (1972), Beauvoir suggests that to the extent that women do not enjoy the same social and economic freedoms as men or, put in ontological terms, because Man is the Subject and Woman the Other (Beauvoir 1972, 16), women's subjectivity or freedom is socially frustrated or forbidden (641). If denied the possibility of self-realization in projects directed toward a world, a woman may seek this in love, either through narcissism, where her subjectivity is directed toward herself, the one self who will not deny it (641), or through a man, whose subjectivity already finds expression in the world. Hence, says Beauvoir, under conditions of social and economic inequality, and insofar as love is about preserving freedom in the wake of the other's look, women and men approach love differently (652– 53). Man demands to be loved in order to take possession of a woman, and in this he gives up nothing for her. But a woman, who thinks she has little freedom to relinquish, will give herself entirely to him in the faith that he will, through his projects, his freedom, justify her existence. This is a tyrannical gift where the woman abandons herself to bodily immanence (or flesh, in Sartre's terms) and the stagnation that this implies and demands of her lover in return that he save her through his power and freedom (666–68). Women's love, under such conditions, is a sacrificial generosity born of desperation, and the resulting love relation merely compounds the inequality from which it springs.

I can find two paths out of this destructive generosity in Beauvoir's work. The first is the obvious one, consistent with radical feminism and with Sartre's account of love, although borrowing something from Hegel's ontology. She posits a "genuine love" based on mutual recognition of two freedoms, where the existence of both is justified through giving the self to the other while remaining transcendent (Beauvoir 1972, 677). But, she adds, if this genuine love is to be realized between men and women, it would require women's economic independence (678) and that men learn to give of themselves. While adding these considerations to Sartre's ideal of love is important for casting suspicion on the egalitarian aspirations of his account, Beauvoir's is no less empty and no less idealistic. "Genuine love" would be the profit at the end of what seems to be an endless struggle. Not only is love not part of the struggle but, as Beauvoir herself admits in her discussion of the independent woman, it is not necessarily won in the end (695–99). Nor is it clear how one would distinguish between what is genuine and what is bad faith in love—bad faith being where a woman deludes herself into taking for love what is in fact a man's desire (669). Finally, taken by itself and grounded as it is in the ideal of transcending bodily immanence, Beauvoir's genuine love is based on the same kind of anti-body logic and distancing from the other as Sartre's, and so it comes with all of the difficulties that that involves.

There is, however, a second and more interesting path out of woman's overly generous love woven through Beauvoir's analysis. Against the sacrificial generosity born of women's social subordination and against the ideal of authentic love, she proposes a generosity born of flesh. What Beauvoir consistently objects to about ideals of love (including Sartre's, one presumes, and perhaps even her own) is the way they separate consciousness from flesh and seek to protect the self from the other. Love at a distance is a fantasy, she says, and it becomes passionate only when carnally realized (Beauvoir 1972, 654). And the problem with man's approach to desire is that in his effort to maintain self-control, he asks woman to make an object of herself while he hesitates to become flesh (413, 423). Woman, on the other hand, being more often positioned as the body-object as a consequence of man assuming his autonomous subject position at her expense, is more sensitive to the fraudulence of separating subject and object, consciousness and body, spirit and flesh (697). Women, therefore, have less trouble becoming flesh (or women are more "psychosomatic," as Beauvoir sometimes puts it).

While it is questionable whether one can confidently distinguish between men and women on these grounds, at least in any essential sense, it is reasonable to suggest that insofar as ideals of love (such as Sartre's) deny the body and that of the other, this is a denial without ontological foundation. On the basis of the impossibility of denying the body, Beauvoir moves to a more general formula for the possibility of erotic generosity. By a mutual generosity of body and soul, I can become flesh through the other's body and achieve a dynamic, ecstatic unity where I move beyond myself without negating the other's alterity (Beauvoir 1972, 422). By flesh, Beauvoir cannot mean the corpse-like flesh that Sartre distinguishes from the body in situation. She does not seem to hold to this distinction. Becoming flesh does not abolish the situation, nor therefore the social, as it does for Sartre. Rather, it *creates* the situation by, as Beauvoir puts it, abolishing the singularity of the moment, of oneself and the other (417).[6] For Beauvoir, the erotic encounter, and its "freedom," is not about self-control or body integrity. On the contrary, it is about the "body at risk," as Debra Bergoffen puts it (1997, 158). The body at risk is a generous body, a body that is opened to the other. And this erotic generosity is creative in transforming the other's embodied situation, and hence existence, through a self-metamorphosis that, if we set aside Beauvoir's motif of unity, does not reduce the other to the self. Becoming flesh is a project directed toward and beyond the other, a giving without calculation that nevertheless gets something in return through the future possibilities it opens.

In finding something generous in the erotic encounter, Beauvoir is gesturing toward an ontology that, while intertwined with Sartre's, challenges his individualism and anti-body logic. She puts this ontology most succinctly as follows:

> The erotic experience is one that most poignantly discloses to human beings the ambiguity of their condition; in that they are aware of themselves as flesh and as spirit, as other and as subject. (Beauvoir 1972, 423)

While Sartre insists, with little justification, that in my concrete relations with others I am either flesh, without any possibilities at all, or transcendent consciousness that leaves its old body behind, Beauvoir, at least here, questions this distinction. And because, for Sartre, relations with others are based on objectification, I am only aware of being *either* an independent subject or a dependent object. While, strictly speaking, I am always both subject and object, Sartre's descriptions of concrete relations suggests that, for him, I cannot live both at the same time nor can I stand for a threat to my independent subjectivity. Beauvoir on the other hand, from her discussion of freedom in *The Ethics of Ambiguity* (1994), suggest that the posture of independent subjectivity is not only a pretense lived at the expense of others upon whom I in reality depend, but also it is a perversion of freedom (Beauvoir 1994, 63).[7] For Beauvoir, I am for-myself as a consequence of being-for-others, rather than the converse. Hence, the freedom of self-realization through projects depends on the freedom of others and so must be directed toward that end (60, 70–72). Therefore, a generous passion does not belong to one who seeks to protect her subject position, nor can it be directed toward one who claims absolute independence (66–67). Generosity belongs to those who would be opened to others without viewing the other's alterity, hence their capacity to transform one's own existence, as necessarily having "hostile implications" (Beauvoir 1972, 422).

On the basis of the ambiguity of our condition, rather than some as yet unrealized egalitarian ideal, Beauvoir also questions the assumption that one is either simply dominant or submissive in an erotic encounter and, therefore, that one can separate "positive" from "negative" feelings in a way that Jeffreys would like. In her discussion of masochism and its equation with femininity, Beauvoir suggests that attributing erotic value to pain does not necessarily imply submission or a masochistic acceptance of absolute alienation and servitude (Beauvoir 1972, 418–20). Nor is inflicting pain exclusively masculine or a sadistic attempt to destroy the other by possessing the other as inert flesh. Rather, she argues, pain always accompanies "bodies that delight to be bodies for the joy they give each other" (418). This is the pain of transfiguration inherent to the generous erotic encounter: the pain of tearing away from self, as Beauvoir puts it; the pain of moving beyond oneself through the other and the "bending" (rather than destruction) of the other that this movement involves. Sex is not safe. Not, as Sartre would have it, because sex necessitates the subordination of the self to the other, and not because it shuts down possibilities in the passivity of flesh. On the contrary, sex is not safe precisely insofar as it opens the self to indeterminate possibilities through exploiting the ambiguity of being a body-for-itself-for-others.

None of this abandons consideration of women's social and economic subordination to men. Beauvoir is aware, for example, that insofar as our social situation promotes man as the subject and woman as other, a woman is in danger of feeling herself positioned as object in an erotic encounter with a man, at the expense of her subjectivity (Beauvoir 1972, 423). However, "passivity is an equivocal concept" and, provided that the relation is consensual (understood in terms discussed in chapter 2), a woman always has the power of retaining the ambiguity of being both subject and object, however submissive she may appear to the outsider (419). Beauvoir's second important qualification about the social objectification of women is the suggestion that "the very difficulty of [the woman's socially subordinate] position protects her from the traps into which the male readily falls; he is an easy dupe of the deceptive privileges accorded him by his aggressive role" (423). That is, because a woman, as a consequence of the social situation, is only too aware that she is for-herself only by being for-others then she is less likely to be deceived into assuming absolute independence from others. Such absolute independence is a posture that denies the ambiguity and therefore the generosity of existence, and in doing so it not only denies the other's possibilities but also cuts off one's own. Beauvoir thinks that just as it would be a mistake for women to affirm images of absolute subordination, so it would be an error to aspire toward this deceptive autonomy. While becoming flesh through the other's body may be unsafe for the possibilities of moving beyond oneself that it opens, feigning independence, whether through a fantastic love or through self-control and body integrity in sex, would be counter-productive for the possibilities that it closes off.

In presenting the possibility of erotic generosity in this way, I have skirted around the contradictions and difficulties present in Beauvoir's account.

Hers is plagued by an ambivalence toward the body, particularly women's bodies, that, as I have indicated, is present in her idea of "genuine love" and that, as others have argued, pervades her whole philosophy.[8] However, to the extent that she does point to a generosity of flesh, this indicates an ontology that departs from Sartre's individualism and from a Hegelian ideal of unity and that moves beyond the anti-body logic of both.[9] Insofar as she has a different understanding of alienation and of the role of the body in sexuality and other relations, Beauvoir does not so much betray a debt to Lacanian psychoanalysis, as Toril Moi argues, but has some common ground with Merleau-Ponty.[10] While her generosity toward Sartre seems to have no bounds, in suggesting as she does that everything she says is already in his work, her generosity toward Merleau-Ponty is of the less sacrificial kind. Both lend to and borrow from the work of the other in raising the possibility of a generosity of flesh.

For Merleau-Ponty, this lending to and borrowing from the bodies of others is a generosity lying not just at the core of the erotic encounter but at the heart of existence itself (Merleau-Ponty 1962).[11] Merleau-Ponty shares Sartre's idea that we encounter others as a lived body in situation for-itself-for-others.[12] But, contrary to Sartre, Merleau-Ponty, for reasons discussed in chapter 3, holds that we do not exist as a singular body that has its world by the objectifying activities of a transcendent consciousness. I am not a singular body, because I am for-myself by being first of all with and for other lived bodies. And rather than consciously transcending my body by objectifying the other, the relation between these bodies is one of prereflective intertwining of body schemas. It is in this intertwining of flesh that Merleau-Ponty finds the kind of ambiguity of existence upon which I think Beauvoir's erotic generosity relies.[13]

The other is my mirror in the sense that it is through the other's body that I am aware of my difference: through the tilt of the other's head, the touch of the other's hand, the look in the other's eye. But the same mirror confuses my body and the other's: by mimesis and transitivism I tilt *my* head, touch *my* hand, and look at *my*self and cannot easily tell the difference between what I live and what the other lives (Merleau-Ponty 1964a, 145–48). So, for Merleau-Ponty, I live my body outside of myself through the mirror space of the other's body. But in contrast to Beauvoir's ideal of unity with the other and without resorting to Sartre's individualism, Merleau-Ponty holds that, in this intertwining, neither body is reducible to the other. "There is thus a system (my visual body [as it appears to others], my

introceptive body [as I live it], the other [as I perceive them]), which establishes itself in the child, never so completely as in the animal but imperfectly,
with gaps" (Merleau-Ponty 1964a, 135). "Syncretic sociability" is what
Merleau-Ponty calls this system of intercorporeal subjectivity "with gaps"
(141).[14] It is by this ambiguity of intercorporeality, where alterity is maintained and existence is transformed through "syncretic sociability," that I
affect and am affected by others, that I engage in projects and am open to
possibilities (118). It is also on the basis of this ambiguity of intercorporeality,
where my carnal existence is given to and through the other's body, that we
fall in love and that existence is given its erotic dimension.

Merleau-Ponty, therefore, unlike Sartre and perhaps Beauvoir, does not
think love or sexual desire is any different in structure to personal existence
in general (Merleau-Ponty 1962, 169). The kind of indeterminate self-transformation through the other's body that Beauvoir seems to reserve for
becoming flesh in the erotic encounter is, for Merleau-Ponty, common to
all projects.[15] I cannot exist otherwise than by risking my body integrity in
an ambiguous situation, and freedom is nothing more or less than this
(Merleau-Ponty 1962, 439–40, 455–56). The pleasure and pain of both love
and the sexual encounter lie in the way that this risk becomes explicit.
While sex may involve being more absorbed in the experience of one's body
than in other projects, this does not imply a state of objectness that severs
ties with the world, the other, or future possibilities.[16] On the contrary, the
corporeal self is opened to a different future through love and sex because
of the ambiguity of being both subject and object, autonomous and dependent simultaneously in relation to the other. Or, as Merleau-Ponty puts it,
both love and the sexual experience play such an important role in human
life, because they provide an "opportunity, vouchsafed to all and always
available," to acquaint oneself with the ambiguity of existence (1962, 167).
Hence, neither love or the sexual encounter poses a necessary threat to one's
freedom to constitute existence, and the generosity of both rests on maintaining the ambiguity of being caught within and opened to the body of
the other without the aim or achievement of unity, entrapment, or self-
possession.[17] As intercorporeal generosity maintains alterity and ambiguity in
the possibilities it opens, it is not based on an ideal of mutual exchange
between equals. There is a reciprocity of giving, but not reciprocity in the
content of what is given, and generosity is only possible if neither sameness
or unity is assumed as either the basis or the goal of an encounter with

another. In sum, conceiving of erotic generosity requires abandoning the anti-body logic, the individualism, and the ideal of mutual exchange between equals (if this implies either unity or sameness) that ground safe-sex discourse.

While erotic generosity can transform existence, I am not suggesting that it can liberate us from ourselves or from social representations of sexual difference and sexuality. Nor am I denying that sex can be violent or a violation of being. Taken by itself, Merleau-Ponty's description of "The Body in Its Sexual Being" does not take into consideration feminist concerns about nonconsensual sex or the effects of the social objectification of women on the sexual encounter. Taken by itself, Merleau-Ponty's discussion of sexuality could be viewed as reproducing rather than accounting for the relation between the socially based differential treatment of the sexes and the body in its sexual being.[18] However, elsewhere, Merleau-Ponty, in his account of the social genesis of the body subject, does find fault with the way the ambiguity, and hence the generosity, of intercorporeal existence is reduced through the social representation of sexual difference: through the treatment of women as absolutely Other in relation to men (an idea he attributes to Beauvoir), or through the assumption that all individuals are the same (Merleau-Ponty 1964a, 103–06). Such "psychological rigidity" is a kind of parsimony that closes off the other's possibilities in direct proportion to the reduction of ambiguity involved. Through this suggestion, combined with Merleau-Ponty's critique of Sartre's model of freedom, it is possible to begin to account for the effects of sociality on sexuality, for why the sexual encounter may transform but not liberate existence and for the circumstances under which sex would be a violation of being.

As discussed in chapter 3, for Merleau-Ponty, the corporeal self is constituted in relation to others who are already social beings (Merleau-Ponty 1964a, 141-55), and the kind of body conducts we develop undergo a process of "sedimentation" (1962, 441). Hence, each of us develops a habitual way of patterning existence, including its erotic dimension, and the character of this patterning depends on the social and institutional setting in which our embodiment, and hence our world, is constituted. Insofar as sexual difference is a body performance and to the extent that women are socially objectified more than men, this will be reflected in differences in body comportment and sexuality.[19] But given that, in the constitution of the body-subject, alterity is maintained in the synchronic relation to the other, women's erotic styles will be multifarious despite any apparent patterns in comportment along the lines of sexual difference. And even though women may be sexually objectified more than men, this does not necessarily destine women to sexual passivity or submissiveness. The most we can conclude about the relation between social representations of sexual difference and personal erotic existence is that while freedom is the indeterminate self-transformation through a generous relation to the world of the other's body, because I am from the start outside myself and open to the world, my freedom to be open to a particular project, including a particular sexual encounter, is limited by my social history and, in the wake of this, my bodily tolerance to the present situation (Merleau-Ponty 1962, 455–56). This history is what I am in the process of what I become as I plunge into the present.

While I will take up the issue of the relation between social norms and affectivity in more detail in the next chapter, there are at least two provisional points to be made from this account of the relation between sociality and sexuality. The first is that, contrary to what I have called new liberation discourses, sex does not liberate existence. While any particular situation we find ourselves in is ambiguous and open, it will tend to call up "specially favored modes of resolution" (Merleau-Ponty 1962, 441–42). We cannot escape what we have been altogether because, for Merleau-Ponty at least, we never leave our old body behind. Second, a sexual encounter can involve a violation of being if it overruns the field of the other's freedom. Sex is never safe if safety means securing one's body integrity. But then nor is any project involving a generosity of flesh, that carnal giving and trans-formation of oneself through the other's flesh that lie at the foundation of human existence. Yet to the extent that sex can be a violation of being does not rest on the degree of domination or submission involved. As Beauvoir's discussion of erotic generosity suggests, these are equivocal concepts in consensual erotic relations. Nor does violation rest on the ratio of becoming flesh implied. If this were the case, we would, on the basis of Merleau-Ponty's ontology, violate the other and ourselves in every encounter. Rather, whether, how, and with whom we are generous depends on the tolerance that our carnal style has to the situation and to the body we encounter (454). What you can tolerate, what you find erotic, the field of your freedom, is stamped with the social history of your existence, and this may not be to another's taste. This history is an indeterminate field that is all too easily overlooked by a parsimonious stranger. Yet it marks what you are, and if another disregards it, he or she violates your being. That the violator may not notice or may even deny his or her appropriation of the other is a function of what Beauvoir would call "the deceptive privileges" accorded to him or her by his or her posture of independence, a function of what Merleau-Ponty would call "psychological" and corporeal rigidity. This privilege and rigidity foster a parsimonious relation to the world that denies the ambiguity of existence in treating the other as being there for the taking in one's own terms.

Granting limits to erotic generosity in this way effectively extends the concepts of violation and nonconsent beyond domination and submission in sex and particularizes the same concepts in terms of the specificity of a person's social, intercorporeal history. This is a necessary move, and not just because "domination" and "submission" can be consensual and hence without violation. Conversely, it also helps account for why a person can feel violated to the core of his or her being (through verbal abuse or physical intimidation, for example) in situations where to others he or she may appear open to anything at all and hence in situations that an outside observer may not consider sexual or serious.

By questioning the anti-body logic and individualism of safe-sex discourse, it is possible to resurrect the sexual encounter from its negative philosophical associations without resorting to the rhetoric of liberation or ignoring the problem of sexual violence. While saying yes to sex does not liberate one's existence, the discourse of safe-sex, as I have outlined through radical feminism and Sartre's existentialism, is inherently conservative. For just as violation amounts to reducing the ambiguity and generosity of existence and hence the other's possibilities, so does an ideal of absolute independence, mutual exchange, self-control, and body integrity.

FIVE

AFFECTIVITY AND SOCIAL POWER: FROM MELANCHOLIA TO GENEROSITY

WE MAY WELL REJECT the old idea of the body as a mechanism that weighs us down and with it the idea of a natural affectivity that is brought under the domain of the social through the taming force of reason. But in the wake of this rejection, the question of the relation between affectivity and social power remains an issue. In chapter 4, I proposed, through Merleau-Ponty's early work, that in the mode of erotic sensibility, affectivity arises through the ambiguity and generosity of intercorporeality, a generosity that transforms existence. I also briefly considered how social norms may condition the limits of erotic generosity. Here the aim is to take this consideration farther with reference also to Merleau-Ponty's later work on perception and by opening up the consideration of the affective dimension of corporeal generosity beyond what we usually take to be erotic or sexual. The question that remains to be addressed is this: If, as I have suggested, the corporeal generosity that constitutes and transforms personal identity and difference is not only nonvolitional but also affective, how can the affectivity of intercorporeality be both conditioned by but thwart the social norms and prohibitions that subject us and devalue difference? Is this affectivity social or antisocial, or something in between? This anger that arises from a dark glance of the eye; this sadness that moves me at the center of a joke; this joy that overwhelms me with the smell of the mundane; this wanting that holds me to the sound of a voice; this affectivity where I am given to the field of the other.

If this affectivity were constant and predictable, we might be satisfied with Foucault's thesis that social power works through me, disciplining and shaping carnal existence so that what I feel is an effect of normative mechanisms that regulate all of our lives (Foucault 1979). Or, if this affectivity would only settle on objects at a distance, we could accept Freud's idea that affectivity is the displacement of cathectic energy from a repressed idea to an external example, a thwarting of the reality principle that has instituted the unconscious and so my alienation from the world. But in both models, while granting the body is a social product, affectivity is explained in individualistic terms: as a second order vehicle of the workings of social power that sets the individual in place (in the case of Foucault), or as the adversary to that process (in the case of Freud). In both models, affectivity extends across the border that already separates us from our objects to either maintain that border in a socially recognizable and calculable manner (in the case of Foucault) or to partially dissolve it through a slight of hand (in the case of Freud).

With Foucault and Freud, we can explain how affectivity, as a product of social power, haunts the way we think and act without us even noticing, and with Freud, and to a lesser extent Foucault, we can account for those affective moments when we seem to lose ourselves completely. But it seems to me that I am hardly ever together enough in the first place to bring off Foucault's docility, the not noticing that is the product of a power that individualizes as it regulates. And I am hardly ever together enough to run Freud's object-cathexis, the dissolving of borders that would reduce me to a melting moment. I could be the exception, but I doubt it. I am pathologically punctual, as Foucault might have it, but in a way that sometimes annoys me; I can go weak at the knees, in Freudian terms, but still grasp at something to stop myself from falling. For the most part, affectivity seems to emerge in ambiguous situation, social but casual, neither as a vehicle of nor a challenge to my individuality, but in strokes, as a corporeality brushes with a world that it is neither a seamless product of, nor a stranger to.

At issue here, in the relation between affectivity and sociality, is the extent to which social power, whether through stimulation or repression, succeeds in individualizing the body so that affectivity would be understood as either a product of that process or its undoing. Judith Butler takes up this issue in *The Psychic Life of Power* (1997) and, through compelling re-readings of Hegel, Nietzsche, Althusser, Freud, and Foucault, she settles for both. Of particular relevance here is the way she combines Foucault's model of power with Freud's model of repression to account for the formation of individual agents whose desire is at the same time the product of normative mechanisms and the agent of their undoing. While refuting individualism in the end, Butler does allow it to take hold of her account of psyche formation. To this extent and insofar as individual sexuality becomes her focus as the exemplary product and vehicle of power, she misses too much, I will argue, about the dynamics of affective and social life. While Merleau-Ponty does not elaborate on an explicit theory of power in relation to affectivity, his account of body motility and perception in *Phenomenology of Perception* (1962) (and his later idea of flesh) does challenge the individuality apparent in these other approaches.[1] For that reason I find that he has something to give an account of the relation between affectivity and social power, and so he has something to offer a politically sensitive account of the generosity of intercorporeal existence.

The sketch I offer begins with the body in its sexual being, not because either Merleau-Ponty or I think that sexuality should hold the monopoly in a theory of affectivity, but because Freud and Foucault do. And so, it would seem, does Judith Butler.

At the heart of her story of psyche formation, in the chapter entitled "Melancholy Gender/ Refused Identification," Butler adapts Freud's concept of melancholia for an account of social reproduction where loss at an individual level can be said to result in the formation of "melancholic" sexualities and identities and in the reproduction of "melancholic" social structures. In "Mourning and Melancholia," Freud describes melancholia as a psychic formation, characterized by dejection, self-loathing, and disinterest, that arises as a result of disavowing, and therefore failing to mourn, the loss of either a loved person or an ideal (Freud 1957). In later qualifications (through "The Ego and the Id"), where he recognizes the ego as a bodily ego, Freud broadens the application of melancholia to ego formation in general by suggesting that the lost object is incorporated as part of the ego, "object-cathexis is replaced by an identification," and by noting how "typical this process is" (Freud 1961, 28). Butler takes up these thoughts and suggests that renouncing or losing a sexual or love object "becomes possible only on the condition of a melancholic . . . incorporation," so that "the lost object continues to haunt and inhabit the ego as one of its constitutive identifications," and attachment to the object is retained in the form of love and aggression directed against oneself (Butler 1997, 134).

Butler is less interested in the constitutive effects of love relations gone wrong than she is in the operation of social power in structuring individual identity and agency. Hence, the losses she attends to are not so much those objects we have had but those possibilities foreclosed by social prohibitions and conventions. The loss of this kind that she thinks governs our contemporary culture is not incestual, as Freud would have it, but the possibility of homosexual attachment. While retaining her earlier idea that gender identity is a body performance subject to disruption through reiteration (Butler 1990), which I have discussed in some detail in chapter 3, Butler adds consideration of how the disavowal and repudiation at the heart of melancholia organize this performance (Butler 1997, 145). She argues that, as a result of social prohibitions, heterosexual gender identities (and homosexual identities, for that matter)[2] are melancholic constructions.

> [A] masculine gender is formed from the refusal to grieve the masculine as a possibility of love; a feminine gender is formed (taken on, assumed) through the incorporative fantasy by which the feminine is excluded as a possible object of love, an exclusion never grieved, but preserved through heightened feminine identification. (Butler 1997, 146)

Heterosexual gender identities, in short, "form themselves through renouncing the *possibility* of homosexuality, a foreclosure which produces both a field of heterosexual objects and a domain of those whom it would be impossible to love" (Butler 1997, 146). The social prohibition of homosexuality "prompts a melancholic identification," so that homosexuality is preserved as it is renounced (142) through the "internalization of the ungrieved and ungrievable homosexual cathexis" (139). This renunciation, then, this disavowed repudiation, becomes the vehicle of desire, "becomes the aim and vehicle of satisfaction" (143), and structures agency in the form of "moral reflexivity," self-beratement, and guilt (182).

That melancholia, characterized by an internalized object-cathexis in the form of a self-berating psyche, could explain the features of a socially constituted sexual identity has already been foreshadowed by Butler earlier in her book. By adapting Foucault's model of the relation between power and the body, Butler offers the thesis that subjection to power involves the internalization of social norms; this process of internalization forms the psyche ("*fabricates the distinction between interior and exterior life*"), and this formation is equivalent to the emergence of reflexivity, the capacity to take the self as an object, which opposes and transforms the desire, power, and norms that constitute it (Butler 1997, 19, 22). To this she adds Freud's model of repression with the qualification that the agent that emerges from subjection, to social prohibitions on sexual aims and objects, finds satisfaction in the renunciation of tendencies that had previously brought libidinal gratification, so that "libido is not absolutely negated through repression, but rather becomes the instrument of its own subjection" (79). It is with this Foucauldian take on Freud, that melancholia (where reflexivity takes the form of self-beratement and therefore self-regulation) becomes exemplary, for Butler, of identity formation in general. And with a Freudian take on Foucault, social prohibitions on sexuality become the exemplary vehicles, for Butler, of the operation of social power, and sexual identity becomes its most notable product.

While retaining the basis of Freud's model of melancholia as an object-cathexis internalized through ambivalent identification and repudiation, Butler departs from Freud's claim that melancholia consists of a disinterested withdrawal from the social realm (Butler 1997, 167, 180). On the contrary, for Butler, melancholia consists of the institution and maintenance of the social at the expense of psychic life: the power that subjects the individual through normative conventions is transformed into the power of agency in the form of renunciation (143); power stimulates as it prohibits; state power in the form of prohibitions and conventions is rendered "invisible—and effective—as the ideality of conscience" (191). Social conventions, however, are not reproduced exactly in this process. Butler applies her idea, developed in *Gender Trouble*, that identity is disrupted through its reiteration, to her analysis of power in *The Psychic Life of Power* (1997, 12–13, 93, 145–47). Just as identity undergoes a change in signification through a change in context (a "perpetual displacement constitutes a fluidity of identities that suggests an openness to resignification and recontextualization" (Butler 1990, 138)), so does the power that constitutes identity. Understood in terms of the unstable structure of reiteration, the power that constitutes the subject is transformed when "taken up and reiterated in the subject's 'own' acting" (Butler 1997, 12–14). Still, despite this potential for disruption and transformation, the subject would seem to become attached to the conventions by which she or he is subjected insofar as psyche formation is melancholic.[3] The impact of the foreclosure of love and sexual objects on personal identity formation in turn reproduces a culture of "heterosexual melancholy" where hetero-sexuality, homophobia, and sexism spill out from agents driven by guilt and self-beratement. Melancholia, as an effect and vehicle of power, characterized by the disavowal of unlived and ungrieved possibilities for love and sexual desire, governs our affective life without us even noticing.

Without denying that losing an attachment one has lived through will impact on the conduct of one's life, Merleau-Ponty would want to ask how possibilities that remain in effect unlived could have consequences of such determinate and tragic proportions. And before this he would ask how object-cathexis could explain what it already assumes: the formation of an individual with objects, ideal or real, possible or actual, external or internal, that it can cathect. While not directly addressing the first question, Butler does attend to the second by suggesting that the turning away from the object that initiates melancholia "produces the divide between ego and object, the internal and external worlds that it appears to presume" (Butler 1997, 170). Still, what is produced is an *individual*: an interiority with exter-nal and internal objects and traces of objects (including an ego of lost possibilities), that are identified with and cathected (173–75). For Merleau-Ponty, on the other hand, it is because the body is *not* closed in on itself and alienated from the stuff of the world that life has its affective dimension. And the perception that characterizes this corporeal dehiscence of Being, which is always affective (and sometimes erotic), does not take the form of objec-tification (neither as object-cathexis or its sublimated forms). Only a body not caught in its world would have objects to consider, identify with, inter-nalize, and renounce, but then such objectification by a personal ("autono-mous") self would involve a retrospective withdrawal from the interworld of perception that is its condition (1962, 352–54). And for this body that attends to objects, the affective and erotic structure of perception would have been reduced (156).[4]

Butler does concede, by occasional qualification, that "phenomeno-logically there are many ways of experiencing gender and sexuality that do not reduce to" the rigid melancholic structure she proposes (Butler 1997,

136). She suggests, for example, through Leo Bersani, that perhaps "only the decentred subject is available to desire" (149) and argues, toward the end of *The Psychic Life of Power,* for a more open, intersubjective model of identity: as melancholia produces interiority through the internalized cathexis of the trace of the lost object, then the ego is always other than itself and its acts exceed the bounds of its "autonomy" (195–97). However, she views this excessive openness not as suggesting a model of the relation between affectivity and sociality that would challenge her own (Freud's and Foucault's) but as a solution to the rigidity of melancholic individualism that she claims is already in place. Melancholic sexualities and the sociality that sustains them can be undone, she suggests, by taking advantage of the tenuous and excessive structure of the melancholic psyche: by avowing rather than disavowing those lost possibilities; by acting out ambivalence instead of sustaining oneself through identification with a particular kind of sexuality (which would only serve to strengthen the structure of repudiation by reinforcing the disavowed loss of other possibilities); and "by forfeiting that notion of autonomy" in remembering the "trace" of the incorporated other in oneself (150, 196).

This is a big ask for an individual if, as Butler argues, the individual is formed, sustained, and affectively driven by that which it is asked to give up. But what if giving up autonomy and identificatory cathexis was not a solution to melancholy but a primordial condition of sensibility? What if this giving is not so much an option open to an individual but a generosity that marks the intersubjective and carnal basis of affective life? What if libido is not a ball of energy with a definite aim and object that links the other to me but, as suggested in chapter 4, the expression of a corporeality already opened to a world? This is how Merleau-Ponty characterizes the body in its sexual being and affectivity in general: the expressive operation of a body that knows nothing of a division between self and world or between the expression and what is expressed.[5] For him, sexuality and existence are "interfused" (Merleau-Ponty 1962, 169), and experience is affective, because perception and motility belong together in an intercorporeal world (1962, 157, 357); existence is endowed "with its degree of vitality" (157), because "the visible world and the world of my motor projects are . . . parts of the same Being" (Merleau-Ponty 1964b, 162).[6] Sensibility (perception and affectivity) does not forge a link between the body and its world and indeed would not be possible if the body was not already caught in the fabric of the sensible (163). Sensibility would not be possible if I were not already given to the openness of being and if, therefore, there were not already a trace of the other in me.

This trace of the other is not left by the incorporation of an object, nor is the trace of the other something to be cathected in an attempt to make up for its loss. Interiority, for Merleau-Ponty, is not characterized by self-reflection, nor by an (unconscious) internalized object-cathexis. Interiority, for Merleau-Ponty, is primordially carnal reflexivity, corporeal self-awareness that emerges "through confusion" "between the seeing and the seen, between touching and the touched, between one eye and the other, between hand and hand" (163). In chapter 3 I discussed this intercorporeal "confusion" in terms of the constitution of carnal identity and difference. The point here is that this intercorporeal field is also the "space" of affectivity and perception, of sensibility. I perceive and feel, because I am perceived and felt by the world of the other, because I am given in my corporeal difference to a common physical and social world of other beings who see and touch me (Merleau-Ponty 1962, 360). It is in this interworld, this "open circuit" established between the perceiving body and its world, this mirror-space of ambiguity, generosity, and intertwining, that the spark of sensibility, of perception, of affectivity is lit (Merleau-Ponty 1964b, 163, 168).[7] This body that I am moves, and the world takes a significant shape as my project establishes an internal carnal echo of the corporeal presence of things (164). So I feel and see in the space of the mirror that is the stuff of the world "outside" my body as my carnality moves into it; but, at the same time, my body is transformed as it assumes segments and gestures from the world that I perceive (168). And this sensibility is done with style— "perception stylizes" (Merleau-Ponty 1964c, 54). What I see and feel carries a trace of prior intertwinings of my body and the world, as an effect of the "sedimentation," discussed in chapter 4, what I see and feel is an "emblem of a way of inhabiting a world, of handling it, and of interpreting it by a face as by clothing, by agility of gesture as by inertia of the body—in short, the emblem of a certain relationship to being" (ibid.). The body thus expresses existence through sensibility, not as a sign of an inner (repressed or conscious) idea, or as copy of an outer (social) idea or thing. The body expresses existence as it realizes it in the "undividedness of the sensing and the sensed" (Merleau-Ponty 1962, 166; 1964b, 163).

This intercorporeal basis of existence and the stylizing feature of perception also account for any erotic aspect of sensibility. The "paradox of expression" is the "labor of desire" (Merleau-Ponty 1968, 144).[8] That an experience is erotic is not, for Merleau-Ponty, a sign that libido has crossed the border of the body to cathect an object, nor therefore is sexuality the habitual external expression of an unconscious representation, of an unconscious object-cathexis (1962, 168, 413). Rather, as I suggested in chapter 4, a sexual experience arises from the ambiguous structure of the body in situation that characterizes perception in general (167). And erotic perception colors the world in the same manner as perception in general: as it is colored . . . with style . . . between the constituting and the constituted. So if I notice, with pleasure, another's "manner of being flesh" (as a total posture or as hand touching skin), it is because it strikes my carnality as a variation, as a resonating echo, of a manner I possess in my incarnate self-awareness (Merleau-Ponty 1964c, 54). But if the other's manner strikes me at all, it is not as a duplication of the carnal style that I already live: there is always a tension in my experience toward another, and "our situations cannot be superimposed on each other" (Merleau-Ponty 1962, 356).[9] The affectivity that arises as an internal carnal echo of another's conduct may be realized in familiar terms, but only because it is the impact of the other's difference that strikes me, moves me, inspires my carnality, and sets up a resonance in my own corporeal style, so that it becomes impossible to distinguish between what sees and feels and what is seen and felt (Merleau-Ponty 1964b, 165, 167).[10] Sexuality, and affectivity in general, is, like painting, an amplification of tensions, resonances, and metamorphoses that take place in the generous, intercorporeal world of perception.

As for what makes a perception erotic as opposed to something more banal, it is almost impossible to tell: "[T]here is interfusion between sexuality and existence . . . so that it is impossible to determine, in a given decision or action, the proportion of sexual to other motivations" (Merleau-Ponty 1962, 169). However, prohibitions on sexual conduct, aims, and objects, along with other social conventions, do play a part in establishing the horizon of what I see, do and feel. As discussed in chapter 4, because of the intersubjective and ambiguous structure of existence my carnal style has a history that consists of borrowing and transforming gestures from the bodies of others who are already social beings. Hence, my perception is always cultural, and its meaning is not constituted personally (consciously or individually) by me (358). Social conventions and prohibitions, then, do effect erotic style, but not in the form of abstract laws that capture the totality of my being. Ideas do not present themselves as objects to be accepted or

rejected in singular determinate conscious acts or as possibilities to be re-
pudiated and repressed as incorporated unconscious representations (162,
362). The body's relation to the social is inseparable from, and of the same
order as, its relation to the world, not a relation of objectification but of
carnal intertwining prior to any reflexive judgement. What I see, do and feel
is thoroughly saturated by social phenomena that transcend and inform my
carnal style but that "exist only to the extent that I take them up and live
them" (363). Based on Merleau-Ponty's account, then, prohibitions on sexual
conduct come to me through incarnated fragments in situation; through gestures
that condemn by the curl of a lip or through words that shame by timbre and
tone. To the extent that, through sensibility, I make a habit of making these
gestures and their meanings my own, insofar as they impinge on my life
through the bodies of others, I will develop an erotic style that tends to follow
the expected in the distinctive way I pattern the world.

But there is nothing certain or predictable here. Every situation is
open, and meaning is indeterminate. Meaning is indeterminate for Merleau-
Ponty partly because, following Saussure, he claims meaning arises in the
interval between terms (1964c, 42), and partly because, by the same logic
and in a way I have outlined, existence is indeterminate or ambiguous in
its very structure (1962, 169)—meaning arises and is actualized ambiguously
"between" bodies. So a slap on the wrist may signal a prohibition to the
body that delivers it, but not to the body that receives and thereby lives it,
or it can mean something different to that same body in a different situation.
For a social prohibition of homosexuality, for example, to foreclose the
possibility of erotic perception of the conduct of someone of the same sex,
the prohibition would need to be enacted by other bodies consistently
across every possible relevant situation, and the meaning of the original and
subsequent gestures of condemnation would have to be taken up, by the
body to which they are directed, unambiguously and finally in the terms in
which they were intended. To claim the foreclosure of possibilities through
social prohibitions would require belief in an original moment of repression
precipitated by an unambiguous act of condemnation, or in the idea that the
meaning adhering to gestures is determinate and translatable between bodies

without loss, or in the assumption that all body styles are exactly the same.
But, for Merleau-Ponty, social conventions and prohibitions, while thoroughly informing personal existence, do not foreclose possibilities, because
"the meaning of an action does not exhaust itself in the situation that has
occasioned it" (1964c, 72), and because, even if I do turn away from a

possibility as a result of condemnation, once the possibility has been raised, I "do not cease to be situated relatively to it" (1962, 362).

That social meaning, including social norms and prohibitions, is incarnate, ambiguous, and indeterminate can explain the unpredictable and transformative character of affectivity. It can explain, for example, why even the most homophobic of us may find a gesture of a body of the same sex pleasurable or even erotic that would be abhorrent in more familiar surroundings. Or it can explain why a woman who has lived with a man for twenty years may find one day, or every day during that time, that another woman can turn her head. In both cases, carnal reflexivity is the locus of the affect. But the meaning of that affective reflexivity is always ambiguous and cannot be determined definitively, within the event, as either guilty or guilt free or even sexual. Self-conscious reflexivity, what Butler calls conscience, may, but not necessarily, follow the perception. If it does, then it is a retrospective perception of the perception, and not the perception itself: "Between the self that analyses perception and the self which perceives, there is always a distance" (Merleau-Ponty 1962, 43). That moment of conscience may, but not necessarily, be moral, self-berating, and consumed with guilt. If it is, this may, but not necessarily, be because of a history of encounters with bodies that would explicitly condemn the pleasurable or erotic perception at issue. But such self-beratement is just as likely to arise through reflection on current commitments to other bodies, and on one's perception of one's own manner of being that the erotic perception may threaten. Even then, even given the distance between the self that reflects (the moment of conscience) and the self of the erotic perception reflected upon, "[R]eflection never lifts itself out of any situation, nor does the analysis of perception do away with the fact of perception. . . . Reflection is not absolutely transparent to itself, it is always given to itself in an *experience*" (Merleau-Ponty 1962, 43).[11] As an experience, the moment of conscience is, like the erotic perception that it analyzes, informed by a carnal history and its meanings. Hence, the moment of conscience is steeped in sensibility and is therefore also open to a world and to the ambiguity that this implies. Sensibility can and does take on a certain rigidity and defensive manner, as I will demonstrate in the following chapter. But it is fundamentally open and transformative of the self, the other, and the social norms that inform it. And sedimentation of style according to convention is not reducible to a guilty conscience closed in on its lost possibilities, otherwise there would be no affectivity, no living of possibilities, that one could feel guilty about.

None of this suggests that losing someone you *have* lived through will not be lived as loss. For Merleau-Ponty, losing someone you love, someone who has been part of the horizon of your affective world, whether through rejection, prohibition, or death, would be like losing an arm.[12] But in such cases, the loss is not lived as an internalized object-cathexis. A memory, the past, is not an object (Merleau-Ponty 1962, 364). If a loss impacts on my life, what is lost adheres to my body as a trace that is present (162, 413). I live that loss like I live my world, not as a self-sufficient individual in possession of its objects but a carnal opening to being. As that loss is lived like a phantom limb, it is *lived* as loss. And so, even as I live a loss, I never succeed in cutting myself off from the possibilities opened though the generosity of intersubjective life.

The sketch I have offered of the sociality of the body in its affective being is consistent with what Butler suggests about the many ways of experiencing sexuality and identity that do not admit to the melancholic structure that she proposes. But accepting the sketch requires forfeiting the model of the relation between affectivity and social power based on object-cathexis and repression in favor of an account of existence that admits to carnal intersubjectivity, ambiguity, and generosity, not as a solution to the unpleasant effects of the workings of social power but as its very basis. This not only helps account for the surprising, flexible, and transformative character of sensibility without recourse to a natural libido, but it also avoids one problematic consequence of Butler's account: that, even if the individual could admit to his or her failure to recognize the disavowal of losses supposedly structuring his or her erotic life, he or she would still be melancholic and therefore deficient on the basis of social prohibitions (such as thou shalt not kill), which are arguably worth keeping and more fundamental and dramatic than those against particular forms of sexuality.

SIX

SEXUALITY AND THE
CLINICAL ENCOUNTER

I ARGUED IN chapter 5 that sensibility (affectivity and perception) takes place in the intercorporeal world of bodies given to each other. This sensibility is informed by social norms through their incarnation, but it is also transformative of those norms and of the modes of being that they infect. This analysis suggests that normalization (and hence discrimination and prejudice) as well as "resistance" are effected through sensibility and take place in concrete relations "between" bodies, "below" the level of conscious intent, and in terms beyond the explicit ideals of moral and legal discourses. In this chapter I both elaborate and demonstrate this thesis through an analysis of a particular concrete encounter between bodies; an encounter with the body of a stranger in an institutional setting—the clinical encounter.

The clinical encounter is a curious event. Through it our body and our life, that which is most intimate and private, is given to a stranger. It involves an offering that we would more usually reserve for a lover, a mother, or a friend. And through this encounter, a corporeal itinerary that is specific to us becomes generalized, subsumed under a medical discourse known better for its promotion of a universal objective body than for its sensitivity to different ways of being.[1] Given the intimate content of the event, it should not be surprising if the patient's sexuality becomes an issue in the encounter. And given the totalizing tendencies of medical discourse, it should not be surprising that the occasion has arisen for critical examination of the relation between medical discourse and sexuality. Perhaps more than any other single health problem in recent times, HIV-AIDS has provided such an occasion, generating charges of latent prejudices within medical discourse against homosexuality in particular and calls for a more generous and sensitive approach to management of sexuality in the clinic.

Notwithstanding the wealth of critical analysis of the relation between medical discourse and sexuality, not just in the context of HIV-AIDS but also from feminist and other perspectives, little attention has been given to the operation of sexuality or affectivity in general in the clinical encounter itself. It is toward such an account that this chapter is directed. Without abandoning insights about how discourses of medical science constitute and normalize sexuality, I will suggest that there are features of the clinical encounter itself that contribute to the mismanagement of sexuality there. Understanding the encounter in terms of the giving of one's body to a stranger, whose own body seems exempt from scrutiny of the clinical gaze yet is an agent of normalization, may help explain parsimonious aspects of the encounter and why better management of sexuality in the clinic is difficult, despite the best intentions of those involved.

I take sexuality to mean the use (in the sense of both capacity and practice) of pleasure and pain.[2] As I argued in the previous two chapters, sexuality is not the social expression of a more original biological instinct. It is the way a person lives her or his pleasure and pain that presupposes a social existence. Sexuality is not contained within a singular body; it is a feature of sensibility lived through a body given to and open to a world of the other. Yet while open to a world, sexuality, as argued in chapter 5, is not reducible to object-cathexis nor therefore definable in terms of object choice (as categories such as pedophile and heterosexual would suggest); nor is sexuality reducible to a single active or passive aim (as categories such as femme and sadist would imply). While sexuality is indeterminate, outstripping a singular body with a definite aim and object, it is also inseparable from social discourses that would constitute and define it in those terms, as the work of Michel Foucault, among others, suggests.

Foucault's analysis of the deployment of sexuality, the elevation in the nineteenth century of the study of sex to a level of a science, points to the central role that medical science plays in the constitution and normalization of sexuality (Foucault 1980a). In this by now well-known account, he indicates how medicine, in concert with other circulating ideas about proper and improper bodies, is deeply implicated not just in the division of bodies into the healthy and unhealthy but simultaneously into the normal and the perverse. And we need not go past the discourses on HIV-AIDS to illustrate the way in which medical science and sexual politics can converge over bodies to siphon off the guilty from so-called innocent uses of pleasure and pain.[3] But it is important to note that such spectacular connections between sexuality and health do not exhaust the medical delimiting of uses of pleasure. Even my seemingly mundane practice of smoking has been transformed (through the intertwining of medical, legal, and environmental discourses with the ever-ready pointed finger of the passerby) from a relatively insignificant use of pleasure to an anti-social, immoral perversion. The work of medical discourse is pervasive, effecting not just who we exchange fluids with and how, but the course of other pleasures and pains inseparable from our manners of being.

While seemingly ubiquitous, it would be a mistake to view the relation between medical science and sexuality as some kind of conspiracy on the part of the few to control the bodies of the rest. The medical reduction and production of sexuality is often as unwitting as it is powerful and may proceed as much by neglect, say by the assumption that the paralyzed body is devoid of pleasure, as it does by obsessive concern, say for my tar-soaked lungs. It would also be a mistake to view the recipient of medical attention as simply a passive body at the mercy of forces that would rearticulate its pleasures and pains in the interests of propriety. Foucault, through his analysis of the technology of confession, also points to our own complicity in constituting ourselves as the subjects of desire in the face of medical discourse (Foucault 1980a, 58-70). And this occurs most obviously in the clinic itself. After all, there seems a no more appropriate place for us to reflect on our uses of pleasure and to connect these to the pains, leakages, spasms, and paralyses that seem to overtake our body. In attempting to locate the origin of disease, asthma, for example, can become, through our own words, a problem of sexual anxiety. Or, in unfolding our medical history, we may link this broken leg to menopause and the sexuality and osteopathology that this now implies.

In this medical examination we are not simply confessing to an already constituted sexuality and unburdening ourselves of a truth that seems to infect us. Rather, as Foucault points out, we are constituting ourselves as subjects of sexuality in the presence of someone with the authority to make of us what she will:

> [T]he agency of domination does not reside in the one who speaks [the patient] (for it is he who is constrained), but in the one who listens and says nothing [the clinician]; not in the one who knows and answers, but in the one who questions and is not supposed to know. And this discourse of truth finally takes effect, not in the one who receives it, but in the one from whom it is wrested. (Foucault 1980a, 62)

The truth of our sexuality is not waiting for exposure in the clinic. Rather, sexuality is constituted through confession, in the body of the spoken word.[4] The clinic, like the confessional in general, incites not just the desire to speak but desire itself. It is a place where pleasures and pains are articulated, formed, and transformed; where a self is dissolved, dissembled, and assembled. And the agent of production is not just the clinician (as some would have it) who, as the executor of medical discourse, examines and therefore objectifies and normalizes the body. The agent of production is also the patient who would have her pleasures and pains represented, to her satisfaction, in the total picture of her medical life.

Since Foucault and others have pointed to medical science as a place where knowledge and sexual politics meet a body, it is no longer possible to simply assume that we encounter medical discourse (whether through television or in the clinic) with our sexuality entirely intact, or that we leave it unscathed. In the meeting, sexuality is reconstituted and normalized with certain uses of pleasure and pain ignored, condemned, transformed, or abandoned.

This kind of analysis has been with us for at least twenty years and has certainly left its mark. After at least two decades of feminist criticism of the medical normalization of bodies,[5] of the way women's health is measured against a male standard, it is more likely that breast cancer, for example, will be treated as a serious infringement on a woman's use of pleasure. And there is some chance that menopause will not be viewed simply as a failure of womanhood, as a lack of usable pleasure that could be rectified by anti-depressants. (Although, as some will be quick to point out, hormone replacement therapy, which has superseded antidepressants as the usual treatment for menopausal "symptoms," does little to shift the old assumptions.) Or, after at least one decade of criticism of the medical discourse on HIV-AIDS, particularly from the gay community, there is perhaps a better chance that a person can live with HIV-AIDS rather than die with the "stigmata of their guilt," to coin Simon Watney's phrase (Watney 1987, 78). In some respects, twenty years of sustained and vigorous critique of the problematic assumptions of medical discourse have produced a generation of consumers and some practitioners attuned to, and critical of, the role that medicine plays in the production and normalization of sexuality.

Yet despite, and perhaps because of, this heightened awareness, there is much to suggest that we are far from dealing with sexuality in the clinic to the satisfaction of all concerned. For the patient, the management of sexuality in the clinic is at best clumsy and sometimes parsimonious with the effect that the clinical encounter is often disconcerting and sometimes alarming. From the patient's perspective, sexuality can become a problem in one of two ways. Either the clinical environment is sexualized by the clinician when there seems no need, or the question of sexuality is elided or evaded when it would seem to matter.

I offer two examples of the first kind of problem.[6] In 1975, Jenny chooses a general practitioner at random to obtain a prescription for her asthma medication. The doctor, a pleasant enough man around age sixty, takes Jenny's blood pressure before returning to his position behind the desk. He then leans back in his chair and asks her three questions: does she masturbate, does she sleep with boys, does she sleep with girls. Jenny is so shocked that the best she can do is squeeze out a "no" in reply to each question in turn. Satisfied with the answers, and commenting that it is gratifying to see that a young woman can still be embarrassed in these times of loose morals, the doctor complies with Jenny's request and writes out a prescription.

We could dismiss this example as extreme, as an isolated incident occurring at a time when liberties were taken that would no longer be tolerated. However, while unnecessary sexualization of the clinical encounter may no longer be so crude, isolated cases of sexual assault aside, it is no less apparent, at least from the patient's perspective. It is now 1995, and Claudia enters a clinic seeking a prescription for her asthma medication. She knows what she needs, and this is all she wants. The doctor, a woman around

Claudia's age and unfamiliar with her case, asks the usual two or three questions about Claudia's medical history before happily meeting her request. But as she is writing the prescription, the doctor asks if there anything else that Claudia would like. Even though Claudia replies "no" several times, the doctor persists: did Claudia realize, for instance, that a simple course of hormone therapy could eliminate her problem of facial hair. Claudia is as mortified by this question in 1995 as Jenny was by those asked of her in 1975.

We could give this doctor the benefit of the doubt by suggesting that she is one of the new generation taught, at our request, to treat, not just the symptom but the patient as a whole person. Perhaps in her world, facial hair on a woman is a problem, a source of anxiety about sexuality and sexual difference. Not in Claudia's world. She has lived with her hair forever; she likes it, as does her partner and friends; it is inseparable from her body given to a world, it is inseparable from her use of pleasure, yet no more relevant to this visit to the clinic than what she had for breakfast. While deeply disturbed at what to her is a challenge to her way of being, Claudia moderates her response, saying only that no, her facial hair is no longer a problem for her, except at times like this, and that the doctor should not assume otherwise given that, if it was a problem she would have already done something about it. Rather than conceding the point, the doctor escalates the stakes, suggesting that, while removal of the hair would normally be advisable, she would simply note in Claudia's records her objections to discussing the issue. Claudia leaves the clinic in despair, regretting her constraint in comparison to the doctor, wishing she had said what to her is obvious: that her own facial hair is no more aberrant than the doctor's severely sculptured eyebrows.

The second, and converse, way in which sexuality can become a problem in the clinic, from the patient's perspective, is in cases where the question of one's own use of pleasure is elided or evaded when it would seem to be the salient point. In 1980, Jael enters a clinic seeking termination of her pregnancy. In order to satisfy the law, it is necessary to first show that continuing the pregnancy would probably result in distress and hardship and second to accept counseling on contraception to prevent a repeat occurrence. Jael can easily meet the first condition and does not need to accommodate the second. Her use of pleasure is such that her usual sexual partner is a woman and in parts of her usual world she would be called a lesbian.

That she finds herself in this clinic of assumed heterosexuality is easily explained: one sexual encounter with an old and trusted male friend, of no lasting significance, at least not to herself or the friend. But to tell the full story, and so properly to prove the need for the termination, would result in as much distress and hardship to Jael's partner, her male friend, and herself, as would continuing the pregnancy. Not only do the relevant facts not sit well with Jael's world, they would be also totally foreign to the counselor she faces. So rather than proving her case beyond doubt, she tells another story more in keeping with the expectations of the clinic and endures the advice about contraception with resignation. The individual is preserved through the art of dissimulation, and she can only be trusted if, to use Nietzsche's words, she fulfills her "duty to lie according to a fixed convention" (Nietzsche 1979, 84).

It is likely that the itinerary of Jael's pleasure and pain would be just as transgressive of convention, both heterosexual and lesbian, now as it was in 1980, and that silence or evasion, both inside and outside the clinic, would be advisable. But while sexuality may exceed convention in this way, where convention is given reductively in terms of a consistent object of desire, it is often not so easy to locate what convention might be, nor therefore to predict the potential to affront its agents. Hence, as the following incident suggests, the impulse to evade, elide, or censor sexuality in the clinic is contingent and unpredictable, as are the effects of this tendency toward self-regulation.

It is 1995. Simone has a problem with anal bleeding and is convinced that she has bowel cancer. But heartened by the discovery, through conversations with friends, that cancer is the unlikely cause, she visits a doctor to have this conclusion confirmed. In the absence of a regular physician, Simone chooses a woman with a reputation among friends for having a good "bedside manner." To assist the doctor, who has admitted to not having the equipment necessary for a proper anal examination, Simone begins to list factors that she thinks are relevant to the case: a prior history of pain from a hernia, although no bleeding; a brief period of constipation prior to the onset of bleeding; no anal penetration. Clearly disturbed at the mention of anal penetration, and before Simone had exhausted her list, the doctor jumps up from her chair, overrides Simone's speech, puts Simone on the table, rubber gloves on herself, and performs a brief examination. While feeling slightly humiliated by the time they return to the desk, Simone does not blame the doctor for her obvious distaste for the procedure. But she is incensed when the doctor washes her hands, not once but three times, while reassuring her that she does not have cancer. And, given the nature of the problem, Simone thinks it strange that a doctor would find mention of anal penetration so disturbing and inappropriate when to her it seems so apt.

These stories of the problematic operation of sexuality in the clinic and of the affectivity it provokes are not particularly spectacular but are noteworthy for that reason. Whether sexuality is evoked unnecessarily or evaded, dissimulation, "misrecognition," confusion, and discomfort are so common that one suspects they are all part and parcel of the clinical encounter itself. But why might this be so? These stories do share features that are consistent with a Foucauldian analysis of the role of medical discourse in the production and normalization of sexuality. It is clear, for example, that in each case the clinician is an agency of domination, a deputy of medical discourse and the conventions it may harbor. As the clinician has the authority to issue a prescription, the knowledge for reassurance and access to technical procedures, then patients must subject themselves to the clinician's questions and interpretations if they are to secure the help they need. And we may agree with Foucault that this game of truth over sexuality seems to take effect in the patient more so than in the clinician, who seems shielded from the medical gaze. Nonetheless, there are indications that disturbing affects are not restricted to the patient and, even there, they are not exclusively in the mode of unification and transformation of pleasures. What Foucault's analysis cannot explain is the extent of dissimulation, agitation, and friction at play in the clinical encounter, nor the way affects are born, not just by the body of the patient but at times by the clinician (Simone's doctor being a case in point). Based on Foucault's account, the constitution of sexuality by medical discourse through the confessional is a much more harmonious and compliant affair than my examples would suggest. In other words, in the absence of a coherent account of resistance to normalization by medical discourse, there is little space for explaining the kinds of collisions that are apparent in the clinical encounter. There also is little space for explaining the surprising, flexible, and transformative features of affectivity, discussed in chapter 5.

Foucault does acknowledge resistance to social normalization of sexuality but without explaining its source, except, as I suggested in chapter 3, with reference to what seems to be a presocial use of pleasure that escapes normalizing regimes. For example, following is one of the few references Foucault makes in *The History of Sexuality, Volume 1* to the possibility of resistance:

> It is the agency of sex that we must break away from, if we aim—through a tactical reversal of the various mechanisms of sexuality—to counter the grips of power with the claims of bodies, pleasures, and knowledges, in their multiplicity and their possibility of resistance. The rallying point for the counterattack against the deployment of sexuality ought not to be sex-desire, but bodies and pleasures. (Foucault 1980a, 157)

Foucault does not explain how such "bodies and pleasures," the "rallying point" against normalization, have escaped the all-pervasive deployment of sexuality in the first place.

However, resorting to a realm of pure bodies and pleasures is not necessary to explain resistance to normalization and, hence, the fractious way in which sexuality is played out in the clinic. There is still another factor to consider. In all of this talk about the body of the patient, its docility as the object of the medical gaze and its stimulation through confession, we seem to have overlooked the body of the clinician. As I argued in chapter 5, we do not encounter social norms in the form of abstract ideas or laws. The clinical encounter is not just an encounter between a singular body (the patient) and the norms of medical discourse in the form of the ear and the pen of the clinician. The clinician may be an agent of medical discourse and therefore an agent of domination, as Foucault suggests, but he or she is also a body. And if sexuality is understood as the uses of pleasure and pain of a body open to a world, and if the clinician is a body, then the clinician's sexuality is also at issue in the clinical encounter. The clinical encounter is an encounter between at least two bodies, two uses of pleasure and pain, two sexualities with different histories. How does the clinician's sexuality figure in the encounter? And how can the meeting of uses of pleasure and pain be better managed?

It does not pay to be coy in characterizing this meeting of bodies: these bodies, if they meet at all, meet through the touch of the medical examination, even when the players stand apart. While everything about the architecture of the clinic (the physician's dwelling behind the desk, the patient's exposure on the table, the location of the physician's plaque on the wall) suggests that only one body examines the other, the examination is in fact contiguous and therefore ambiguous: bodies that touch are also touched. For every eye or hand on skin, there is skin on hand or eye. Every body, including the clinician's, while a subject for itself is also an object for others. For Merleau-Ponty, for example, the person could not be otherwise: I can only touch or see, because I am touched and seen (Merleau-Ponty 1968, 133). I exist for myself in the hands of the other. So while the clinician transforms a de facto situation into medical significance, through examination of the patient, the itinerary of his or her own body conduct is open to the other, rendering the encounter indeterminate and ambiguous. For Merleau-Ponty, this ambiguity, and its attendant affectivity or sensibility, is the essence of existence, and whatever transformations may occur in an encounter can never be eliminated (Merleau-Ponty 1962, 169).

While not reducible to personal existence in general, sexuality, as I argued in chapter 4, has the same ambiguous structure. For Merleau-Ponty, like Foucault, sexuality is not a pure fact, not a bodily instinct hidden behind, and driving, existence, nor a conscious representation at its perimeter. But nor, as Foucault sometimes implies, are there bodies or pleasures exempt from passing through the other and the sociality that this involves. Of erotic perception, Merleau-Ponty says, "through one body it aims at another, and takes place in the world, not consciousness" (Merleau-Ponty 1962, 157). And, he suggests, sexuality occupies such an important place in human life, because sexual experience affords an "opportunity, vouchsafed to all and always available to acquaint oneself with the play of autonomy and dependence," with the ambiguity of corporeal intersubjectivity (167). Sexuality, then, differs from other modes of personal existence, not in structure but in being an explicit indulgence in the pleasure and pain arising from the uncertainty of being caught in the open circuit of ambiguity, generosity, and intertwining characterizing existence and from the metamorphosis that this allows. And, because sexuality shares the ambiguous structure of personal existence and is inseparable from the distinctive way a person patterns and gives meaning to his or her world, it is, as I argued in chapter 5, "impossible to tell, in a given decision or action, the proportion of sexual to other motivations" (169). At the same time, it would not be inconsistent to suggest that whether an encounter could be considered sexual would depend on the extent that sexuality is an explicit theme and on the specific ways in which the bodies involved have lived their affective patterns of existence as sexual.

The clinical encounter, then, shares with both the sexual encounter and personal existence in general the same structure of corporeal generosity, where I am given to the world of the other's body in an indeterminate, ambiguous relation. However, the clinical encounter differs from the sexual encounter in that sexual pleasure is not the dominant theme. As there is no agreement here to indulge in the pleasures and pains of body ambiguity, then any sexual aspect of that ambiguity is less preeminent. Yet the clinical encounter stands out from expressly nonsexual conducts, insofar as the itinerary of pleasures and pains of one body—at least—is explicitly given to the other. And while the other's body, the clinician's, may seem exempt from scrutiny, it is, as I have suggested, implicitly open to the patient. I believe it is because the clinical encounter stands on the cusp between personal existence in general and the sexual experience that it is so often alarming. As I will go on to describe in more detail, it is the opening of one's body to a stranger, whose own body, while apparently invisible, is no less in play, that makes the clinical encounter so often fractious and the play of sexuality there so open to mismanagement.

I am suggesting in the first place that understanding the clinical encounter in terms of an encounter between bodies requires abandoning the idea that human bodies are singular, self-contained entities standing apart from one's agency and apart from others. When engaged in the world, the person, whether acting, observing, doing, or knowing, is not a disembodied thinker. Rather, the person is her or his body, its gestures, movements, and habits, its uses of pleasure and pain. It is as carnal openness to a world that the clinician and the patient orient themselves, incorporate the surrounding field, and engage in the situation. The clinician performs the examination this way. She does not calculate the distance between her body, the stethoscope, and the skin of the patient, and then consciously direct her movements. Rather, her body, its gestures, and its spatial orientation are given to a situation through which the instrument and the other's body become part of her body spatiality.

Perception of the other's body, then, is not the capacity to intellectualize its needs across the gulf that would seem to separate us. All perception, knowing, and understanding is informed by prereflective intertwining of corporeality. Or, as Merleau-Ponty puts it:

> Whether it is a question of another's body or my own, I have no means of knowing the human body other than that of living

it, which means taking up on my own account the drama which is being played out in it, and losing myself in it. (Merleau-Ponty 1962, 198)

On this understanding of an encounter between bodies, the clinician is a body given to a world of the other and immersed within it. And just as sexuality presupposes a social existence and is inseparable from it, being a body immersed in others is not fortuitous; as discussed in chapter 3, it actualizes one's social identity. The capacity to use a stethoscope, for example, is a skill mimetically borrowed from another body. Similarly, Claudia's doctor's discomfort about facial hair is not an arbitrary, conscious representation of uniform significance, but an unease belonging to a body with a tradition of immersion in a world of other female bodies devoid of body hair. In short, the clinician brings to the present encounter not just an abstract medical model of a "normal" body but a history of interlacing with other bodies, skills, gestures, and uses of pleasure and pain, all pregnant with meaning, and all of which inform her carnal style and hence her perception of the situation. And, insofar as the clinician is an agency of domination, her perception of the situation involves living that history through the body of the patient, imposing that history on the other's body, and making it familiar and hence similar to her own.

While as a corporeal subject the clinician operates through the other's body with the absence of singularity that this implies, she is maintained as a separate existence, however, by the feeling of difference from the other. This difference emerges in the first instance because the clinician, while a body-subject with the power of perception, is also a nonthematic "object" for the patient. Through the touch of the patient's skin, the look in her eye, through their gestures and speech, the clinician feels the difference in her own identity. In other words, the constitution of the body subject through the other, while based on possession of the other's body, also involves a sense of a difference between the two. As discussed in chapter 5, this difference between bodies is irreducible, not because of an original or final individuality but because of the ambiguity of coexistence as I have just described it. And the difference is irreducible, not because one body has escaped the deployment of sexuality or the normalizing work of social discourse in general. Rather, it is because, added to this irreducible difference in the present, is the condition that the drama played out in the body of the patient—while perhaps familiar to the clinician in some respects—is of a body with a different history.

This picture of the clinical encounter suggests two immediate points about sexuality under clinical management. First, in order to appreciate the needs of a different body, the clinician's body must have already lived through that experience, or must at least be open to it. It is unrealistic to expect that a particular clinician could be open to every possible body history and every experience of a particular patient, unless we assume that the clinician is a god without a body at all. If the clinician is not a god, then her ability to know the other's body is limited insofar as her social history, and therefore uses of pleasure and pain differ from that of the other. It should not be surprising then that as patients we so often encounter what seems like the shock of the new. We, like Jenny and Jael, manage this by dissimulation or, like Claudia, by refusal. This dissimulation is not a mask, deliberately worn to hide the truth of one's sexuality, but a refusal to open the indeterminate, any more than necessary, to the body of a stranger for his or her final possession. And/or we shop around, but not for a use of pleasure and pain that matches our own. Carnal style is not open to objective analysis, and no list of habits, skills, or sexual preferences would give us a match, however similar to our own that that list of attributes may appear to be. The best we can do is find someone with whom we feel comfortable for no determinate reason. But given that oscillation between dissimulation and familiarity and difference and indistinction is already a feature of the ambiguity of existence, these contributions by the patient bring nothing new to the management of sexuality in the clinic. The medical profession could also manage the problem better by first granting that the clinician is a body. It is this body, including its uses of pleasure and pain, more so than that of the patient and as much as the normalizing body of medical discourse, that is generalized illegitimately in the medical examination with parsimonous effects.

Second, and somewhat paradoxically, while an understanding of the other implies immersion in her or his body, it is just as critical to maintain the difference. The indeterminate ambiguity of existence suggests this alterity, and our ethics demands it. Too much familiarity on the part of the clinician or the patient may transgress the indistinguishable line marking off his or her difference, threatening the security of the identities of both. The sexual encounter may be an opportunity for indulgence in the ambiguity of intercorporeal existence; the clinical encounter is not. Simone's doctor, for example, may have been threatened by the mention of anal penetration in a context where it seemed appropriate, not necessarily because it fell outside of her sexual experience, but perhaps because it did not. That is, the problem may have been that the patient inadvertently sexualized the very part of her body that the doctor sought to put at a distance. This is how we all deal with uncertainty in the face of body ambiguity: we build a partition between our body and the body of the other without any thought at all.

In the end, absolute resolution of the ambiguous relation between bodies is impossible, unless we assume that all bodies are the same. Hence, complete understanding of the patient's sexuality in a clinical setting is also impossible. A more generous and sensitive approach to sexuality in the clinic does not require resolution of this ambiguity but recognition that the clinical encounter involves corporeal generosity and an attendant clash and transfiguration of uses of pleasure and pain. Rather than attempting to better manage the patient's sexuality with the parsimonious incorporation of them that this implies, perhaps a more constructive starting point would be acknowledgment of the clinician's sexuality and its constitutive role in the clinical encounter.

Attending to the dynamics of an encounter with a stranger in an institutional setting provides us with a case where social norms and conventions are most likely to operate through bodies to efface differences. This, I have argued, operates at a prereflective, nonvolitional level of intercorporeality. Here, openness to others, characteristic of corporeal generosity, is mediated by a closure to the other effected by a body that is a product of convention and an agent of normalization. However, as I have also suggested, because social norms are incorporated and perception is intercorporeal, affective, and ambiguous, it is difficult to locate convention and parsimony, and it is difficult to predict the circumstances under which convention could be transformed toward different modes of being. Further, not only is corporeal generosity indeterminate and unpredictable, it is also impossible. Unconditional openness to otherness, as the analysis of the clinical encounter suggests, is impossible, given how sedimentation of corporeal style closes off possibilities for existence for both oneself and the other.

If, as I have suggested, both openness and closure to alterity operate primordially at a prereflective level, then so does a politics of generosity. That is, if social ideas and their corporeal instantiation effect normalization and discrimination at the intercorporeal level, then so would the transformation of sociality toward fostering different ways of being. But the nonvolitional and unpredictable character of this operation of generosity raises a number of questions about a politics of difference. What, for example, is the relation between intercorporeality and conscious intent, thought, and judgment? Under Merleau-Ponty's formulation of intercorporeality, conscious reflection and intent, while informed by corporeal affective perception, cannot catch up with the perception it attempts to think. How then might social norms and consciously held ideas be transformed in a way that is open to difference? And, related to this, how might the community that this conventional thinking supports be transformed in a manner that fosters different ways of being? These are the questions addressed in the third and final part of this book, beginning in the next chapter with an account of the generosity of critical thinking—a thinking that seeks to transform the social concepts that seem to dictate our modes of existence to the advantage of some and the detriment of others.

PART III

GENEROSITY AND COMMUNITY (TRANS)FORMATION

SEVEN

THINKING THROUGH RADICAL
GENEROSITY WITH LEVINAS

The self says to the ego, "Feel pain here!" Then the ego suffers and thinks how it might suffer no more—and that is why it is *made* to think.

The self says to the ego, "Feel pleasure here!" Then the ego is pleased and thinks how it might often be pleased again—and that is why it is *made* to think. (Nietzsche 1978, 35)

WHAT MAKES ME THINK? In particular, what makes me think in a way that would be critical of existing ideas? If, as I suggested in chapters 5 and 6, existing ideas (including social norms and prohibitions) come to me in the form of incarnated fragments that color the horizon of what I do and feel, what opens me to the generation of different ideas and to the transformation of my horizon of being that this would entail? What makes me think differently and against the conventions that normalize and discriminate against different ways of being? Nietzsche, in the opening quotation, suggests a connection between affectivity and thinking. Affects of the self (which for him is a body) make me think. Something gets under my skin. Something disturbs me, makes me think in a direction that may not be altogether different from what I thought initially, but different all the same.

The disturbance that has made me think the question of thinking comes from at least three directions. The first is from the guardians of economic rationalism in Australian universities who reward the productivity of an instrumental reason that would teach for vocational purposes in accordance with student interest and in response to the demands of industry. The second comes from a current trend of dismissing the ideas of contemporary cultural theory (particularly what its critics call postmodern or poststructural theory) on the grounds of its apparent inaccessibility and lack of reason.[1] The third is a recent attack on academic feminism, especially that which might be considered "deconstructive" and that which is critical of scientific concepts, for sacrificing the idea of liberation in favor of seeking power for itself and for the madness of its method, for its "systematic and pervasive confusions, logical slides, and the mode of argument which . . . refuses to meet the tests of genuine reason" (Curthoys 1997, 10).[2]

What I find disturbing about all three provocations is that they locate proper thinking and the proper dissemination of ideas in that which does not disturb, in the domain of the familiar. Ideas and their teaching that are unfamiliar, that distort the boundaries of existing ideas (particularly those of classical economics, liberation politics, and the natural sciences), or that are not immediately and obviously useful to further predetermined ends, are dismissed as failing to meet the tests of reason. What I will argue in this chapter, using feminist philosophy as characteristic of critical thinking, is that it is in the generation of new ideas that thinking is productive in its political task of transforming both the self and the social realm. While such new ideas are open to criticism that they may be difficult to comprehend at first, in the context of long-held beliefs, or that they may not obviously fit the explicit ideals of a liberation politics, this does not constitute grounds for dismissal. A second feature shared by these three sources of disturbance, and a central target of the thinking in this chapter, is that they explicitly or implicitly hold that proper thinking is an autonomous exercise, carried out by an independent agent prior to communication to another. It is this idea of autonomous theorizing that, I will argue, works against the creation and transformation of ideas necessary to feminist and all critical thinking, a process that takes place not in isolation but within the field of the other. It is a disturbance arising within this field of the other to which I am given that makes me think; the other affects me, gets under my skin, and that is why I am made to think. Finally, I will claim that this production of ideas against convention involves corporeal generosity, a generosity central to teaching, learning, and thinking, which seems absent from the ideal of instrumental, autonomous reason espoused by these provocateurs who have made me think.

In positing a connection between affectivity and critical thinking, my aim is to harness an idea raised in Part II for a politics of generosity. The idea is this: Our relation to existing ideas that govern social relations and are instantiated corporeally is ambiguous and open so that the transformation of existing ideas is possible. How though, given this ambiguity and its prereflective, nonvolitional character, can a politics that aims for social justice be enacted? To better imagine what such a politics might look like requires arguing initially, as I do in this chapter, that existing ideas and the sociality they support are opened to new paths of thinking through a generous response provoked by the other's alterity. This generosity involves a dispossession of self and is born of an affective, corporeal relation to alterity that generates rather than closes off sexual, cultural, and stylistic differences.

As I take feminist thinking to be exemplary of this generosity, the work of feminist philosophers who question the maleness of reason provides the foundation of this account, as do Deleuze's and Guattari's thoughts about the creation of new ideas. However, it is Levinas' work on the generosity of sensibility that I find particularly conducive to an account of how generosity transforms thinking that otherwise would be closed to otherness. Levinas, more explicitly than either Nietzsche or Merleau-Ponty, bases a sociality that would be open to difference on giving to the other without thought of return. And insofar as his work challenges the ideals of instrumental reason and autonomy that sustain male domination, it provokes thoughts about thinking that are consistent with feminist thinking. But Levinas is equally provocative and disturbing for what he leaves out, presenting a strangeness within which new lines of thought will open. As will be noted toward the end of this chapter, Levinas, unlike Merleau-Ponty, tends to locate radical generosity outside of ontology and therefore outside of politics. This is a tendency that inspires some revision of his ideas and is a problem that will be addressed more directly in the following chapters.

We begin this account of the generosity of critical thinking then with the claim that feminist philosophy operates through the production of new ideas. Deleuze and Guattari have argued in *What is Philosophy?* that what distinguishes philosophy from other enterprises, namely, science and art, is its "art of forming, inventing, and fabricating concepts" (Deleuze and Guattari 1994, 2). "Philosophy does not contemplate, reflect or communicate," as more conventional definitions of philosophy might claim (6). These activities are "mechanisms for constituting Universals," not just in philosophy but "in every discipline" (ibid.). What is more fundamental to philosophy is the production of new concepts, "singularities," prior to any universalization (7). By "concept," Deleuze and Guattari do not mean a proposition that represents a thing or state of affairs: representation is the aim of science (23). Nor, by concept, do they mean a medium for expressing feelings: affective expression is the work of art (164). Rather, concepts address problems that they are designed to resolve; they are incorporeal expressions of events; the "concept speaks the event, not the essence or the thing" (21). But the event does not precede the concept; the event is itself constituted through the fabrication of the concept, through the "condensation" or gathering together, in a particular way, of the components of the concept (20). Central to Deleuze's and Guattari's concept of the concept is that it is a "becoming," involving realignment of its heterogeneous components and recasting of relationships with other relevant concepts (21, 18). Through its becoming, the concept "assigns conditions to the problem it addresses," tracing "the contour of its components" in an "undecidable" way (20–21). The resulting condensation or event is fragmentary, unstable, and subject to transformation.

Just as the event does not precede the concept, nor does the philosopher, at least not in any stable form. The concept is given voice by a conceptual persona, a philosophical figure, such as Nietzsche's Zarathustra or Plato's Diotima, that is constituted through the speaking. And the concept emerges in a "plane of immanence" or "image of thought": a historically and socially specific milieu of presuppositions about what thought involves (e.g., transcendence, universals, discursiveness) that acts "like a sieve stretched over . . . chaos" (Deleuze and Guattari 1994, 43). This sieve, this plane or image of thought, necessitates or motivates the creation of concepts and lays out paths in which their creation will take place.[3] As Paul Patton suggests, along with the concepts of the conceptual persona and the plane of immanence, Deleuze's and Guattari's concept of the concept generates a model of philosophical thinking as experimental, "a dice-throw," concerned with recasting problems in new and interesting ways with a view for opening new possibilities for life (Patton 1996, 324–25).

Irigaray's concept of the "two lips," by now well known, at least in feminist theory, might serve as a useful illustration of Deleuze's and Guattari's concept of the concept (Irigaray 1985). The problem that Irigaray addresses through this concept is the way in which woman's social subordination is supported by dualistic representations of sexual difference so that woman is viewed as the same as man (a sexed unity or one) or as a lack (none). "Two lips" does not represent an alternative essence of woman or woman's sex as an anatomical thing. Rather, it figures woman as event, a composition of postures, lines of potentiality. The concept has at least three components: two lips (although it remains ambiguous which two—whether genital or oral) and their relation. Other preexisting concepts (equating sexuality with genitalia, woman with lack) are recast through a condensation of the components of the concept so that woman is figured as not one sex, not a lack, at least two, and maybe more, perhaps genitally oriented, perhaps not. Whatever you think of Irigaray's two lips, it is a concept in Deleuze's and Guattari's sense, as is Genevieve Lloyd's "man of reason."

Lloyd's concept "the man of reason" not only illustrates the concept of the concept but also indicates why the production of new concepts is important to feminism. Lloyd demonstrates, through a reading of the history of philosophy, that philosophical conceptions of reason are male. Not that men by *nature* embody reason; rather, men by *definition* embody reason: "the male-female distinction has been used to symbolize the distinction between reason and its opposites," Lloyd argues, so that "our ideals of Reason have historically incorporated an exclusion of the feminine, and that femininity itself has been partly constituted through such processes of exclusion" (Lloyd 1993, x, xix). The concept "the man of reason" recasts the relation between the male-female distinction and ideals of reason not to suggest a feminine alternative to reason nor to reject claims to women's irrationality on the basis of empirical evidence. What is interesting about the concept "the man of reason" is that it makes concepts of reason, rather than "woman," the problem to be addressed, and it does so by questioning their means of symbolic production and sexually neutral status. Why such questioning has been necessary is indicated by Lloyd's claim, in her preface to the second edition of *The Man of Reason*, that while exclusion of the feminine or the female from concepts of Reason is a "contingent feature of western thought, the elusive but real effects [. . .] are still with us" (1993, x). One such effect is that what a woman may count as a philosophical problem and the concept that emerges from her exploration of that problem may be dismissed as irrational, simply because she is a woman and by definition does not embody reason.

Insofar as philosophy has been a male-dominated enterprise then, it should not be surprising that the problems addressed in the production of concepts are those of particular concern to the lifestyles of the men who address them, and that the concepts that emerge affirm the existence and status of the men through whom they emerge.[4] Even when the conceptual persona that gives voice to the concept is a woman, Plato's Diotima, for example, we find that the concept, in this case a concept of love, not only speaks little of women's concerns but is likely to exclude women altogether. Not only has the male domination of philosophy guided the selection of problems addressed in the creation of concepts, but the "maleness of reason" has infected the plane of immanence that lays out the paths of thinking, favoring the emergence of exactly the kind of concepts it has. Michèlle Le Doeuff suggests such a relation between a plane of immanence, the particular social situation of the philosophers who inhabit it, and the type of concepts likely to emerge. In addressing the sexism of philosophical thought, she claims that any theoretical enterprise is structured by an "axiology," a set of values "concerning that which is or is not 'done' in this enterprise, [. . .] a whole series of theoretical orientations and also the trace left in the theoretical language by people's practical and concrete interests" (1991, 11–12). That the axiology of philosophy (and the humanities in general) has been infected with male ideals of reason and has addressed problems of concern to men is not to say that men and women do not share paths of thinking, or that the problems and interests of men and women do not overlap, for they clearly do. But there will be problems that some women would address, including the sexism of a plane of immanence itself, that a man may not even notice. To address such problems requires new concepts, concepts that may at first seem foreign to the plane of immanence from which they emerge; concepts that may seem unreasonable within an axiology that they will necessarily transform and that may seem obscure to the "man of reason" whose life they may bypass or whose security they may challenge.

I have suggested that feminist philosophy requires new concepts in order to address problems that may have been overlooked in an axiology that has deemed women unreasonable. But how do these concepts arise, and what motivates their creation? Deleuze and Guattari do not really answer this question, at least not in a way that I find completely convincing. For them, the concept is produced through a "conceptual persona," a historically contingent figure through which the philosopher's plane of immanence passes and which, rather than being the philosopher's representative, is that which the philosopher is in the process of becoming (Deleuze and Guattari 1994, 63–64). The conceptual persona is the concept's "friend," its "potentiality," the site for the "deterritorializations" and "reterritorializations" of thought, who emerges with the concept in a field of rival claimants (4–5). One problem I have with this formulation is that the production of concepts is described as a solitary affair where the philosopher, or his or her conceptual persona, in his or her own isolation, seems to be the only friend the concept has. Second, and related to the first problem, there is little consideration of how the history of the philosopher's social experiences (his or her encounters with other social beings) informs the production of concepts. While Deleuze and Guattari grant that a conceptual persona is related to the historical milieu in which it appears, the existential mode and social status of the philosopher who thinks it has little or no bearing on the creation of concepts. Rather, according to Deleuze and Guattari, thinking, the creation of concepts, wrests the thinker from the "historical state of affairs of a society" and from his or her own lived experience in order to transform him or her into a conceptual persona on a plane laid out by thought (70). It is as if the plane of immanence motivates the creation of concepts, irrespective of the philosopher's location in it. Without denying that thinking seems like a lonely venture, and that in it we get carried away by paths of thinking beyond our control, it seems to me that the creation of concepts has more to do with the philosopher's social constitution in relation to others within a plane of immanence than Deleuze and Guattari allow. The philosopher needs other friends necessary to the production of concepts. Rivals for sure, but also companions, mentors, students, lovers, mothers, and brothers might put us on the path of thinking. I want to suggest that the philosopher's specific experiences within his or her social milieu, which includes a plane of immanence, directly motivate the creation of new concepts; a woman philosopher's experiences within a plane of immanence that embodies traces of the interests of men directly prompt the opening of those paths of thinking that we call feminist.

Erika Kerruish suggests a connection between a philosopher's social experience and her or his response to existing concepts when arguing, with and against Derrida and with reference to Nietzsche's theory of affect, that a woman's "embodied social history" makes all the difference to how she will read, accept, and criticize Nietzsche's ideas on woman (Kerruish 1997, 11). A philosopher's *response* to concepts of "woman" found within a plane of immanence involves an experience that is never as sexually neutral or interchangeable with the experience of others, as Derrida's reading of Nietzsche's ideas of "woman" suggests. And Genevieve Lloyd points to the role of such experience in the *creation* of concepts, such as the "man of reason": "[t]o bring to the surface the implicit maleness of our ideals of Reason [. . .] means for example, that there are not only practical reasons, but also conceptual ones, for the *conflicts* many women experience between Reason and femininity" (1993, xix, emphasis added). There is something, a conflict, a disturbance, in the female philosopher's experience of reason and of other concepts, as they are usually defined, read, and institutionalized in and beyond a philosophical community that motivates their reconceptualization. Indeed, Emmanuel Levinas suggests that such an unsettling experience lies at the heart of the formation of new ideas: this "experience deserves its name only if it transports us beyond what constitutes our nature. Genuine experience must even lead us beyond the Nature that surrounds us" and in which we may normally feel our selves "to be at home" (Levinas 1987a, 47). Something gets under my skin, something disturbs me, something elates me, excites me, bothers me, surprises me. It is this experience that sets off a movement that extends my world beyond the intimate and familiar. A disturbing experience motivates the creation and transformation of concepts.

At the very least then, our relation to ideas is not only mediated by our corporeal history but is also affective. Levinas describes our primordial experience of and relation to ideas in terms of "living from . . . ," just as we "[l]ive from acts [. . .] we live from ideas and sentiments" (1969, 113). That we live from ideas does not mean we already exist as a separate being who uses ideas for some purpose: "what we live from is not a 'means of life' " (110). Ideas are "not objects of representations" of a self-conscious existence (ibid). What characterizes living from ideas, acts, bread, and so on is not impassionate contemplation but enjoyment, where enjoyment refers to sensibility or affectivity in general and so includes joy, pain, and suffering. Before or beyond reflecting on ideas we live them "as a body that feels itself affected and affective" (Peperzak 1993, 156). And what "living from . . ." accomplishes is separation from what one lives from: there is a basic relation to life, including to ideas, by which the self is constituted as separate on the basis of an affectivity that it cannot share with others.

To characterize our relation to ideas, elements, life in terms of prereflective sensibility, or enjoyment is to suggest that there is something that exceeds any act of living that propels the activity; there is an affective aspect of thinking, eating, sleeping, reading, and warming oneself in the sun, which nourishes that activity and makes it possible. Enjoyment explains why we bother at all: we bother to live, to think, and to act, because we enjoy it and suffer from it. For Levinas, ideas or concepts are not incorporeal expressions of events, as Deleuze and Guattari suggest; ideas are corporeal and affective, distinct from our substance but constituting it, contributing to our becoming and to the worth of our lives by moving us through sensibility (Levinas 1969, 112). And while we live from ideas at the level of prereflective sensibility, this enjoyment is not presocial. The structure of *Totality and Infinity* might suggest otherwise insofar as Levinas discusses enjoyment there prior to consideration of relations with others, prior to dwelling, labor, erotics, and the ethical relation. However, he also indicates that each order presupposes the other (170, 216). In *Otherwise Than Being or Beyond Essence,* he removes any doubt that enjoyment, or what he by then more consistently calls sensibility, is inseparable from sociality. There sensibility is a condition of subjectivity and is exposure to the other in the ethical relation (Levinas 1981, 50–51). Or, in the terms of *Totality and Infinity*, our relation to life is based on an irreducible affectivity without which thinking, doing, and indeed living would not be possible.

While "living from . . ." or enjoyment may explain the affectivity of ideas, why we find life worth living, and why we bother with ideas, and while I have suggested why ideas about "woman," for example, may affect some of us and not others, this sensibility, taken by itself, is prereflective, egoistic, immediate, and fragile. As enjoyment is immediate, self-constituting gratification, living for and from the moment, it has no past and no guaranteed future. Further, enjoyment, as Levinas formulates it in *Totality and Infinity*, is always assimilation, consumption, appropriation, and possession of what one lives from, and while it accounts for the production of a separate self, this is a prereflective, nonproductive autonomy. If this self-serving egoism alone characterized our relation to ideas, then ideas would be what we consume, enjoy, and suffer from rather than something we produce. Still, the consumption and regurgitation of ideas by an autonomous self is what characterizes the production of knowledge in much of Western philosophy, with the qualification that, unlike Levinas' formulation of the egoistic living from ideas, the usual model of autonomy is given in terms of a reflexive self without consideration of the affective dimension of ideas. Without this consideration, along with consideration of the social specificity of one's carnal experience within the plane of immanence, there is no explanation for why some ideas might hold us, bother us, and move us more or less than others. And while the idea of an autonomous self may account for the possession and consumption of ideas, it does not account for their production, nor therefore, for feminist or other critical thinking. Yet it is this idea of a self-reflexive autonomous self that dominates thinking about thinking.

Jean Curthoys, for example, supports her charge that the bulk of academic feminism does not meet the "test of genuine reason" and her thesis about what should count as proper feminist thinking with such a model of autonomy. For Curthoys, liberation theorists are exemplary of genuine feminism and are held up by her as the paradigm of wisdom and virtue (Curthoys 1997, 38–54). Liberation feminists are wise, according to Curthoys, because the concept of liberation that they hold is based on self-knowledge, the discovery within the self of an irreducible concept of human nature (to be human is to need recognition as human) (49).[5] This wisdom is a virtue in that the discovery of this concept of human nature within oneself objectively grounds the moral claim that this need for recognition must be equally met for all humans and leads its discoverer to reject aspirations for status and power in favor of listening to others and caring for their needs (45, 50, 53–54). These are worthy ideas that one would certainly be unwise to reject. It is the means by which they supposedly arise that I find problematic. Curthoys' model of the production of ideas is one that, I will argue, would make no difference to social relations at all and so cannot provide the basis for feminist or any critical thinking.

Curthoys, by her own admission, holds to a Socratic model of the production of knowledge, where ethics is based on epistemology (the more you understand, the more virtuous you are), and genuine knowledge arises from within the self. The getting of wisdom is based on the doctrine of anamnesis (recollection), and ignorance and lack of virtue arises from amnesia, a forgetting of ideas (particularly the concept of human nature that grounds liberation theory) that Curthoys attributes to the bulk of academic feminism. Curthoys' Socratic model of feminist thinking speaks of a kind of philosophical ideal that Levinas calls "autonomy," a philosophy that aims to ensure the freedom and identity of the beings who produce it, where the knower seeks to understand and integrate his or her external world in terms familiar to the self (Levinas 1987a, 49). Indeed, Curthoys reserves the word "autonomy" for such a thinker: the one who, having discovered the idea of human nature within herself, recognizes her dependence "on the proper recognition and respect of others" (1997, 53). This knowledge of the human need for recognition makes the knower autonomous, according to Curthoys, because it breaks "the link which binds us to others only to seek their confirmation" (presumably because if you know you depend on another's recognition, you will not demand it). And such autonomy fosters generosity as an individual virtue by allowing one to be more open to the other's needs (54).

While Curthoys champions this idea of autonomy, there are at least two reasons for advising caution. First, this idea of autonomous thinking ignores the possibility, discussed in chapters 5 and 6, that ideas come to us not from inside the self but as incarnated fragments through the bodies of others in an ambiguous, intercorporeal field. Second, Levinas advises caution against this model of autonomous thinking precisely because concepts discovered within the self would not alter the self or the world. Rather, they would mediate one's relation to external being (including one's assessment of the other's needs) by dissolving its alterity (Levinas 1987a, 50). This meditation of one's relations to the singularity or alterity of others through the generality of concepts discovered in oneself is where

> every power begins. The surrender of external things to human freedom through their generality does not only mean, in all innocence, their comprehension, but also their being taken in hand, their domestication, their possession. . . . To possess is, to be sure, to maintain the reality of the other one possessed, but to do so while suspending its independence. . . . Reason, which reduces the other, is appropriation and power. (Levinas 1987a, 50)

In this exercise of reason, of power, there is nothing disturbing, at least not in the end. Hence, there is no teaching or learning, no production of new ideas, in such a model. One's mentor, student, companion, or rival is reduced to an intellectual midwife (through the exercise of maieutics in the name of virtuous care), someone who merely helps brings to consciousness "the already-known which has been uncovered or freely invented in oneself, and in which everything unknown is compromised" (Levinas 1987a, 49). And, as Norman Wirzba suggests, while in this model the other, through his or her questioning, may contribute to a change in my understanding, my understanding only changes "with reference to my prior understanding" (1995, 131).[6] Philosophical autonomy involves a kind of intellectual imperialism that might explain why Curthoys, while offering an ideal of listening to and caring for the other in her own work, cannot, in the end, hear others' unfamiliar ideas (particularly those of the academic feminists she censures). Philosophical autonomy also describes the paradigm of education currently favored in Australian universities where, under the pressure of economic rationalism, the teacher and the student are reduced to vehicles for the consumption and repetition of familiar ideas valued for their utility in allowing easy appropriation of our world. But philosophical autonomy does not explain how new ideas, central to feminist and other critical thinking, evolve.

What is it then that disturbs the confidence of autonomy and any egoism in enjoyment? What experience transports us beyond what constitutes our ways of being and beyond the familiar worlds we inhabit? What experience sets us on the path of thinking differently? It is not just the content of what is said, written, or embodied in the institutions I inhabit that disturbs me; it not just the idea itself that gets under my skin. It is its saying, the strangeness of the event of expression by someone who remains beyond my self-understanding and so beyond my attempts at assimilation. It is the other's alterity that disturbs me, that difference in proximity generated by his or her own separation, his or her own sensibility. This alterity implies not only that the other cannot be possessed, but that her or his presence contests my possession (not just my possession of things and ideas but my self-possession). The other's strangeness, the feeling that he or she cannot be known, puts my autonomy into question.

Levinas calls this putting into question of autonomy teaching, and he explicitly contrasts it with Socratic maieutics (1969, 51, 171, 204; 1987a, 49). The other, through her or his strangeness, teaches me nonpossession, that there is an element of the unknowable in every known; the other teaches me alterity, exteriority, or "infinity," as Levinas calls it. This is a teaching, because it breaks the "closed circle of totality" (Levinas 1969, 171), the imperialism and violence of self-knowledge that would limit the other through the imposition of familiar ideas. It is a teaching that opens me to the infinity or alterity of the other and so "invites me to a relation incommensurate with a power exercised, be it enjoyment or knowledge" (198). The other's alterity is also a teaching, because it opens me to think beyond myself and therefore beyond what I already know. This thinking provoked by the other's alterity is not outside of reason; it is its condition. Through this teaching, "reason [. . .] is found to be in a position to *receive*" (51), "[i]n thinking infinity the I from the first *thinks more than it thinks*" (Levinas 1987a, 54), and "[t]o think is to have the idea of infinity, or to be taught. Rational thought refers to this teaching" (Levinas 1969, 204).

The other's teaching opens me to transform what I know by founding my responsibility, meaning literally the other's teaching of alterity solicits a response and is the basis of my ability to respond at all to anything. Through the expression of alterity another being presents itself not in the "neutrality of an image," not as a representation of "an interior and hidden world," but as a solicitation, an appeal that "obliges the entering into discourse" (Levinas 1969, 200–01). Accompanying any exercise of autonomy, any attempt to represent or objectify the other, any feeling or thought that would possess the other through one's own ideas, is this disturbing expression of alterity that solicits one's response and is its condition and potential undoing. This "order of responsibility [. . .] is also the order where freedom is ineluctably invoked" (200), the order that gives rise to my being affected, my agency, my reflexivity, my capacity to think (and to the egoistic enjoyment and self-knowledge that would dissolve it). Contrary to the model of difference that governs liberal individualism, where the other limits my freedom to think and act, or to Hegelian dialectics, where alterity is dissolved through thought in the service of totality, the other's strangeness, for Levinas, is "the first rational teaching, the condition for all teaching" (203). The other's otherness is what makes me feel and makes me think what I feel.

I could respond to this teaching by forgetting the other and seeking refuge in my own egoism (Levinas 1969, 172–73) (a forgetting of the other that would ground feminist or any critical thinking in self-knowledge, as Curthoys does). But there is a moral dimension to my responsibility. According to Levinas, the disturbing experience of the other's alterity urges me not to turn my back.[7] Certainly I am urged not to attempt to possess the other through my own concepts. What drives this urge is sometimes described by Levinas in terms of the naked vulnerable humanity expressed in the other's face, the primordial expression "you shall not commit murder" (Levinas 1969, 199), or in terms of the idea that the teaching of alterity is a concil-iatory rather than a hostile gesture (171). Such descriptions, while meta-physical rather than ontological (hence, referring to the general and fundamental basis of responsibility rather than to the content, conciliatory or hostile, of what I respond to), seem to belong to the experience of a secure ego unused to hostility and faced by a more humble other rather than to a feminist philosopher dealing with conflict between her self-possession and the saying of concepts embodied in a world that would exclude her. There would be situations, it could be argued, where we would be wise not to respond to the other at all. In the face of hostility or indifference, it could be said, we have no ethical obligation to respond and hence no obligation to think again.

However, Levinas' point is that even the most secure ego cannot efface the other's alterity that is its condition, and even the most fragile ego faced with the other's strangeness is nevertheless "autonomous" as a result. Hence, a feminist philosopher would not differ from any other kind of philosopher in her self-possession, in her capacity for reflexivity, agency, or autonomy in Levinas' sense. Nor, therefore, would she differ in the "structure" of her subjectivity as a reponse to the teaching of alterity, to the disturbance that inspires sensibility as a condition of thinking. The content of what is said as the vehicle of that disturbance, the content of what provokes the response, will, as I have suggested, have some bearing on the itinerary of her sensibility and her response. And to consider this content will require moving beyond the terms of Levinas' work in ways I will return to. The point I wish to emphasize here is that the woman philosopher will not differ in the urge to respond, in the order of responsibility. In accounting for the urge to respond to the other's strangeness as a command I cannot escape, Levinas is gesturing toward the idea that even my turning away from the other, that is, even the egoism of enjoyment and the self-knowledge and self-possession of autonomy, presupposes another who cannot be possessed and for whom my possessions are destined. While "living from . . ." or sensibility is the basis for separation or interiority, it is given the security of a future through "recollection" or "habitation," through incarnate reflexivity. But this with-drawal from the elemental, this thinking, this acting, this labor of possession, presupposes "a relation to something I do not live from" (Levinas 1969, 170). This is the relation to the other whose alterity not only puts my autonomy in question and so solicits my entry into discourse but also welcomes my possessions. Thinking, subjectivity in general, the gathering and storing of the fruits of enjoyment, presupposes a social world of others who welcome me, and to whom I will give what I possess. So while I live *from* ideas through sensibility, I only do so because it is *for* others that I live. Or, as Levinas puts it in *Otherwise Than Being or Beyond Essence*, "I exist through the other and for the other, but without this being alienation: I am inspired. This inspiration is the psyche," where the "psyche" is the animated body of sensibility exposed to the other (Levinas 1981, 114, 70). It is the other whose alterity, both questioning and welcoming, animates the body as a precondition to thinking, lifts me above "immersion in the elementary enjoyment of my surroundings" (Peperzak 1993, 165), sustains "enjoyment as the body that labors" (Levinas 1969, 165), and gives enjoyment time, a future. That responsibility in the face of the other's alterity is an obligation I cannot avoid rests on the conviction that it is to the other's alterity, his or her teaching, that I owe/give my sensibility, interiority, and "autonomy" in the first place (216).

It is necessary to acknowledge that I have just collapsed two dimensions of alterity that Levinas tends to keep apart in *Totality and Infinity*: the alterity of the ethical relation, which I have argued disturbs my complacency and so inspires creative and critical thinking, and the alterity that welcomes rather than questions and is a precondition to recollection. This distinction itself provokes feminist thinking insofar as Levinas describes the alterity that welcomes as "feminine" in terms consistent with the sexism of the plane of immanence, and he separates it from the alterity that disturbs and questions my autonomy by saying explicitly that this "feminine alterity" is *not* the alterity of the ethical relation (1969, 155). This, as well as his treatment in *Totality and Infinity* of the feminine in the erotic relation, has provoked charges that Levinas is "masculinist," and/or that he excludes women from the both the realm of subjectivity and from the alterity of the ethical relation that is the condition of that realm (see, e.g., Beauvoir 1972, 16n; Sandford 1998). Without denying the import of those charges, but in the wake of the feminist thinking that Levinas' sexism has provoked, it is possible, as Tina Chanter suggests, to move beyond that sexism without abandoning the idea that alterity might indeed be marked by sexual difference

(Chanter 1995, 207–13) and without abandoning Levinas' insights about creative thinking through the field of the other that I am borrowing and transforming here. Such a move is indicated not only by the feminist thinking already done[8] but also by aspects of Levinas' own work with which this thinking is engaged. First, while in *Totality and Infinity* Levinas deals with the face-to-face relation separately to habitation and recollection (allowing him to posit the two orders of alterity at issue) and apart from enjoyment and the phenomenology of eros, he also indicates, as I have already mentioned, that each order presupposes the other. This circularity tends to undermine the distinction he makes between the alterity that questions and the alterity that welcomes and any sex specificity tied to that distinction that would exclude women from either subjectivity or the alterity of the ethical relation. Second, as Derrida argues, while the order of responsibility that is subjectivity (and is itself a welcoming of the other) presupposes the other's teaching of alterity, the face, which signifies this teaching of the other, is also a welcoming (Derrida 1999, 23). This suggests that the welcome that responsibility presupposes is not confined to the silent, discreet alterity of the Woman in the home, but that this feminine alterity is consistent with, and perhaps exemplary of, the welcoming of the alterity of the ethical relation. Third, Levinas abandons the stratified analysis of *Totality and Infinity* altogether in *Otherwise Than Being or Beyond Essence,* so that it is clearer there that all modes of subjectivity (thinking, sensation, perception, eroticism) consist in a welcome, an openness to the other, a movement predicated on a relationship with alterity steeped in sensibility that is not sex specific. It is in the spirit of these considerations that I have described the relation to the other as consisting of a welcome as well as a contestation by the other, that I have attributed both subjectivity and otherness to women, and that I read, retrospectively, Levinas' thinking on creative thinking as being applicable to feminist thinking.[9]

To be "responsible," then, that is, to respond to teaching and therefore to learn, "I must know how to give what I possess" (Levinas 1969, 171). The calling into question of my self-possession requires that what I possess is given to the other, not just the tangible products of my labor, but myself. And this giving of one's self-possession amounts to the opening of myself beyond myself through discourse, conversation, language. Language, or what Levinas later calls the saying of the said, designates my possession to the other; it is, in Levinas' terms, "a primary dispossession, a first donation" (173).

Rather than attempting to fit the other into my scheme of things I am put in question, effecting the transformation of what I enjoy and suffer from into concepts. This creation of concepts is neither an exteriorization of "a representation preexisting in me" nor a thematization of the other; it is a "conversation" where I offer a world put into concepts and "in which at each instant [the other] overflows the idea a thought would carry away with it" (174, 51).[10] This is a dispossession because, in designating myself and the world to the other, my egoism, my self-possession, is given over to the other. It is "radical generosity," a giving of myself that I do not choose, a movement toward the other that does not return to itself the same (Levinas 1987b, 92; 1969, 50, 208). And as concepts, while perhaps singularities in their enjoyment, become generalities when speaking the world to the other, my responsibility effects a gift of the possibility of a common world (Levinas 1969, 173).[11] Thinking is a welcoming of the other and a gift, inseparable from sensibility, an initiative through which responsibility is "exercised" without choice, and it is motivated by alterity, by both its questioning and welcoming dimensions (Levinas 1981, 6, 16).

While the other's alterity transports me beyond myself, this does not imply that I accept the other's ideas, the content of what is said. It implies only that I think again. Just as the other's teaching sustains rather than cancels enjoyment, it sustains rather than cancels autonomy. While a condition of autonomy, the teaching of alterity directs autonomy outward into modes of living and paths of thinking beyond what I think I am and beyond what I think I know. And whether the content of what the other says, the ideas that he or she embodies, is hostile to or happy with the concepts I offer makes no difference to the possibility that my complacency will be disturbed. The other's teaching and its ethical dimension, whatever the content, initiate meaning: it is the precondition of representation and objectification, and that which puts this under erasure. Ethics (the interruption of autonomy and of the imperialism that this implies) is a precondition to knowledge (the creation of concepts). It is the other's alterity that makes me think, rather than ideas I live from and that seem to make me what I am. It is this alterity that provokes any gesture of expression, is necessary for its production, and is not subsumed by the incarnate thinking that results.

But why might this experience set me on a path of thinking that is feminist? As Levinas is concerned with the order of responsibility rather than with its content, with ethics understood in terms of radical generosity rather than ontology and politics, it is necessary to move beyond his thinking and to return to points made earlier in order to answer this question.[12] While what is said is not reducible to the alterity of the saying that is its condition, the content of what is said by the other matters (whether spoken, written, or as a corporeal attitude that I perceive). It matters as the vehicle of that alterity that contests my self-possession and as that which may appear to absorb the difference by subordinating the saying to its theme (Levinas 1981, 6, 62). Hence, if the saying of the other's alterity expresses a said that embodies traces of the interests of men and so exhibits the world in a way that conflicts with ideas I live from and that contribute to my existence as a woman, then the path of thinking that this disturbance provokes is likely to be feminist. Further, whether or not the other, male or female, is hostile to the ideas I offer in response may make a difference in how I put myself on the line for *his* or *her* sake. While autonomy in general is produced and put into question by the other's alterity, a woman who inhabits a plane of immanence of concepts that denigrate or exclude her would find herself doubly in question by the other's expression of these concepts. In the face of such hostility, there is a necessary limit to her generosity that does not limit her responsibility of being-in-question nor the thinking that it inspires, but that would direct what is given in response toward a "third party" as much as toward the other who solicits it. The other who contests her is in relation to a "third party" to whom the other is responsible and who treats her, alongside the other she faces, as someone to be concerned about and welcomed (Levinas 1981, 161). The feminist thinking that conflicts within a plane of immanence inspire needs the welcoming of those other others to be sustained. I cannot help but be given to the other in sensibility, but the creation of concepts that this opening solicits needs other friends besides hostile rivals, friends who through their own responsibility and generosity would welcome those concepts and give them time without assuming that they emerge from something in common.

To characterize feminist thinking in terms of the creation of concepts in the face of the disturbing experience of the other's alterity is not to suggest that women or women who call themselves feminists are any better at this way of thinking than anyone else. Rather, it is to say, against those provocateurs with whom I began who would understand and assemble the world in a self-serving way, that any philosophy, to be critical, must be open to the teaching of the other, including the teaching of feminism. With respect to that philosophy we might call feminist, only by responding to the strangeness of the others with whom we dwell by giving through incarnate thought can we produce, and indeed have produced, the concepts that transform not just ourselves but the maleness of the planes of immanence that we inhabit. To remain living within what we think we know would be to relive an unproductive autonomy that exhibits the world in a way that is familiar but doubly contests us and so haunts our lives over and over again. To open ourselves to thinking through the affective field of the other and to the transformations that this implies does not lessen that inspirational sensibility, the passion for thinking, the enjoyment of ideas. But it would and has given us time to address other problems that touch our lives that may not be explicitly feminist.

There are countless people who have brought me the teaching of the other: teachers, students, colleagues (both friendly and hostile), friends, family, and children—colleagues (both male and female) without whose interest or indifference I may not have asked myself the questions: "What is feminist philosophy?" "What is generous thinking?"; Jean Curthoys, without whom I may not have thought about the relation between autonomy and generosity and before any of these, the vehicles of economic rationalism in my own university, who more than anyone else in recent years have set me off on this path of thinking through their inability to count enjoyment, the teaching of the other, and responsibility among their performance indicators. In response to the disturbing experience of these others, my body said to my ego "Feel pain here!" and my ego suffered and wondered how it might suffer no more. And that is why I was "*made* to think."

EIGHT

TRUTH, CULTURAL DIFFERENCE, AND DECOLONIZATION

IN THE PREVIOUS CHAPTER I explored the production and transformation of ideas in terms of what Levinas calls "radical generosity," the giving of my self-possession in response to the other's teaching of alterity. Both the teaching of alterity and this generosity, this responsibility, are necessary, I argued, to open modes of living and paths of thinking beyond the imperialism sustained by familiar ideas. In this chapter I explore this relation between alterity, generosity, and responsibility further toward a politics of generosity. This involves, first, elaborating in some detail, through Nietzsche's ideas of truth and language, how familiar ideas, concepts, and social conventions effect a closure to difference in cultural as well as self-formation. The imperialism at issue here is the European colonization of indigenous peoples through "truth," through the concepts of belonging that sustain the colonizing culture. That such imperialism is an affront to alterity is manifest, I will argue, in the "lying" involved in maintaining the "truth" of the colonizing culture. The teaching of alterity, though, issues from the testimonies of the colonized that contest that truth. That contestation raises the question of what this teaching of the other teaches us and how decolonization might proceed in the interests of social justice. The claim guiding the analysis is that decolonization, the opening of modes of living beyond the imperialism sustained by the truth of colonization, rests on the ability of the colonizers to respond to this contestation of their "truth" generously, in Levinas' sense. This is a generosity born of an affective corporeal response to alterity that generates rather than closes off cultural difference. To elevate this generosity to the status of a politics, however, requires some departures from Levinas' understanding of radical generosity as passive and unconditional giving to the other.

I begin with a testimony from an indigenous Australian that contests the "good" of colonization, in particular, the assimilation policies of the twentieth century that encouraged the removal of indigenous children from their communities. The testimony also attests to the lying involved in maintaining those policies:

> So the next thing I remember was that they took us from there and we went to the hospital and I kept asking—because the children were screaming and the little brothers and sisters were just babies of course, and I couldn't move, they were all around me, around my neck and legs, yelling and screaming. I was all upset and I didn't know what to do and I didn't know where we were going. I just thought: well they're police, they must know what they're doing. . . . And I think on the third or fourth day they [the police] piled us in the car and I said, "Where are we going?" And they said, "We are going to see your mother." But then we turned left to go to the airport and I got a bit panicky. (HREOC 1997, 2)[1]

This is part of a testimony describing the forcible removal of an indigenous Australian and his/her seven siblings from an Aboriginal community on Cape Barren Island, Tasmania. The eight children were not taken to see their mother, as the police had promised, but were flown off the island and placed in separate foster homes. This occurred not in the nineteenth century but in the 1960s. While the incident was sanctioned by welfare policies that still seek to protect children from neglect or abuse and under which we are all in principle equally at risk, it was driven by highly interventionist government and missionary policies of assimilation explicitly aimed at absorbing Aboriginal Australians into the nonindigenous community.[2] The case cited is not isolated, nor necessarily the most disturbing. Between 1910 and 1970, as many as one in three indigenous children were forcibly removed from their families and communities and placed in the care of nonindigenous families or in state- or church-run institutions.[3] These children are collectively called the "Stolen Generation," and the time these children spent apart from their families has been referred to as the "stolen years." Not only were Aboriginal children deprived of their families, suffering from isolation and sometimes abuse and exploitation with damaging long-term effects (HREOC 1997, 177–211), but the communities from which they were taken were robbed of the means of cultural reproduction and transformation.[4] This was the aim of forcible removals, and few Aboriginal families and no Aboriginal communities have escaped the effects of what has been described as cultural genocide (HREOC 1997, 218).

The National Inquiry into the Separation of Aboriginal and Torres Strait Islander Children from Their Families was conducted between 1995 and 1997 as part of the process of attaining reconciliation between indigenous and nonindigenous Australians. Reconciliation, in general, is defined as the restoration of harmony and friendship between persons who have been estranged and, in keeping with this definition, the Council for Aboriginal Reconciliation aims, through the process of reconciliation, toward "a united Australia which respects this land of ours; values the Aboriginal and Torres Strait Islander heritage and provides justice and equality for all" (CAR n.d., 2).[5] Within the eight issues the council outlines as essential to the reconciliation process, reference is repeatedly made to the need to "share history," to bring to light the history of violence, dispossession, and racism suffered by indigenous Australians and for indigenous peoples to tell their own stories. This emphasis on testimony, telling the truth about and bearing witness to the past, is also what shaped the National Inquiry into the Separation of Aboriginal and Torres Strait Islander Children from Their Families. Following the "van Boven principles" for the restitution, compensation, and rehabilitation of victims of gross violations of human rights and fundamental freedoms,[6] the Report of the Inquiry, called *Bringing Them Home*, emphasized the importance of "full and public disclosure of the truth" about forcible removals (HREOC 1997, 3, 284). Indeed, *Bringing Them Home* opens by lamenting over the fact that the Inquiry could only hear a limited number of testimonies from indigenous witnesses (535), and its first recommendation is that governments make full provision for the recording, preservation, and distribution of testimonies from indigenous peoples affected by forcible removal policies (21, 22). Equally important, according to the Report of the Inquiry, is that such testimony be met with an appropriate response, beginning with a formal "apology" to indigenous peoples from all Australian Parliaments (287).

In this chapter I examine the role of truth, testimony, and apology in the reconciliation process, although decolonization rather than reconciliation might be a more appropriate description. It is highly unlikely that reconciliation as defined would ever be fully realized given that this would require restoration of an original harmony that to my knowledge has never existed between indigenous and nonindigenous Australians.[7] On the contrary, estrangement rather than unity characterizes cultural difference, and violence rather than harmony marks the origin of colonization. Further, reconciliation based on an ideal of restitution implies what would seem to be impossible: the ability to give back time. As one testimonial in *Bringing Them Home* suggests, "[T]he stolen years that are worth more than any treasure are irrecoverable" (HREOC 1997, 3). Still, if in retrospect we think that colonization is characterized by theft, then decolonization requires that something be given back if justice is to be realized. The purpose of this examination into the role of truth, testimony, and apology in the reconciliation process is to explore the extent of what was taken with the stolen years and to suggest what form of response, what form of giving back, would foster a productive operation of cultural difference rather than the continuing assimilation of the colonized into the cultures of the colonizers.[8]

That the truth about the past must be told for reconciliation to begin implies that the history of colonization of Australia, and our present knowledge of it, is based on lies. The principle of *terra nullius* is arguably the lie that started it all. *Terra nullius*: land belonging to no one, the perception that, with the exception of the coastal fringe, Australia was uninhabited at the time of the arrival of European colonizers. That this was a land belonging to no one was a perception that precluded acknowledgment of the land rights of indigenous Australians for 200 years until the *Mabo (No. 2)* judgment in 1992[9] and that justified their dispersal and annihilation. But was the idea that Australia was a *terra nullius* really a lie or more a perception based on historically and culturally specific concepts of belonging? Just as it is still a common perception that Australia has an empty heart, it is likely that Joseph Banks, the first European to officially make the judgment, really could not see anyone or anything beyond the coastal fringe. No life could possibly be sustained beyond the fringe, it was and still is thought, hence, Australia must have been a land belonging to no one. Of course, as the European settlement crept inward, life-forms were encountered requiring some adjustment to Banks' initial perception. It turned out that Australia was inhabited by strange flora and fauna and strange people. While these life-forms were named, catalogued, and allowed some measure of cohabitation, their discovery did not weaken the hold of *terra nullius*. The land was inhabited but did not belong to its inhabitants in a way recognizable to the European eye. The land was not fenced or cultivated, the flora was not planted, and the fauna was not bred or tended. To a European sense of belonging, to European law, there was no law; the land therefore belonged to no one. Such European concepts of belonging guided not just the European possession of land in the eighteenth and nineteenth centuries but also the assimilation policies that justified the forcible removal of indigenous children throughout the twentieth century. Just as the land did not belong to its indigenous inhabitants, those indigenous inhabitants, from a European perspective, did not belong to the land. Living barefoot under bark, sleeping on the ground ten to a patch, learning from the elements—this was no way of belonging to those who lived in private houses, slept in single beds above the ground, and learned from books.

Terra nullius is based on a concept of belonging that is not so much a lie but a dominant perception. Like every concept, it begins from an impression and a word for an impression then, through habit where the word is applied to numerous dissimilar cases, the word for the impression becomes a convention. At least this is how Nietzsche claims we arrive at truth. Truth is an agreement between individuals about what word will stand for the thing: "a uniformly valid and binding designation [. . .] invented for things" (1979, 81). Or, if we take Nietzsche's account of the metaphoric transfer of a nerve stimulus into an image and then into a word, truth, the word, is a designation invented for an experience, a perception, rather than a thing (82). The word, an arbitrary designation invented for an experience, evolves into a concept through repetition and takes on the status of truth when the history of its invention is forgotten (84).

But if truth is an arbitrary invention, this can only be part of the story; the arbitrary status attributed to truth does not explain what binds us to it. According to Nietzsche, what binds us to truth are the "pleasant, life-preserving consequences of truth" (81). We are bound to truth because we are bound to a way of life that truth sustains. Truth is more about shared meaning and hence social identity than it is about "adequate expression: otherwise there would not be so many languages" (82). Truth is relative not to an individual but to a culture; more exactly, truth is relative to language or to the concepts or linguistic conventions that a culture embodies. Language, for Nietzsche, is not an instrument for retrieving the truth of an "inaccessible x." It is a convention that constitutes and maintains a culture. Language provides the terms of an agreement between members of a social group by designating their relation to a world (ibid.). Language gives us a world by facilitating understanding between members of a social group, by giving a measure of common meaning to experience. This connection between language and social identity is echoed in a submission from the Kimberley Language Resource Center to the National Inquiry into forcible removals:

> Language and identity are closely linked, and for many of us our language is a symbol of identity central to our self-esteem, cultural respect, and social identification. Our languages provide more than just a way to talk to each other. They provide a way for us to interpret the reality we see around us. The words we use to name things, to describe feelings, understandings, and each other, carry meanings particular to us. If we lose these words, we lose part of ourselves. (HREOC 1997, 299)

Truth may be arbitrary, but it endures through the work of fabricating social life and preserving the individual within the cultural group that that individual inhabits. To say one sees otherwise than the majority is to disqualify oneself, or be excluded, from that way of life.

But this cannot be the full story either. Can truth be constituted through an agreement between individuals of the kind Nietzsche implies, where individuals seem to have a choice whether to agree with linguistic convention or get carried away by their own first impressions? If the impression is not an error and its expression is not a willful lie, if Banks really saw nothing, if the social workers of the twentieth century really saw poverty, ignorance, and dis-ease among indigenous peoples, rather than just a different way of belonging, then these perceptions were already informed by a concept and the ethos to which that concept belongs. We could not be bound to truth if an impression is separate from its linguistic designation, so that as individuals we could choose, after the event, which word belongs to a perception and then which moral value belongs to the word.[10] Rather, as Nietzsche suggests in his later work, the impression, the experience, must already be informed by the word and the concept and moral value that it carries. That meaning, embodied in linguistic convention, precedes and informs experience, is why Nietzsche says in his later work: "All experiences are moral experiences even in the realm of sense perception" (1974, 174), "everything of which we become conscious . . . [has been] interpreted through and through" (1967, 263–64), and:

> To understand one another it is not sufficient to employ the same words; we have also to employ the same words to designate the same inner experiences, we must ultimately have our experiences *in common.* (Nietzsche 1973, 186)

As I discussed in more detail in chapter 1, it is through the social education of bodies or through the mnemotechnics of pain, as Nietzsche calls it (1969, 61), that linguistic convention constitutes a shared memory of what an experience means and so fabricates our experiences in common. However, it is necessary to add the qualification that while linguistic convention or meaning may precede and shape experience, the relation between the word and the experience cannot form a seamless whole. There must be the possibility of a lapse in memory, otherwise there would not be uncommon experience, misunderstanding, or transformation of meaning within the same cultural group. Merleau-Ponty adds this kind of qualification to Nietzsche's thoughts on the relation between meaning and experience (or between meaning and perception, to use Merleau-Ponty's terminology) by establishing in some detail a model of the intercorporeal world of perception as the site of expression. As discussed in chapter 5, for Merleau-Ponty, the body, through the inter-world of motility and perception, expresses both culture (or meaning) and being. As a consequence, also argued in chapter 5, the body, while informed by cultural convention, is, through the generosity of intercorporeal existence, creative in its evocation of existing cultural formations in its particular assembling of being. Hence, no members of a social group will have their experiences exactly in common. Still the salient point here, about the relation between meaning and perception/experience, is that,

Then what is a norm? 4

unless we are going to conclude that every encounter between indigenous and nonindigenous Australians in the past 200 years involved pathological lying, self-deception, and willful violence by the colonizers, then we need to suggest that nonindigenous Australians not only believed what they saw but also saw what they believed and, hence, that what they said they saw had the status of truth. _POWER   NIETZSCHE_

This is not to excuse the violence that has been done in the name of truth. Rather, it is to suggest that such violence could have only been done in the name of truth understood as "honest" expression of socially bound experience. Telling the truth matters, not because it simply sets the record straight but because truth is central to cultural formation and self-preservation. It has been the life-preserving consequences of truth that have allowed the proliferation of European cultures in Australia and in other European colonies. We nonindigenous inhabitants have built our ways of life under the shelter of the truth that sustains it. But this brings us to the question of the cost to indigenous cultures of the truth that drives us. To quote Nietzsche again:

> The importance of language for the development of culture lies in the fact that, in language, man juxtaposed to the one world another world of his own, a place which he thought so sturdy that from it he could move the rest of the world from its foundations and make himself lord over it. To the extent that he believed over long periods of time in the concepts and names of things as if they were *aeternae veritates*, man has acquired that pride by which he has raised himself above the animals: he really did believe that in language he had knowledge of the world. . . . [I]t is *the belief in found truth* from which the mightiest sources of strength have flowed. Very belatedly (only now) is it dawning on men that in their belief in language they have propagated a monstrous error. (Nietzsche 1984, 18-19)

On Nietzsche's model of truth, the error of colonization is not so much that it is based on wrong perceptions but that it is based on the belief that these perceptions belong to a truth that is found rather than cultural convention, and that this truth is universal and eternal rather than socially and historically specific. Put another way, in the words of Levinas, the error of colonization is the belief in a Platonic model of truth: that "the world of meanings precedes language and culture, which express it; [and] is indifferent to the system of signs that one can invent to make this world present to thought" (Levinas 1987b, 84).[11] This belief in found truth justifies colonization in that, for Plato, there is a privileged culture that has access to the world of meaning, of truth, and so can bypass historically specific cultural conventions. This privileged culture is that of Western reason, that of the lovers and guardians of absolute truth who by their claim to access apparently eternal Ideas win the right to rebuild the world in the image of these Ideas. But from the perspective of an anti-Platonism, to build a way of life upon the basis of the assumption that truth is found, eternal, and universal involves lying. It is this other side of truth, the lying involved, that characterizes colonization, that attests to the alterity that colonization offends, and that supports the destruction of the cultures of the colonized.

On the basis of a Nietzschean model of truth, there are three kinds of lying. The first is unconscious lying "according to fixed convention" (Nietzsche 1979, 84). This kind of lying is central to truth. Being bound to truth involves lying in several ways: linguistic convention informs experience by universalizing different perceptions under a single concept; giving the expressed perception the status of truth involves forgetting that truth is constructed; and imposing one's own cultural perspective on others involves denying the possibility of other perspectives. But this kind of lying is unconscious and to a certain extent "innocent." It proceedes through conventions that one has inherited, and if preservation of social life is the consequence of truth, then one would have a social duty to lie unconsciously in this way (ibid). The second kind of lying involves "misus[ing] fixed conventions by means of arbitrary substitutions or reversals of names" (81). Again, this can be "innocent," a matter of just seeing things differently to the majority because one's experience is informed by different conventions or is in some other way uncommon. What Foucault calls "reverse discourse," where power and knowledge realign to reverse the value of categories in strategies of resistance, would fall under this kind of lying (Foucault 1980a, 100–01), as would the views of the minority of white humanitarians whose voices of protest, based on uncommon perceptions of the injustice done to indigenous peoples, have accompanied 200 years of colonization in Australia— what Henry Reynolds calls "this whispering in our hearts" (Reynolds 1998). Or, misuse of convention may be a deliberate misreporting of one's experience.

In any of these modes, such misuse of convention is destructive of convention rather than life preserving and, as Nietzsche suggests, a social group will exclude the liar, the colonizers will revile the humanitarian dissident, not so much because of the "deception" itself but because of the harmful effects that such lying has on the stability of the dominant culture (Nietzsche 1979, 81). The third kind of lying, which Nietzsche tends to overlook, is willful lying in order to preserve truth.[12] While it may seem paradoxical to say preserving truth requires willful lying, it is precisely this kind of lying that Plato recommends to the guardians of truth who seek to embody eternal Ideas in the structure of the state. Medicinal or noble lying is necessary to implement absolute truth in the face of the expression of bodily appetite, as opposed to "reason" or to counter what is taken to be entrenched opinion and belief.[13]

It is this third kind of lying that attests most obviously to the presence of cultural difference and is perhaps most symptomatic that colonization is taking place. *Bringing Them Home* notes the extraordinary amount of willful lying, sanctioned by law, that was necessary to support the policies of forcible removal of indigenous children. "We are going to see your mother," rather than "We are going to fly you out of here," "Your parents are dead," rather than "I'm not going to tell you where they are," "Your family is free to visit you," rather than "We've told them it would be better if they don't." In the mouths of those who are bound by European modes of belonging, such willful lying is not necessarily designed to harm. Rather, it is designed to sever others from foreign ways of life deemed harmful to what is perceived to be the common good. But precisely because the good is not common, truth is not universal and eternal, such willful lying has been as harmful to its targets as any "misuse of convention" is to the dominant culture. What looks, from a European perspective, like medicinal lying to counter mere opinion, belief, and myth has effectively undermined the threads of truth that hold together these other ways of life. So while such lying may have enabled European life, it has served to disassemble indigenous cultures in Australia through the sense of abandonment it bestowed on the stolen children and through the doubt, shame, and sense of inadequacy about indigenous ways of belonging that it has fostered in the communities from which they were taken.[14] In the final analysis, if we admit to more than one set of cultural conventions, there is little to separate the noble or willful lie from misuse of convention, insofar as destruction of culture is characteristic of both; "misuse of convention" undermines the colonizing culture while the "noble lie" erodes the cultures of the colonized. Finally, such destruction could not take place if it was not supported by the forgetting characteristic of lying "innocently" or unconsciously according to fixed convention. Truth is likely to become more life denying the more it forgets it is convention and hence the more inflexible it becomes. Belief in found truth involves absolute forgetting, a totalizing gesture requiring a force of lying and possession so insistent and immoderate that one has to question the strength of the belief in found truth that underpins it.

Terra nullius, then, while true to one law, is really, as Robyn Ferrell argues, an "admission of ignorance" of other laws, other truths, other ways of belonging and, most important, of the aesthetic qualities of the law itself (1998, 316). And if truth has these aesthetic qualities of establishing, transforming, and preserving social relations, then we need to admit that the truth of *terra nullius* has been a judgment that has passed sentence on any original indigenous cultures, to such an extent that it is hard to tell the difference any more, at least from the perspective of the colonizers. Beyond the truth of any pure origin, what has been taken with the stolen years is the truth of indigenous experiences of colonization, and with this the possibility of cultural formations emerging beyond poor relatives of the dominant culture. So given the extent of cultural annihilation effected on the word of *terra nullius,* what is the point in soliciting and witnessing in the present indigenous testimonies of their experience of the past? The answer, as I will go on to argue, lies in a particular understanding of how the present is tied to the past. With this understanding, witnessing indigenous testimonies about the past in the present would allow us to give back the stolen years and thus give cultural difference a chance.

The truth of colonization, its social and individual embodiments, has a history that ties the present to the past. If we consider history to be linear or horizontal, where everything seems to progress as if the present is a product of the past, then just as individuals are the result of previous generations, of their errors, passions, and crimes, so the current state of Aboriginality as well as the privilege enjoyed by many nonindigenous cultures in this country are the product of the truth of *terra nullius* upheld by the related errors of colonization. Moira Gatens (1997) argues, partly on the basis of this horizontal notion of history, that insofar as the past endures in the present social imaginary, then we have a collective responsibility for the past and therefore for any harm to indigenous cultures that endures in the present. But Gatens also suggests that on the basis that the meaning of the past is contested in the present, we have a responsibility to engage with these other self-constituting narratives, these other truths, and to thereby "open the past to its own latent possibilities for change in our present" (12). That the way the past constitutes the present could be altered in the present implies that history is not only linear but also vertical, an idea of history upon which I believe the possibility of the promise of decolonization rests.[15]

Behold this eternally recurring gateway called the moment, says Nietzsche, from which a path leads backward to eternity and another contradictory pathway leads forward to eternity (Nietzsche 1978, 157–58). This is the idea of vertical history, where the past and future extend out of the present and where the future contradicts the past. As I argued in more detail in chapter 1, through this formulation of eternal recurrence, Nietzsche is suggesting a return to the self, a self-relation, involving a kind of temporality where the self neither escapes the past (linear history) nor simply repeats it (cyclic time). By defining history as extending from the present moment, Nietzsche is suggesting that one temporalizes oneself by recreating the past in a projection toward a different future. However, the future only contradicts the past, the self only returns differently to itself, if the truth that constitutes the self and its culture in the present moment is unsettled. This unsettling of truth involves a reinterpretation of the past that constitutes the present, and this reinterpretation is mobilized through the operation of memory and forgetting.

In "On the Uses and Disadvantages of History for Life," Nietzsche makes much of how a healthy culture, that is, a culture that is stable but open to change, needs both tradition (a memory) and forgetting. But he says little there about the actual operation of forgetting and how, in conjunction with memory, forgetting could be a positive activity. Contrary to the usual understanding of forgetting as a passive and negative force where the past recedes through a loss of objects and images, forgetting along with a selective memory, as I have already indicated in the earlier account of unconscious lying according to convention, can be understood as a creative activity that constitutes truth. The idea that present perception involves both memory and forgetting can also be put in terms of vertical history. To rephrase Galen Johnson's account of Merleau-Ponty on forgetting: Remembering is a figuring of the past that includes differentiation of the past from the present, a differentiation that produces a perception of the past; forgetting is a figuring of the past without differentiation where the past is not lost but subsumed within the present without being actually perceived (Johnson 1993, 204–05).[16] Or, as Merleau-Ponty himself puts it: Memory "spreads out in front of us like a picture, a former experience, whereas this past that remains our true present [by adhering to the body through habit] does not leave us but remains constantly hidden behind our gaze instead of being displayed before it" (1962, 83). Forgetting by itself may be therapeutic for the way it allows past meaning to inform present perception and hence cultural activities without effort. (Forgetting, on the part of the colonizers, allows their own habitual perception to dominate without noticing and without the possibility of being open to the new and the different.) And memory, by itself, may install personal and social stability by allowing perceptions of the past to reinforce confidence in the present. But, by themselves, memory and forgetting are ideal functions that change nothing. Rather, like the relation between truth and lies, there is a passage between memory and forgetting, forgetting and memory. Together and in this passage, memory and forgetting enact a rearticulation of differentiation of the past from the present, altering present meaning and hence perception, self-identity, and cultural formation.

This suggests that the expression of indigenous memories, testimonies of their experiences of colonization, does not consist in raking over the past for its own sake but represents a positive activity of self- and cultural reformation, a taking back of the stolen years. This is a memorialization of a past that is forgotten by the colonizers but that contests the truth that holds the colonizers in their dominant position. But this reinterpretation is occurring in a climate of the absolute forgetting that characterizes colonization. Either these testimonies are met with denial by the colonizers of this other past, and with this absolute forgetting there is a "disarticulation of past from presence" (Merleau-Ponty 1968, 197), a closing up of differentiation, so that the truth of *terra nullius* informs the present habitual assembling of being so thoroughly that nothing new can be seen—or, indigenous testimonies are not disputed but are countered with the memories of white Australians who remain proud of their own past, their own culture, and who claim a present supposedly uncontaminated by the assimilation policies that have done damage to indigenous cultures.[17]

Levinas, like Nietzsche, not only points to the creative aspect of such a self-serving memory in its constitution of truth and the self, but he also points to its colonizing aspect. In *Otherwise Than Being or Beyond Essence* he, in a manner not inconsistent with Merleau-Ponty, equates memory with representation, consciousness, and the assembling of identity in the language of the said. But in a departure from Merleau-Ponty, Levinas suggests that memory, caught in the domain of ontology, belongs to a consciousness that would disclose being by reducing what is other to the same. Time is the difference between present and past and, for ontology, "time is reminiscence" (Levinas 1981, 29). Reminiscence is the exposition of being that assembles "the dispersal of duration into nouns and propositions" (26–27), into the clarity and security of the said, into themes. While reminiscence is prompted by an "ex-ception," a difference in being between past and present and between the "who" speculating and the "what" disclosed, a "getting out of phase of the instant" and the "divergence of the identical from itself" (28), memory recuperates this difference, gathers the past into the present project, the other into the same (29). Understood in these terms, the subject of memory, who is also the subject of truth, establishes itself as an entity (a "who" that is a "what"), recovers from any "disruption of identity that the movement of temporalization provokes," and secures itself in the present of the said (Durie 1999, 47).[18] In such an operation of memory as a response to indigenous testimonies, nothing about the colonizing subject or his or her culture is altered or lost in the process: the subject just represents, rediscovers itself simultaneously with the totality of being, and returns to itself the same. This subject endures in the self-identity of consciousness and is closed in on and at home with itself.

I have suggested that in a Nietzschean model of truth, any expressed perception, any testimony, must be repeated before it can begin the work of truth and hence the work of cultural formation and self-preservation. And to be iterable, a testimony, bearing witness, must in turn be witnessed, acknowledged by others. What is missing from the truth that mobilizes colonization is a particular kind of strength required to bear witness to indigenous testimonies, a strength that enables the admission of the new and the different without violence, a strength born in the passage between memory and forgetting. Bearing witness in the interval between memory and forgetting involves being bound to truth in a way "delicate enough to be carried along by the waves, strong enough not to be blown apart by every wind" (Nietzsche 1979, 85). For the truth of *terra nullius,* for this eternal recurrence of the same, to be unsettled, for the future to contradict the past, indigenous testimonies must affect the fabric of dominant culture. Indigenous Australians are creating waves; the rest of us must bear witness and respond.

Pity, a sympathetic emotion directed toward another's pain and suffering, has, along with expressions of regret, been the most common response in Australia, both official and unofficial, to indigenous testimonies about the forcible removal of indigenous children. A notable exception is the government of New South Wales, on behalf of which the premier, Bob Carr, has extended a full apology to Aboriginal peoples for its "own role in endorsing policies and actions . . . [that] continue to inflict grief and suffering upon Aboriginal families and communities" (HREOC 1997, 287). Other official responses have tended to express pity and regret without responsibility, acknowledging how past mistakes of governments have adversely affected Aboriginal cultures and admitting that in taking land and children we, through ignorance and prejudice, failed to "imagine these things being done to us . . . [and so] failed to see that what we were doing degraded all of us" (286).[19] But this recognition of past mistakes, of a failure of imagination, and of the suffering that has resulted comes with a refusal to acknowledge "inter-generational guilt," as current Australian Prime Minister John Howard puts it. And it comes with the kind of self-serving memories mentioned earlier. For the vast majority of us, those indigenous memories do not seem to intersect with our own: they mark times and places where we were not present and recount suffering caused by acts that were not our own. Moreover, those acts of theft of land and children sprang from attitudes about cultural difference that we supposedly no longer hold. In staking a claim for our own memories against those of indigenous Australians, we are implying that there are at least two histories, two sets of memories that do not intersect, at least not any more. To stand accused, to suggest that indigenous memories do have something to do with me, to apologize for past acts and attitudes of others, would be to take responsibility for acts that were not my own; it would be to take a "black arm-band" approach to history, to dwell in the past of colonization rather than the present of multiculturalism, pluralism, and tolerance of difference. Or at least this is how the argument that would avoid responsibility proceeds. We are sorry but not responsible.

Martha Nussbaum points out that pity, insofar as it is endorsed as a beneficial human emotion from the Stoics through the egalitarian thinkers, such as Rousseau, is understood to rest on three beliefs: that the suffering of the other is "significant rather than trivial"; that the "suffering was not caused by the person's own fault"; and the belief in some kind of community or sense of commonness between myself and the other so that the other's suffering suggests a possibility for me (Nussbaum 1994, 141–42). It is this third aspect of pity, that the other is like me, hence, their suffering could be mine, that perhaps explains why shedding light on the impact of forcible removal policies on indigenous Australians has touched more nonindigenous Australians than the issue of land rights has or ever could. (As we all are or have been either a child or a parent or both, then we can "imagine these things being done to us.") But it is this assumption of commonness that suggests that pity is neither a sufficient nor an appropriate response. Pity, according to Nietzsche, is the most egotistical and self-serving of all the human sentiments. Not only is pity of little benefit to the sufferer but, he says, it is a vehicle of domination and appropriation of the other (Nietzsche 1974, 175–76). Pity is egotistical, because it interprets the other's suffering in terms of one's own experience and so "strips away from the suffering of others whatever is distinctly personal" (269). What is distinctly personal about suffering, for Nietzsche, is that it is, like any self-expression, an aspect of self-temporalization and, hence, self-reformation: a process of reinterpreting one's past, of healing wounds, of shedding the old and opening the new (ibid.). To respond to indigenous testimony of their own suffering with pity and without responsibility, without generosity, would be to risk subsuming this emerging truth and its accompanying cultural formation under the truth of the dominant culture. Pity, so understood, is just another mode of assimilation.

Pity, as a mode of assimilation, exemplifies a self that denies its openness to the other. In pity, the self is disturbed by its own possibilities but remains undisturbed by any alterity that the other's suffering might suggest. Also undisturbed is the self-knowledge, the truth, that holds the pitier in place. But this denial of one's openness to the other is just that: a denial. It is a denial that the privilege and stability many Australians currently enjoy is based on a history of assimilation and a degradation of the difference of indigenous cultures. Pity, with its assumption of commonness, along with policies of land acquisition and forcible removal of children and their assumptions of absolute truth are in Levinas' words denials of "the trace of the other in me," as are those responses to indigenous memories that affirm one's own relation to the past and deny any connection to the plight of others. But of this self-serving memory, Levinas asks: What accounts for the "getting out of phase of the instant" that provokes the gathering of reminiscence in the first place? What disrupts identity and so prompts memory? Levinas' provisional answer is that there must be a "temporality beyond reminiscence," "diachrony," an immemorial past, a lapse of time that cannot be recuperated through memory (1981, 30). That I do reminisce, that I am out of phase with myself, attests to this past: not to my historical past or to the historical past of others but to a relation to alterity that has never been present (24). That I am, that my identity is disturbed, that I reminisce and speak, attests to the saying that is a condition of the said, to "a being affected by the other whom I do not know" (25). I am this exposure to and movement toward the other that cannot be put to rest by the memories, the said, that it provokes. So while in response to indigenous memories many nonindigenous Australians would assert their own and so cleanse themselves of fault, those very responses contain what they would deny: a trace of the other in me.

This trace of the other, of alterity or irreducible difference, is Levinas' explanation for how multiple meanings and hence multiple cultures arise at all. In "Meaning and Sense," Levinas argues, in an analysis of different models of the relation between reality and meaning, that it is through exposure to the other's alterity that multiple meanings and hence multiple cultures arise (Levinas 1987b). He poses this thesis about the production of meaning and culture not just against the intellectualism and its notion of absolute truth that has justified colonization and assimilation but also against the multiculturalism that would now regret colonization and deny responsibility for it. Insofar as we may now regret the imperialism of indigenous cultures and the suffering it has caused in favor of cultural diversity and multiculturalism, then, according to Levinas, we would hold to another model of the relation between reality and meaning than the Platonic, one more in keeping with the phenomenology of Heidegger and Merleau-Ponty. While not addressing Nietzsche's anti-Platonism, what Levinas says of the phenomenological model of the relation between reality and meaning is also true of what I have discussed about Nietzsche's model of the relation between reality and truth. For this anti-Platonism, as with Nietzsche's, there is no common world, no prelinguistic reality that would justify the assimilation of different cultures under the way of seeing and belonging of the colonizers. Language, for Merleau-Ponty no less than for Nietzsche, assembles meaning and being, including the being of the one who speaks and is dependent on the sociohistorical context of the speaker and the listener (Levinas 1987b, 77). The corporeal expression of meaning is therefore creative of being and culture. For both Nietzsche and Merleau-Ponty, being is thus assembled and expressed in diverse ways. This diversity of cultural expression, this multiculturalism, "is not, for Merleau-Ponty, a betrayal of being, but is responsible for the glitter of the inexhaustible richness of its event" (Levinas 1987b, 83). All of these expressions, all of these cultures, are on the same plane and equally true, for truth on this account "is inseparable from its historical expression," without which it would be nothing (ibid).

Without denying that meaning and culture are created, that cultural expression is a work rather than a given, Levinas questions the indifference to cultural difference that he claims this phenomenological model of the production of cultural diversity implies. A work, a cultural gesture, does not arise at random in isolation from others and would not arise at all, Levinas insists, if there were not an "orientation . . . a leap, an outside-of-oneself toward the *other than oneself*" (90). This radical alterity toward which the work is orientated is "not only the collaborator and the neighbor of our cultural work of expression or the client of our artistic production, but the interlocutor . . . whose presence is already required for my cultural gesture of expression to be produced" (95). Without this orientation toward alterity, we would have to assume that culturally bound meanings arise at random, that different cultures are incommensurable, and that we are indifferent to cultural difference (88–89). On the contrary, says Levinas, colonization is testimony to the interpenetration of cultures, we are obsessed with cultural difference and, as I have argued with reference to Levinas in chapter 7, the production of knowledge, truth, and culture arises from our orientation toward it. This alterity cannot itself be known or eliminated, but it is felt in our experience of the other's strangeness. I am, my culture, bears witness to this alterity that disturbs it and without which I would be nothing. As this exposure to alterity is a condition of self-constitution and cultural production, there is always a trace of the other in the work that I am in the process of becoming. And this trace marks a debt to the other that cannot be repaid (Levinas 1981, 111). White responses to indigenous testimonies of the past in the present, whether expressing pity or recalling another more familiar past, are works of orientation toward the alterity that disturbs and solicits the response.

It can also be argued that those indigenous testimonies would be nothing without the witness that I am in response. This claim may mark a departure from Levinas, insofar as he insists that the orientation toward the other that produces cultural expression is one way and not reversible (i.e., the other comes first and is not dependent on my response, and the obligation to respond is not recpirocal). However, without resorting to reciprocity, Levinas does suggest repeatedly in *Otherwise Than Being or Beyond Essence* that while the alterity to which I bear witness "does not show itself to me, save through the trace of its reclusion, as the face of the neighbor," it also "becomes present only in my own voice" (1981, 140). My response matters for the cultural reformation that these testimonies would effect to find fertile ground. If decolonization is to proceed, it matters that my response does not deny the other, even if my voice, and the said it speaks, would attempt to settle the matter. For, as Derrida argues in exploring the undecidability of who comes first in Levinas (the other's face or my welcome as exposure to alterity), just as there is no welcome without the other's face, there is no face without the welcome, without the being-given to the other, without the witness to alterity that I am (Derrida 1999, 25).

In Levinas' model of the relation between reality and cultural meaning, then, beneath what is perceived or said, beneath the categories of language that suppress and totalize differences in the formation of culture, is the condition of the said; not a commonness but an exposure to alterity that is inseparable from articulation of a multiplicity of cultural meanings yet unsubsumed within them (Levinas 1981, 45–60). That I bear witness to cultural difference even as I would recover myself through pity, regret, or memory suggests the possibility that the meaning of *terra nullius* that secures my culture and soothes my ego can be unsettled. And I am suggesting that this disturbance issues from the strangeness of the testimonies of others I have not literally faced. The content of what is said in those testimonies matters not in terms of proof, or of evidence, or of the truth of indigenous experience. In any case, these testimonies cannot be judged in terms of evidence by a law that has been built on their erasure, or by memories for which they are out of reach. Rather (although Levinas would not put it this way), the content of what is said in these testimonies matters as the vehicle for the contestation of my truth, as the means by which the contestation of the truth of the dominant culture is effected.

This may mark a second departure from Levinas (or at least from some of his commentators) insofar as Levinas describes the alterity that calls me into question in terms of the "nudity" of the other's face (1981, 140; 1987, 96), and insofar as his commentators describe this in terms of "another's looking at me" rather than "any text or work" (Peperzak 1993, 164). This suggests that the condition for orientation toward the other may be immediate contact with the invisible within the visible of the face rather than contact with the invisible in words or other vehicles of cultural expressivity. After all, Levinas insists that this alterity is not a representation of the other but a "bareness without any cultural ornament," a surplus that breaks through his or her form. Still, this alterity is a surplus of form that breaks through "in the midst of the production of its form" (Levinas 1987b, 96), which can be said to be in the midst of the production of form through words. While the "signifyingness of the trace" of alterity is exemplified in a face, Levinas also admits that it can lie in a cultural form after the face has receded: it "lies in, for example, the writing and the style of a letter, in all that brings it about that during the emission of a message, which we capture on the basis of the letter's language and sincerity, someone passes, purely and simply" (105). The other manifests herself to me in divesting herself of form through words by which she would speak to me. And the other can still divest herself through words after a face as such insofar as these words have the power to touch me, in her absence, through the epiphany of the other they carry. What disturbs is the alterity that is surplus to and the condition of those indigenous testimonies. The saying of the stolen generations to which we bear witness, the strangeness of indigenous testimonies by which I am affected and that solicit my response, is testimony to the truth of alterity and hence testimony to my lies, to the way that not everything can be captured in my present, in my truth, by my memory. That these testimonies solicit a response is testimony to an immemorial past, testimony to a difference that cannot be remembered nor absolutely forgotten (Levinas 1981, 51). The eternal recurrence that Nietzsche suggests characterizes the self's relation to itself is, for Levinas, the eternal recurrence of this relation to alterity (110–11). In moving outside myself in the face of the other's testimony, I return to myself disturbed; the truth that constitutes my present is unsettled.

Neither pity nor regret for the past mistakes of others allows this unsettling to take effect in any concrete way. Regret for the acts of others gives nothing other than a shelter for oneself. For the other's testimony to strip our egos of their "pride and the dominating imperialism characteristic of [them]" (Levinas 1981, 110), we need to accept that the testimonies about forcible removals, for example, contest our truth, put into question our affirmation of ourselves and our confidence in our culture. To endure this contestation without evasion, without denying the trace of the other in ourselves, requires that we pass from pity for the other's suffering to questioning ourselves. This response of being-in-question amounts to responsibility for the other; a being-given to the other without thought of return; a movement toward the other that answers, without annulling, the debt to the other incurred in the constitution of oneself and one's culture.

In *Totality and Infinity*, Levinas considers this being-given to the other in terms of apology (1969, 240–47). Based on this, I want to argue that a full, open apology to indigenous Australians would be a minimal condition of such a response of being-in-question, an initiative through which responsibility could be enacted. But to say that responsibility could be an initiative enacted through an act of Parliament risks departing from Levinas a third time. The apology that Levinas refers to is that characteristic of the self open to the contestation and accusation issuing from alterity, the self of infinite responsibility in its apologetic position (ibid). The "I" disturbed by the other is apologetic because, while it "cannot renounce the egoism of its existence [that colonizes through the said] . . . the very fact of being in conversation [of responding] consists in recognizing that the Other has a *right* over this egoism" (240). Apology, as Levinas understands it, is a movement toward the other that, while asserting itself, inclines itself before others that call it to infinite responsibility, and that would judge it as not the origin of itself but responsible for others. This apology is a "risky uncovering of the self" (Levinas 1981, 48), an exposure to others, that "empties the I of its imperialism" (Levinas 1987b, 97), a witness to alterity that commands me "to give to the other taking the bread out of my own mouth, and making a gift of my own skin" (Levinas 1981, 138). But apology is not an attitude I will, a position I elect, or a response I consent to. This apology, this bearing witness to cultural difference as the disturbance that I am, this responsibility of being-in-question, is a *passivity*, a being affected by the other that I do not choose. On the other hand, an apology enacted deliberately in the theme of the said would be, like those self-serving memories discussed earlier, where consciousness attempts to regain self-control (102), as if to discharge the debt, annul the guilt, and so betray the apology by which I would welcome cultural difference.

The difference between the nonvolitional, unconditional apology called for by the other and the apology elected by me is the difference, remarked by Levinas, between ethics and politics, where ethics is not reducible to but a condition of politics (1969, 64). As I will discuss in more detail in chapter 9, politics for Levinas lies in the realm of the said, conscious judgment, and memorialization that effect an ontological closure to the other. This distinction between ethics and politics is problematic. Just as there is no face without the welcome and no surplus of the other's form without the production of form through the words the other leaves behind, there is, as Bernasconi argues in his account of the "third," no ethics without politics and no saying without the said (Bernasconi 1999, 86).[20] While Levinas says that the witness of "bottomless passivity of responsibility" is betrayed by the said, by thematization in the form of a spoken apology, for example, he also says that "[t]hematization is inevitable," and that it is "[i]n the play activating the cultural keyboard of language . . . [that] witness signifies by the very ambiguity of every said" (1981, 151–52; c.f. 164). There is no witness to cultural difference, no apology as responsibility, without the said, without the act of apology that would betray it. In other words, there is no unconditional generosity, no being-given to the other that is not also caught in cultural self-expressions. These expressions are ambiguous and not essentially destined to serve the self to the other's detriment. The other inspires, provokes, accuses, and contests, and I cannot help but respond. And while apology as a political act may risk converting exposure to the other into "egotistical pride" (142) it would also, if open without expectation of return, dismantle the shelter to myself and my culture provided by those official expressions of pity and regret accompanied by self-serving memories.

Such open apology to indigenous Australians would bear witness to the trace of the other within our cultural formations, without thematizing what it bears witness to (146). It would put our culture, our truths, our ways of belonging in question without insisting on controlling where that questioning would lead. Apology, in other words, is consistent with the radical generosity discussed in chapter 8: a primary dispossession, a giving back, not simply of land and children and other acquisitions but a giving of oneself and one's culture. This is a generosity provoked by the other, a movement toward the other that does not return to itself the same. As responsibility of being-in-question, apology is a "work" that envisages a future without me, a work of cultural formation for a world beyond one's own time, one's own memory (Levinas 1987b, 92–93). The question remains, though, whether we are strong enough to endure indigenous memories, whether we are bound to truth in a way open enough to be carried along by the waves, strong enough to not be blown apart by every wind.

NINE

GENEROSITY, COMMUNITY, AND POLITICS

IF WE TAKE UP one thread of Nietzsche's thinking, community is a sociohistorical formation built by truth, by language, which, through the mnemotechniques of pain, through the discipline of a body-memory, constitutes our experience in common. By concepts we share, those of us who belong to the one social body will see the same leaf and share an understanding of its nature, we will build bridges together and understand their purpose, and we will look at each other with recognition of the passions and reasons that drive us. In such a community, the leaf, the bridge, and the other, no less than the self who perceives and understands them, are cultural works built from linguistic concepts that we share and that give us our experience in common. Nietzsche, as indicated in chapters 1 and 8, is not happy with the exclusion of unique experience that this community requires. He would admit a kind of multiculturalism, a tolerance of difference based on the generosity of those individuals and communities strong enough to endure transgression of the concepts upon which their experience and cultural works are built.

Levinas, on the other hand, thinks that the generosity that welcomes cultural difference is of a different order, as is the experience that provides the basis of community formation. He is critical of any conception of community that bases sociality on shared experience. This, he says, grounds our relation to exteriority in knowledge we already embody, knowledge that strips the other of its alterity in building a culture in which nothing remains foreign (Levinas 1998, 180). For Levinas, on the other hand, community formation is based on generosity. But, as we have seen in chapters 6 and 7, generosity for Levinas is not a virtue belonging to a volitional subject or an excess of power that, through self-overcoming, enhances the existence of those secure in their form; generosity is the passivity of exposure to the irreducible difference of the other that both bases subjectivity in disturbed sensibility and opens that subjectivity to discourse through which cultural works are given. Beneath the community of commonness grounded in the said of language is the community of the saying, of exposure to alterity, or to borrow the words of Alphonso Lingis, "the community of those who have nothing in common."

> Before the rational community, there was the encounter with the other, the intruder. The encounter begins with the one who exposes himself to the demands and contestations of the other. Beneath the rational community, its common discourse of which every lucid mind is but the representative and its enterprises in which the efforts and passions of each are absorbed and deper-sonalized, is another community, the community that demands that the one who has his own communal identity, who produces his own nature, expose himself to the one with whom he has nothing in common, the stranger.
>
> This *other community* is not simply absorbed into the ratio-nal community; it recurs, it troubles the rational community, as its double or its shadow.
>
> This *other community* forms not in a work, but in the in-terruption of work and enterprises. It is not realized in having or producing something in common but in exposing oneself to the one with whom one has nothing in common: to the Aztec, the nomad, the guerrilla, the enemy. The other community forms when one recognizes, in the face of the other, an imperative. An imperative that not only contests the common discourse and community from which he or she is excluded, but everything one has or sets out to build in common with him or her. (Lingis 1994, 10–11)

How are we to understand the connection between these two communities? What is the connection, if any, between the community constituted by shared linguistic concepts that would admit cultural difference only through the generosity of those who, secured by a cultural identity, can afford to overlook, and so make good, the disruption that difference brings, and the other community where generosity, as passive sensibility, is born of that disruption and is not subsumed in the cultural gestures that are produced as a result? The connection between the two has been hinted at in previous chapters but will be addressed more directly here. The question of the connection between the two is the question of the politics of generosity that would produce rather than close off cultural difference in the transformation of community.

Politics, like morality, whether international, national, local, or personal, is fundamentally about the organization of society for the improvement of human survival (Levinas 1986, 29). It is about the regulation of differences and of exchange, the prevention of harm from one's enemies, the promotion and maintenance of some values over others. Politics therefore presupposes judgment, decision, and knowledge; judgment about what is good for one's survival and knowledge of the other, of the difference between an enemy and a friend, and of the difference between the source of harm and good.[1] That politics presupposes judgment, decision, and knowledge, and that judgment, decision, and knowledge involve consciousness, is why Levinas distinguishes politics from the ethical relation to the other and therefore from the generosity of exposure to alterity. He makes the distinction in order to save alterity from reduction to the Same that is characteristic of conscious judgment. The moral-political order is inspired and directed by ethical responsibility to the other ("the ethical norm of the interhuman"), and not the other way around (30).

In one of his many formulations of the relation between the political and the ethical orders, Levinas suggests that it is by the human capacity to *repress* the passivity of exposure, nonvolitional generosity, saying, that we are political:

> [M]an can repress his saying, and this ability to keep silent, to withhold oneself, is the ability to be political. Man can give himself in saying to the point of poetry—or he can withdraw into the nonsaying of lies. Language as *saying* is an ethical openness to the

other; as that which is *said*—reduced to a fixed identity or syn-
chronized presence—it is an ontological closure to the other.
(Levinas 1986, 29)

Politics, the organization of society for the improvement of human survival
that presupposes judgment, is an ontological closure to the other, reduction
of difference, parsimony. If politics presupposes withholding oneself in a
moment of judgment, then the politics of generosity, the decision and judgment about whether to welcome the other's difference, is a suppression of
the generosity of exposure to alterity that I am, despite myself. Just as the
political act of apology, discussed in the previous chapter, risks "repressing"
and so betraying the apology of exposure to the other that is its condition,
so does any generous act risk betraying the generosity that exposes me to
those with whom I have nothing in common. But this separation of politics
and ontology from ethics, the said from the saying, implies that the said of
language that organizes the social and constitutes our experience in common comes after and does not inform the saying that bears witness to
alterity in my encounter with the other. Similarly, the separation of politics
and ontology from ethics implies that the realm of the said, conceptualization,
knowledge, and judgment comes after, and may be inspired and interrupted
by, the affectivity or sensibility characteristic of exposure to the other, but
does not inform that sensibility. I have already suggested in chapter 8, by
questioning this separation and following Derrida, Bernasconi, and others,
that just as there is no said without the saying, no politics without ethics,
there is no saying without the said. Here I will tackle this question in a
different, although compatible, way by arguing (with reference to Merleau-
Ponty's ontology) that just as the generosity of exposure in the saying of
alterity inspires and directs the politics of generosity of the said, the community constituted through the said of the political-social realm informs the
generosity steeped in sensibility, that is, exposure to those with whom we
have nothing in common. The "passive" generosity of exposure is already
active and political, even if the "judgments" made are of the order of affective sensibility rather than conscious or thematized.

Moira Gatens' work on "imaginary bodies" is helpful in demonstrating
what is at stake in the question of the politics of generosity. What Levinas
calls language as the said and what Nietzsche calls truth is also what Gatens
calls the social imaginary: "those images, symbols, metaphors, and represen-

tations which help construct various forms of subjectivity" (Gatens 1996, viii). Included in a social imaginary are not only "imaginary bodies," ideas about bodies, but also ideas about the value of these bodies and how they are or should be related: "the (often unconscious) imaginaries of a specific culture [consist in] those ready made images and symbols through which we make sense of social bodies and which determine, in part, their value, their status, and what will be deemed their appropriate treatment" (ibid.). Gatens demonstrates in her critiques of various philosophical imaginaries, and of legal, journalistic, and everyday expressions of ideas about bodies, that the social imaginaries that organize Western communities systematically devalue, exclude, and justify violence toward some bodies on the basis of sex, race, and class. Hence, contrary to the thread of Nietzsche's thinking with which I began, insofar as social imaginaries, embodied in our language, laws, and theoretical and other social texts, construct various forms of subjectivity, they do *not* constitute our experience in common. As various analyses in previous chapters have indicated, we wear these social imaginaries differently depending on the value and meaning our bodies accrue within our social context. Nor, therefore, do these social imaginaries realize the organization of society for the improvement of the survival of all humans equally well.

With regard to ideas about the regulation of the relation between these bodies, I have suggested, in the Introduction and chapters 1 and 2, that the idea that dominates Western social imaginaries is contract and exchange between individuals. On the basis of this idea of sociality, social relations are subject to calculation and expectation of return in terms of values that favor the bodies that already dominate the sociopolitical sphere. This is an image of sociality that does not allow a generosity that would foster multiculturalism, nor therefore the improvement of survival of anyone other than those bodies that already dominate. Gatens formulates this aspect of social imaginaries in a different, although compatible, way. Taking into account that our social imaginary consists in ideas about bodies that denigrate and exclude different bodies, then, Gatens argues, insofar as "the modern civil body was instituted by and for a particular politico-economic group of men and explicitly excluded women (and others), [t]he historical relation of that body to women's powers and capacities [and those of "indigenous peoples, working-class men, and others"] has been one of 'capture' and 'utility' " (1996, 120). In rejecting this idea of sociality, Gatens argues, with reference to a complex reading of Spinoza's ideas of conatus and natural and civil law, which I do not have the space to do justice to here, that the responsibility for the effects of this image of sociality lies with the civil body whose laws and institutions, which embody this image, constitute the bodies of its citizens who then reproduce it in their behavior (115). The responsibility for changing this social imaginary would also therefore lie with the civil body: rather than blaming the individual whose violent behavior (against women and others) is consistent with the idea of "capture" and "utility" embodied in civil law, it is down to the civil body to become aware of and so to transform its principle of sociability into one that ensures the safety and security of all of its citizens (120). To this end, Gatens favors an idea of sociability based not on the capture and utility of the capacities and powers that have been excluded by the civil body but on her reading of Spinoza's principle of ethical community, where individuals thrive by combining with those whose capacities and powers agree with and enhance their own, under conditions where those traditionally excluded from the civil body are given civil power through this process of combination (111, 120).

Attending to the politics of generosity is a matter of attending to the source of any potential transformation of social imaginaries that, as Gatens has demonstrated, continue to do the damage to difference. Without denying that the civil body is responsible for the damage, this civil body is inseparable from the individuals who do its work (a point I do not think Gatens would deny). Hence, the possibility of transforming social imaginaries rests with the potential of these bodies who benefit from the ideas and values that structure the civil body to be open to different ways of being. This possibility rests not so much with accepting an alternative image of sociality but with an openness to others already operating within intersubjective relations. It is within the generosity of intercorporeality, I will argue, that the potential to open social imaginaries to different manners of being lies. This generosity is born not so much with the combining of bodies whose capacities and powers agree but with the possibility of those dominant bodies remaining open to and transformed by alterity without effacing that indeterminate difference. Such a politics rests in part on Levinas' insight that sociality is based on exposure to irreducible alterity. But it also rests on insisting with Merleau-Ponty, and contrary to Levinas, on the inseparability of the politico-ontological from the exposure to alterity of sensibility.

Attending to the politics of generosity that would foster rather than close off different ways of being in the formation of community involves an examination of a twofold role that bodies may play in the formation and transformation of community: how "imaginary bodies" (social ideas about different bodies and their relations manifest in the political organization of society) constitute different kinds of subjectivities and, second, how the generosity operating in relations between bodies can transform those subjectivities and thus open social imaginaries to new possibilities. My argument (which proceeds via a comparison of Merleau-Ponty's ontology and Levinas' ethics) is that the two are inseparable, that the generosity of intercorporeality is where politics (the organization of society for the improvement of human survival) takes place.

The political organization of society for the improvement of human survival proceeds through the constitution of subjectivities by social ideas and images about bodies and their interrelation. The political is ontological. But how are we to understand this process of constitution by the sociopolitical realm, and so how far does the political extend, where does the political take place? While Levinas tends to restrict politics to the realm of conscious judgment and knowledge, Merleau-Ponty's ontology would suggest that judgment and hence politics takes place where subjectivity is constituted, i.e., in prereflecitve perception. As I have argued in previous chapters, with reference to Merleau-Ponty's thoughts on the matter, the ideas embodied in our laws and social institutions do not constitute us from above at the level of consciousness. His is not an idealism that would have nonmaterial images capturing and molding the material; we embody social imaginaries insofar as we live through the bodies of others who are already social beings. Subjectivity is constituted on the basis of intersubjectivity, which for Merleau-Ponty is intercorporeality. I have already discussed in chapter 5 how, for Merleau-Ponty, subjectivity (which to him is equivalent to perception) assumes that the perceiving body is already caught in the perceived world, and that this ambiguity of corporeality is such that what is seen and felt is at the same time a being seen and a being felt. To perceive, speak, or act is to touch one's being-touched; the felt is a feeling. Hence, "subject" and "object," "culture" and "nature" (although the distinctions are only abstract), are articulated together through the perceiving body, through sensibility (Merleau-Ponty 1964d, 167). I will return to that point of ambiguity, which is also the point of generosity. The point about perception as sensibility that I wish to stress initially is that "our perception is cultural-historical," as Merleau-Ponty puts it in his notes (1968, 253). So, referring to *The Visible and the Invisible*,

I perceive red, for example, in terms of "a fossil drawn up from the depths of imaginary worlds," in terms of the social imaginary of redness, "which includes the tiles of roof tops, the flags of gatekeepers, and of the Revolution, [. . .] red garments, which includes [. . .] the dresses of women, robes of professors, bishops and advocate generals" (132).[2] Perception and, hence, subjectivity, which takes place in the "interworld" of affective sensibility, is "cultural-historical," because "the imaginary [. . .] is in my body as a diagram of the life of the actual" (Merleau-Ponty 1964b, 164). Hence, judgments and decisions that affect the political organization of society are not restricted to consciousness. They inhabit the body and so the perception of the subject. Perception is political, even if the judgments and decisions made there are not mine. The judgments and decisions made in perception are not mine in two senses: in the sense that perception is prereflective and therefore nonvolitional, and in the sense that perception is already informed by social imaginaries that come before me. Perception is not my doing: "I do not perceive any more than I speak—Perception has me as has language" (Merleau-Ponty 1968, 190).

That perception is cultural-historical suggests not only that social imaginaries that devalue and/or exclude different bodies on the basis of sex, race, and class operate through the constitution of carnal subjectivities but also that the judgments and decisions of the makers and guardians of the laws that regulate society are never abstracted from the imaginaries that are "in their bodies" and that they live to maintain. Based on Merleau-Ponty's model of the sociopolitical constitution of subjectivity, there is no "rational community" if by this we mean a community of "lucid minds" abstracted from their bodies, passions, and personal interests. Insofar as the makers and guardians of the laws are representatives of a "common discourse," their judgments and decisions will be informed by that discourse, by the "social imaginary" that is "in" them and that "has" them through perception. Given that this discourse is not so much about what we have in common but that it already devalues and excludes different bodies and ways of being, this devaluing and exclusion will be prolonged in every judgment made by the perceiving bodies who dominate in the legal and political realms. The white, middle-class government official or high court judge presiding over the granting of land rights to indigenous peoples will see black and white in a way that depends on the meaning, the imaginary worlds, of black and white (land and rights) from which his or her perception extends. This perception is prereflective, affective, and thoroughly corporeal, and while subject to reflection and modification after the event, the subsequent reflection, as perception of perception, never lifts itself completely out of the cultural-historical situation that informs it. Similarly, male philosophers presiding over the admission of a woman to their field may see "red" and reject her application in the end, not on the basis of purely "objective" criteria but on the basis of philosophical and sexual imaginaries from which their perception and judgment draw. (The philosophical imaginary, as I argued in chapter 7 with reference to Michèlle Le Doeuff, contains ideas and values about what counts as philosophy, as well as traces of the interests of men who are its vehicles.) Again, the perception and judgment that it contains can be "rationalized" after the event (her publications are not prestigious enough, she will not "fit it"), but such justifications are still bound to the philosophical and sexual imaginaries that inhabit the initial perception and keep the subject of philosophy closed to other meanings and values.

So far, Merleau-Ponty would be in agreement with Levinas' claim that perception (and its "judgments") can effect an ontological closure to the other. But, as discussed initially in chapter 3, for Merleau-Ponty this closure of perception to otherness is effected not simply through consciousness but through a cultural sedimentation of corporeal style according to the gestures and their meanings that one has inherited and embodied through habit. But as also discussed in previous chapters, for Merleau-Ponty, each perception and the judgment it contains, however rigid, is infected with ambiguity. Just as the body realizes "culture" through its expression in perception, perception also realizes "nature" or the "world" through its impact on the body. Perception takes place in the interworld of affectivity, "between" body and world, in the intertwining and reversibility of flesh. This ambiguity of perception is also its generosity where I am given and opened to a world as it is given to me. The generosity of perception effects a transformation of meaning and so a metamorphosis of my style of being and the world it actualizes. So, while "perception has me as has language," my perception and my speech do effect a transformation of meaning, insofar as my body, with reference to the imaginary worlds of meaning from which it draws, favors a pole of redness, depending on what I am doing and in what context, and depending on the *impact of the world on me* in that context (Merleau-Ponty 1973, 131–33). While it is in my own way, with reference to cultural-historical meaning, that I move and touch "red," I am also moved and

touched by "it" and, as it is in this ambiguity that "imaginary worlds continue to *make themselves*, the red is not *finished*" (Castoriadis 1997, 292). It
is the impact of the world on me, and the affectivity of that impact, that
lights the spark of perception or, as Merleau-Ponty also puts it, effects the
transgression of the world upon its meaning so that the red is not finished
(this acknowledgment of the impact of the world on me in perception
effects "the ontological rehabilitation of the sensible" (Merleau-Ponty 1964c,
167)). To see things in black and white or red, as if they are finished, is a
denial of the ambiguity of perception, and with this a denial of the impact
of the world on me. More important for my purposes here, the denial of
the ambiguity of perception, and with this the possibility of transforming
imaginary worlds, is also a denial of the other's alterity who animates perception and who therefore animates subjectivity. This brings me to a second
point about the sociopolitical constitution of subjectivity, besides the point
that perception is cultural-historical.

The second point about the sociopolitical constitution of subjectivity,
and the one toward which the first point has been heading, is that the
relation between the perceiving body and (cultural) meaning and between
the perceiving body and its sensible world is not a private or direct relation.
Rather, perception and language "have me," my body is only open to the
sensible world, and the imaginary is only "in my body," because my body
is also open to the bodies of others who are already social beings. Merleau-
Ponty's answer to his own question, "What is it that, from my side, comes
to animate the perceived world and language?" (1968, 190) is this: "We shall
completely understand this trespass of things upon their meaning [. . .] only
when we understand it as the trespass of oneself upon the other and of the
other on me" (1973, 133). The political is ontological, but only insofar as it
is always intersubjective. The trespass of intersubjectivity that animates perception and language is, for Merleau-Ponty, beneath reflection, the consciousness of the "I think," and what Levinas calls the "said" of language.
Intersubjectivity, like the perception of the world it animates, belongs to the
reversibility of flesh. While prereflective, this intercorporeality is no less
inflected with judgment, nor therefore politics. Intercoporeality and its
sociability is where the political begins. A further and related point I want
to draw out in what follows is that the intercorporeality at the heart of
sociability and community formation is essentially generous. The closure of
the other effected by the government official who sees in black and white

and the male philosopher who sees red is first of all an offense against the generosity of intercoproreality, an offense that continues the habit of social imaginaries that makes refugees of other ways of seeing and being.

The question is, how might the generosity of intercorporeality be harnessed against this closure to the other that, through a rigid perception, sees the other as finished? On the way to attempting an answer to this question, I will consider two ways of understanding Merleau-Ponty's model of the trespass of intersubjectivity, insofar as it relates to perception, meaning, and community formation. The first is the understanding highlighted by Levinas in his critiques of Merleau-Ponty, emphasizing Merleau-Ponty's tendency to base intersubjectivity, community formation, and sociability on an agreement between bodies that share the same language, knowledge, and cultural world.[3] In a paper that addresses Merleau-Ponty's reading of Husserl in "The Philosopher and His Shadow" (1964d), Levinas, while admiring the way Merleau-Ponty accentuates in Husserl's *Ideen II* "everything that makes the relation with others depend upon that carnal structure of sensibility," is critical of the way Merleau-Ponty sets up that structure so that intersubjectivity eliminates anything foreign to it (Levinas 1994, 100). Merleau-Ponty does this, according to Levinas, by firstly modeling sensibility or perception (where the felt is also a being felt) on the model of two hands of one body touching each other (Levinas 1994, 99). This, says Levinas, becomes Merleau-Ponty's prototype of intersubjectivity (where "I shake another man's hand") so that, insofar as the meaning of the sensible content of perception presupposes the constitution of intersubjectivity, this is by *agreement* between the other and me where, through the handshake extended from my body to the other's, both become elements of a single intercorporeality (100). To put Levinas' criticism of Merleau-Ponty in terms of the issue I am addressing, while I am given to and borrow myself, and hence the meaning of my experiences from the bodies of others and vice versa, while the social imaginary is "in my body" and "in" the other on the basis of intersubjectivity, intersubjectivity accomplishes community by establishing common ground between different bodies, so that they belong to one social body of shared meaning and knowledge. Levinas summarizes this, his interpretation of Merleau-Ponty's model of intersubjectivity, as follows:

> Intersubjectivity, constituting itself in sensibility, described on the basis of the "reflected touching" of two hands touching one

another, is structured according to the community between the "touching" and the "being touched," "the common act of feeling and being felt." It is a community that is affirmed in its agreement about [*autour de*] being—about things and the world. (Levinas 1994, 101)

Levinas' objection to Merleau-Ponty's model of intersubjectivity (as he interprets it) is that, despite Merleau-Ponty's claims that this is a "pretheoretical" structure based on the "I can" rather than "I think," his model effectively grounds the constitution of community in "shared" knowledge which is based on prior knowledge that I already embody. "Thus, sociality does not break the order of consciousness any more than does knowledge [*savoir*], which, cleaving to the *known* [*su*], immediately coincides with whatever might be foreign to it" (Levinas 1994, 101). What this means for the politics of generosity is that, based on Levinas' reading of Merleau-Ponty's understanding of the structure of intersubjectivity, there is no room for admitting difference without erasure in the constitution of subjectivity, nor therefore in the formation of community. On Levinas' reading of Merleau-Ponty's model of the tresspass of intersubjectivity, the exclusions and valuations of bodies that Gatens finds in modern social imaginaries are already operating and are reproduced in the sociality "between" bodies. Decisions and judgments, although prereflective, are made about difference in the formation of one intercorporeality, so that the reversibility of flesh, that is, perception of the other, subsumes what is foreign under terms already established in existing social bodies.

Against Merleau-Ponty's model of intersubjectivity (as Levinas understands it), based on the transmission of mutual knowledge in the constitution of one social body, Levinas posits his ethical order of sociality based on the gift. This has been discussed in chapters 7 and 8 in different terms. In the handshake, Levinas suggests, there is "a *radical separation* between the two hands, which in point of fact do not belong to the same body" (1994, 102). The other's "ineradicable difference," "*signified* in the nakedness of the face [. . .] in the expressivity of the other person's whole sensible being, even in the hand one shakes," is what initiates the handshake (ibid.). And the handshake signifies not the transmission of knowledge but the gift of myself for the other, the saying, "going from myself to the other" with "a certain indifference toward compensations in reciprocity" (101). For Levinas, only by understanding intersubjectivity in these terms, in terms of a "spirituality of the social" "beyond being" (beyond ontology and politics), in terms of a bond lying in "the non-indifference of persons toward one another," can we conceive of a sociality that "does not absorb the difference of strangeness" (103). This sociality is provoked by the other's difference of strangeness that founds my uniqueness as the "here I am" for the other (hence, the radical separation between two hands). This sociality is manifest in the generosity of exposure where I am given to the other unconditionally through the passive sensibility that is the saying of the spoken word, and the difference of strangeness that provokes my movement toward the other is not absorbed by what is said as a result.

For Levinas, politics does not extend to this inaugural moment of sociality, at least not at first glance. This sociality is without politics because, as Levinas has argued earlier in *Otherwise Than Being*, it is without problems, and it is without problems because it is without decision or judgment about differences (1981, 161). There are no decisions or judgments here, because the ethical relation to the other is neither ontic or ontological (144): the alterity that commands me to the other does not appear in the other as a cultural gesture (there is no significant gesture by which comparisons and judgments could be made), and the generosity of my response is neither a cultural gesture nor an act based on a decision or judgment I make (140, 144). The generosity of exposure is a having been given to the other, "not the generosity of offering oneself, which would be an act" (75); this sociality of the one-for-the-other is prior to any decision, judgment, and every (political, moral, and social) position (144), and this sociality precedes the empirical order of the state (116).

But can this be right? If existing social imaginaries favor the bodies and modes of being that dominate the social and political sphere, this implies that the unconditional generosity of exposure is already distributed inequitably by the political organization of society, demanding of the subordinated self-sacrifice and openness to the privileged who would leave the black, white, and red finished. Merleau-Ponty has pushed sociality, community formation, and politics back from the ontic realm of reflection and calculation (which for him does not exist in any pure form) to the ontological realm of intersubjectivity where prereflective judgments are made in the intercorporeal expression of culture that is actualized through that expression. Levinas, convinced that this understanding of intersubjectivity effaces difference no less than the ideal of community between rational minds, appears to take the origin of sociality back even farther to an ethical openness to the other that is no longer political or ontological. While thereby establishing the ethical and affective basis of sociality, the potential problem with separating radical generosity from ontology and politics is that who the other is and what he or she has done (as a corporeal expression of a social imaginary) make no difference to my responsibility for and openness to him or her. And it would make every decision, action, and judgment I make, and every word I utter, *equally* a betrayal of exposure to the other that precedes it and is its condition and *equally* a closure to the other who provokes it. All acts and judgments (whether despicable or not) of all persons (whether beneficiaries of current social imaginaries or not) would be equally a closure to alterity.

But if the ethical relation is really outside of ontology and therefore the cultural-historical dimesion of perception, what are we to make of Levinas' claim that the other's "ineradicable difference" is not just "*signified*" in the nakedness of the face" but also in "the expressivity of the other person's whole sensible being, even in the hand one shakes"? Does not this expressivity belong to the ontological expression of imaginary worlds by a body, and hence to the politics, that ethics is meant to exceed? And if the ethical relation is really outside of politics, what are we to make of Levinas' claims that justice (involving concern for all other others, consciousness, comparison, coexistence, thematization, etc.) "is shown from the first" in the ethical relation (1981, 159), and that "there is a question of the said and being only because saying or responsibility require justice" (45). Justice is always called for in the ethical relation because, according to Levinas, conscious judgment, perception, and comparison are there from the first, in that the other who inspires and accuses me is in relation to a "third party," to other others to whom they are responsible and who treat me, alongside the other I face, as someone to be concerned about and welcomed (161). The here I am one-for-the-other of radical generosity always also refers to other social beings and, hence, is mediated by the political, by the organization of society for the improvement of the human survival, and so by the need for reflection, comparison, and conscious judgment.[4]

While Levinas thus acknowledges that the inaugural moment of sociality is perhaps inseparable from politics and justice, he also depersonalizes politics by assuming it operates only through grand themes and conscious decisions and judgments. He does not seem to grant that the political is personal, and that perhaps politics is also inseparable from sensibility, from the prereflective being-given to the other by whose alterity here I am. If justice is called for from the first, then this is because other others are there from the first, not by conscious judgment (to which Levinas reduces politics and justice) but in the expressivity of the other person's whole sensible being, that is, in the ontological expression of cultural-political-historical imaginary worlds that is inseparable from the nonindifference to difference of sensibility. This suggestion, that the ethical and the politico-ontological are inseparable in the formation and transformation of community and that this does not imply a closure to alterity is indicated in a second way of reading Merleau-Ponty's idea of the trespass of one upon the other in perception, a reading that Levinas' critiques overlook.

That intersubjectivity conceived in politico-ontological terms remains indifferent to difference would be a consequence of Merleau-Ponty's understanding of the trespass of intersubjectivity if we accept Levinas' reading. Merleau-Ponty does say enough to allow Levinas' reading, and not just in "The Philosopher and His Shadow." In another paper, "Dialogue and the Perception of the Other" (which has the advantage of not being burdened by a reading of Husserl's *Ideen II*), Merleau-Ponty seems to confirm Levinas' criticism of him as follows: "The other's body is a kind of replica of myself, a wandering double which haunts my surroundings" (an anonymous generalized corporeality), and "we encroach upon one another inasmuch as we belong to the same cultural world, and above all to the same language, and my acts of expression and the other's derive from the same institution" (Merleau-Ponty 1973, 134, 139). But if we follow this paper through, we find the kind of generosity and nonindifference to difference that Levinas claims is the basis of sociality: an openness upon and giving to the other, provoked by the other's alterity, that is not also a closure to the other. Just as Merleau-Ponty effects an ontological rehabilitation of the sensible, he effects an ontological rehabilitation of the other. Levinas misses this, insofar as he reads a linear progression into Merleau-Ponty's account of intersubjectivity: first carnal reflexivity (my two hands touching and being touched), then perception of the world, then intersubjective agreement about the content of perception through the formation of one intercorporeality. Levinas reads Merleau-Ponty's account of intersubjectivity as the formation of one body that "breaks egological isolation" while maintaining the primacy of the self (Levinas 1994, 101). But, upon close scrutiny, it is not so clear that for Merleau-Ponty the self as a perceiving body comes before and so dominates the other.

Having said, in "Dialogue and the Perception of the Other," that the experience of the other is of a replica of myself, Merleau-Ponty adds that, "[I]t is not enough simply to say that henceforth I inhabit another body" (1973, 135); there is a "mysterious slippage," a "decentering" of myself, so that "the other is not I" (134–35). And having said that each body encroaches on the other in as much as we share the same language, Merleau-Ponty adds that "this 'general' usage of speech presupposes another more fundamental practice" (139). The shared gestures that would make us part of the same intercorporeality and the words (or what Levinas would call the "said" of language) that provide our common cultural background are built up through "cultural sedimentation" (141) which, as discussed in Part II, effects an ontological closure to the other. But accompanying all institutional language and its corporeal support is an operation of intercoporeality where the other impacts on me as there is a "catch" of my gestures toward them. Merleau-Ponty does admit that this "more fundamental practice" attempts to produce a common culture, but he is less certain of its success. This more fundamental practice of intercorporeality, "the trespass of oneself upon the other and of the other on me," involves being disturbed by alterity. This disturbance by what my body does not "catch" is what animates perception and language and, most important, allows for the transformation of meaning and ways of being.

> If the other person is really another, at a certain stage I must be surprised, disorientated. If we are to meet not just through what we have in common but in what is different between us [this] presupposes a transformation of myself and of the other as well. (Merleau-Ponty 1973, 142)

Merleau-Ponty also suggests in the same passage, and problematically, that, in this transformation of meaning and being in response to the other's indeterminate difference, "our differences can no longer be opaque qualities. They must become meaning" if the other's indeterminate difference that surprises, disorients, and so animates perception is not to be dismissed as nonsense. The issue is to what extent this becoming meaning through intercorporeality is a totalizing gesture that subsumes the disturbance of the other under the social imaginaries that inhabit the bodies that dominate our culture. The most promising thread of Merleau-Ponty's thinking here suggests that, in order for the other's alterity to animate and transform perception without being absorbed in the process, it is those dominant imaginaries that must give way. The animation of perception and meaning by the trespass of the other rests on allowing oneself to "be lead by the flow" of the other's discourse, "especially at the moment he withdraws from us and threatens to fall into non-sense," so that what does not fall so easily into the catch of familiar gestures is capable of transforming us into the other and opening "us to another meaning" (Merleau-Ponty 1973, 143). While Merleau-Ponty also assumes, at least in this paper, a kind of communion between different bodies as an ideal end point to this intercorporeal relation, it is still the other's difference that inspires that attempt at communion, and this alterity cannot be absorbed. In Merleau-Ponty's own terms, this disturbing "spontaneous" operation of speech (what Levinas might call the "saying" of language), "the first 'human' signification [. . .] surpasses our common prehistory even though prolonging its movement" (141); this spontaneous power (which is "not a god") "pulls significations from us," "destroys the generality of the species, and brings [man] to admit others into his deepest singularity" (146).

On the issue of which comes first for Merleau-Ponty, my corporeal reflexivity, perception of the world, or the spontaneous power of intercorporeality, this is equally uncertain. While Merleau-Ponty speaks of "a carnal relation to the world *and* to the other" (1973, 139, emphasis added) that would put perception of the world on the same plane as perception of the other, either as two examples of the same operation or where the carnal relation to the other would give sensibility its significant content by agree-ment after the event, he also says that "the other always slips in at the junction between the world and ourselves" (138). This suggests that perception in general and, hence, the disturbance that animates perception and transforms imaginary worlds is opened by and dependent on the sociability of intercorporeality. And while it can seem as if my corporeal reflexivity is already in place before the world or the other, which would allow the imaginary in my body to dominate, it is also the case that it is the other's body entering my field that "multipl[ies] it from within," and it is through this multiplication, this decentering, that "as a body, I am 'exposed' to the world" (ibid.). This exposure to the world through the disturbance of the other's body "is not an accident intruding from outside upon a pure cognitive subject [. . .] or a 'content' of experience among many others but our first insertion into the world and into truth" (139). In this way Merleau-Ponty, through his model of intercorporeality, makes prereflective perception and judgment political without assuming that the politico-ontological effects a closure to the other.

The importance of Levinas' claim, that the other's alterity, the other's "ineradicable difference," is the basis of sociality cannot be overstated. This bases subjectivity and all cultural works on nonindifference to difference, on the generosity of being open to the other without seeking compensation. However, to suggest that this movement toward the other could be outside of ontology and politics and therefore passive and unconditional is a problem. It is essential it seems to me to still think of this strangeness that disturbs, inaugurates subjectivity, and surpasses and transforms existing imaginary bodies, within ontology and therefore within politics, as Merleau-Ponty does, albeit in the tentative way that he does.[5] To do so does not return us to the idea of sociality reducible to an exchange economy of "rational minds" where generosity, as a virtue built by habit informed by existing imaginaries, and justice are subject to calculation and expectation of return and so would effect an ontological closure to the other. But figuring subjectivity within the politico-ontological in a way that bases the disorientation of perception and subjectivity on the sociability of intercorporeality, does point to how and why this exchange economy has persisted with its parsimonious effects by indicating why the bodies that dominate and extract privilege in this exchange economy continue to see the other in black and white and red, as if the black and white and red are finished. Such rigidity and closure to different ways of being do not need to be a deliberate withholding of oneself in a moment of conscious reflection (which is the terms in which Levinas defines justice and politics), although it could also be that. But, based on Merleau-Ponty's ontology, such rigidity would first of all be the effect of sedimentation of the social imaginaries that inform perception in a way that I do not choose.

While attending to injustice, the ontological closure to the other, at a prereflective level, Merleau-Ponty's understanding of how alterity animates perception also allows for the possibility that this sedimentation could be disturbed not from outside of the intercorporeal, cultural-political-historical basis of perception but from within the sociability of intercorporeality, from the disorientation effected by the other's body that is the basis of perception. It is this disorientation that animates perception, inspires subjectivity, is our "first insertion into the world," and while therefore prolonging the cultural-historical imaginaries that have my body in perception, it also surpasses them. The other's alterity does not have to become meaning in this process, in a way that immediately subsumes "whatever might be foreign" under existing social imaginaries, as Levinas' reading of Merleau-Ponty suggests. Rather, the alterity that animates perception allows for the possibility that the black, white, and red are not finished and so opens my movement toward the other without promise of returning the same and allows the other into the singularity of subjectivity that it has inspired. Being "led by the flow" of this disorientation, toward the other without promise of return, which would transform meaning and so admit other ways of seeing and being, is no more or less an act or a gesture subject to choice than the sedimentation, the return to the imaginaries in my body, that is also inherent in perception. This disorientation troubles perception and its tendency toward sedimentation from the first. Alterity therefore troubles existing social imaginaries within every act and gesture (both prereflective and volitional). Both openness toward the other that transforms meaning and its closure through sedimentation of imaginaries are prereflective and corporeal, both are part of the ambiguity of subjectivity that is opened by the other, and both are manifest only within that subjectivity, its perceptions, acts, and gestures, that have me and that I am, not by choice but by the grace of the other's alterity.

To relegate this disorientation and its ethical import to the realm of extreme passivity outside of an act, perception, or gesture and therefore outside of the cultural-political-historical is unnecessary and possibly counterproductive. If ethical openness to the other is prior to the political as a passive, unconditional generosity, and if the political is a repression of the ethical relation, as Levinas sometimes suggests, so that every perception, action, and judgment is equally a closure to the other that provokes it, then it is difficult to envisage how transformation of meaning and therefore of the social could occur in such a way as to remain open to other ways of being. However, allowing that the ethical relation, my disorientation toward the other, falls within perception, acts, and gestures does not render alterity reducible to existing social imaginaries, nor does it cancel Levinas' important idea that nonindifference toward others is the basis of sociality. On the contrary, only if alterity always troubles social imaginaries from within their expression, through intercorporeal perception, acts, and gestures, could it be said that these imaginaries and the bodies that gain privilege from them are open to transformation and to different ways of being.

This does not suggest any particular program of political practice that could better regulate unconditional generosity, ethical openness to the other. Rather to admit that alterity troubles social imaginaries *within* their cultural-political-historical expression suggests that unconditional generosity, of the kind Levinas envisages is at the basis of sociality, is never present in any pure form. As Derrida suggests, "[n]o matter what Levinas might have said, the determinability of this limit [between the ethical and the political] was never pure, and it never will be" (1999, 99). To admit this is not to be defeatist about the possibility of changing what is nor is it to deny that nonindifference to difference underlies *every* encounter, every perception, and is the basis of subjectivity and community. Rather, it is to acknowledge, as Levinas increasingly does, that the "ineradicable difference" that animates and disorientates me is signified in "the expressivity of the other person's whole sensible being, even in the hand one shakes," and that this expressivity is cultural-historical so that neither I nor the other is ever innocent or free of the social imaginaries that already position us, to our benefit or detriment, in relation to other others and these other others in relation to me. Justice, and therefore politics, is called for from the first in the ethical openness to the other, not just because nonindifference to difference is a precondition to justice (in being the condition of, inseparable from but not reducible to, every act, whether "good" or "bad"), but because the ineradicable difference that calls me to the other is inseparable from the other's cultural baggage as I feel it being felt. I will feel the indeterminable difference, the disorientation, accordingly. So it is no accident that Levinas (and Lingis) do not include the white, middle-class businessman, the philosopher, or the high court judge in their list of concrete others who are most likely to signify this alterity that calls me to the other. These others do not rate a mention, not because they do not move me (for they do, if I encounter them at all), but because the expressivity of their sensible being contests less, benefits more from, and has more in common with corporeal and institutionalized expressions of existing social imaginaries (including my own) than the "Aztec," "nomad," "guerrilla," "refugee," or "orphan." Without denying that nonindifference to difference underlies *every* encounter and is the basis of subjectivity and sociality, it makes a difference to the gesture that necessarily expresses or accompanies that nonindifference if the other, presenting herself for a job in philosophy or for native title in court, is someone who is already felt to be out of place within a philosophical imaginary or within the law of the land. And the cultural-political-historical makeup of those sitting on the selection panel or on the high court makes a difference to whether they will be "led by the flow" of the other's discourse, to whether they remain open to the other or effect an ontological closure.

That the expressivity of the other person's whole sensible being and of mine makes a difference to the nonindifference to difference is not to return Levinas' ethics to the realm of existing knowledge, calculation, or the domain of the "ought." To admit that the expressivity of social imaginaries makes a difference to the nonindifference to difference is to admit that politics makes a difference to any encounter with the other in terms of what is felt rather than known, and in terms of what my (indeterminate) response already is in disturbed sensibility rather than in terms of what my response ought to be. However, if we are serious about our responsibility for the refugees our social imaginaries continue to effect, then we ought to take heed of the contestations that haunt us. To grant that "ineradicable difference" disturbs the political from within and also that generosity of being-given to the other it prompts is never unconditional is also to admit that "being led by the flow" of this disorientation is not a question of passivity prior to any particular act. This is not to deny the aporetic structure of generosity. Recognizing that subjectivity as sensibility animated by the other's alterity is inseparable from the act, from politics, and so from the danger of doing damage to difference is to suggest that an ethico-politics of sexual and cultural difference is to be found not in the self-serving collection of debts nor in an expectation of unconditional self-sacrifice in the service of the other but in the indeterminacy of generous acts that lie somewhere in between. That generosity born of exposure to alterity is necessarily also a closure to the other is not an excuse for inaction or passivity, nor a license for justifying the most other-denying acts. On the contrary, to paraphrase John Caputo, this aporia of generosity underscores a passionate politics and an impatience for justice embodied in acts that risk oneself now for a justice that is never here.[6] To stay open to other ways of being, to see red, black, and white as not finished, to remain troubled by the other takes work. While the possibility of being led by the flow of alterity is already there in perception and in every act and gesture, to make good this possibility would require a break with old habits, an unsettling of sedimentation, particularly by those who benefit from existing social imaginaries. The politics of generosity begins with all of us, it begins and remains in trouble, and it begins within the act.

CONCLUSION

WHILE IN THE PROCESS of finishing this book, mindful of the daunting prospect of writing a conclusion to a topic as impossible as generosity, I was asked if I would respond to a plenary address at a Women's Studies conference. The address in question was to be a joint paper by Helen Keane and Marsha Rosengarten entitled "The Biology of Sexed Subjects," and I was told by the convenors that they were chosen as plenary speakers on the basis of being relatively new to their field but on its cutting edge.[1] I had admired their work for some time for the way it (separately and differently) addresses the ambiguities and contradictions of scientific biological discourse—Keane on addiction (1999) and Rosengarten on blood and other body matter (2001)—harnessing these ambiguities and contradictions to demonstrate that even in scientific terms body-matter thwarts our sexed and species boundaries and unsettles any attempt to fix our identities in unsavory, discriminating, and singular terms. At least this is how their work impacts on me. To respond to such work in the context mentioned provided the opportunity to think through the possibility of responding generously—in a way that would be neither self-serving nor patronizing; that would not endorse myself by finishing them off in passing judgment on their work, but that would acknowledge the impact of their work on me, while giving it the more elevated public status, within an academic institution, that I feel it warrants.

To take up this offer provided the challenge of practicing the generosity I write about, but squarely within my own profession. (But already, in saying that if I had achieved these objectives my response would be generous, I have failed, as I have, no doubt, throughout this book in responding to other's writings on the body.) At the same time, the content of what I was asked to respond to provided the opportunity to suggest that the matter Keane and Rosengarten write about (called, variously, blood, hormones, tissue grafts, neurotransmitters, etc.) is itself generous as is the way their responses to it, their writing about it, animates it without finishing it off.

It took some time and some other inspiring encounters to make this connection between concluding by saying what I might mean by corporeal generosity, the possibility of practicing generosity as a respondent in an academic context, and the content of what I have been asked to respond to, the demonstrated generosity of intercorporeality.[2] Through a somewhat convoluted route, part of which I have just relegated to a note, I have settled on one sentence of Nietzsche's, from *Thus Spoke Zarathustra*, in an attempt to capture what I might mean by "corporeal generosity." I say, paraphrasing Nietzsche, and in response to Keane's and Rosengarten's paper, and to all of the others who appear in and have inspired this book: of all that is written, *I love most what is written in blood* (Nietzsche 1978, 40). What I mean by corporeal generosity, as I have developed the idea throughout this book, is, in a sense, writing in blood and love of that. Corporeal generosity is writing passionately in blood, writing in matter that defies the culturally informed habits of perception and judgment that would perpetuate injustice by shoring up body integrity, singular identity, and their distinctions between inside and outside, culture and nature, self and other.

But what does it mean to say "I love most what is written in blood?" I did not say I love what is written *on* blood, or *about* blood, but *in* blood. So to say that corporeal generosity is writing in blood and love of that is not to evoke a metaphor of writing or of generosity to suggest that the two are similar to each other and similar to blood. To say generosity is writing in blood and love of that does imply something that plays off what I think is meant by "blood"; it implies that generosity is a kind of life force, a passionate defiance of corporeal borders in response to being cut, touched, or wounded, an overflowing that is neither simply active or passive. And it implies that there might be some violence involved in this generosity. But the definition of generosity as writing in blood and love of that is just as literal as metaphoric. To understand the word, language, meaning in terms of a metaphor that stands above, on, or about the work being addressed or above the body that the work is about is to miss what matters. The word, and its socially sanctioned meanings (spoken, gestural, or written), is not *on* or *about* its matter, as if separate from it. The word, social meaning, does come before a particular body, but not to shape it simply into a seamless, socially recognized whole (which would be idealism, or what I gather some mean by "social constructionism"—where the body would be a "somatic fact created by a cultural effect"). And the word does come after a particular body, but not to describe its truth in commonly accepted terms (which would be realism or empiricism—where the word and its meaning might be described as a "cultural fact created by a somatic effect").[3] Rather, the word, the meaning of my response to the matter that moves me, is also always *of* a body, written in blood.

We do not have to write *about* the body, its gestures, cells, and fluids, to write *in* blood. A response to a person in the street, to a picture, a poem, or to a historical or a political event can also be written in blood. In a sense we cannot help but write in blood, even the scientist, the lawmaker, and the judge, although she or he might deny it. We cannot help but respond to the other in matter that overflows any perceived integrity of the self. And, as in this response our self-possession is given over to the other, we cannot help our generosity. If we understand the author in terms suggested in this book, as animated flesh, fluids, forces, and affects, opened by and to the other's palpable difference signified in the strangeness of her or his actions or words, then the discourse and the actions that the author offers in response to this strangeness are of that author's body as a trace of the alterity that provokes it. We perceive, speak, and write to touch what touches us, to touch our being-touched. What we perceive, think, or write is written in our blood, is an affective material offering of our body to the other whose difference inspires and moves us. And in that blood donation, that perception and its verbal expression, the skin that holds our self-possession is broken; we cannot tell the difference between what touches and what is touched. My body, and its expression, is real-ized, ambiguously and open, in this writing for the other, between the touching and being touched, between inside and outside, culture and nature, self and other.

The words and concepts that would express, as it writes, this body that touches its being-touched in response to another, are cultural-historical for sure. I do not invent these words or their meanings; these actions and their morality come before me and are incorporated in the social and political institutions into which I am born and in which I dwell. And, as I have argued in different ways, these words and their meanings have my body through habitual ways of being. Or, to summarize this point again in Nietzsche's words, a person has "selected and breathed life into their means of expression, not by chance but of necessity, in accordance with [their] morality" (1986, 242). But if that were the end of the story about corporeal expression in response to another, generosity would be a virtue, a habit of giving some of what I already have to others in my own terms, a habit of expressing at the same time as confirming my own socially bound way of being as if it were finished. However, as I have attempted to demonstrate throughout this book, such an understanding of generosity (and the relation between the body and its meaning that guides it) would have us already secure in our social identities before we encounter another, a security that would set the meaning and value of the gift, of the donor and of the donee, and that would thereby prolong cultural-historical conventions and their favored ways of being. The social imaginaries that have our bodies through habitual ways of being, and that are called upon in perception in response to the matter at hand, already memorialize the generosity of the privileged and forget and do not actively perceive the giving of others. It is this selective blindness that, for example, affords me the privilege of the position of respondent at an academic conference, that makes this response seem generous, and that extends to me the right to judge what I am responding to, without acknowledging what it may have given me. It is precisely this kind of privilege, and the way it is generated, that is contested by the corporeal generosity examined in this book.

While insisting that my response to another is saturated with the cultural-historical, the writing in blood that describes the generosity of intercorporeality unsettles the security of those positions and perceptions that derive privilege from dominant social conventions. This disturbance arises not from outside but from within the response. Because perception, and its verbal or written expression, is animated by another body (by the difference of the matter at hand that touches me by words, gestures, pictures, events, or whatever), then the meaning of what I write in my blood in response is opened and transformed by the difference that provokes it. This generosity of intercorporeality, and the transformation of meaning and being that it effects, is not a purely passive being-given to the other that lies outside of cultural conventions. It is a prereflective activity mediated by the cultural-historical that haunts my perception, but an activity that surpasses that perception and the modes of being it supports. Something that matters moves me in its difference and, while I find, from within the social imaginaries that have my body, the words and prereflective judgments to respond, I also find that my body, my blood and its meanings, is opened by, and flows toward, the other, and so is not yet finished. It is this generosity of intercoporeality, the "unfinishing" of my self-possession provoked by the gifts of others, that would open and transform cultural conventions to admit different modes of being.

But then this brings us to a paradox, to the impossibility of writing in blood and getting it right. This is the impossibility of a generosity that achieves justice. It is impossible to respond to another matter in a way that finally settles the differences between us with justice. This failure is not because the body that writes and the matter responded to are ineffable, as if everything else could speak for itself and be understood. The intercorporeality of my response to the other is not outside the meaning that it would surpass. Rather, this failure to write in blood about another matter and get it right arises from the way that this writing in blood, as suggested above, is animated by that alterity that it would write about, the alterity that is a condition of the response it provokes and that, by moving me beyond what I already perceive, ensures that the writing is not yet finished. I feel a difference that touches me and compels me to speak and act, but find I am a bit lost for the usual words that would confirm my habitual perception and my usual manner of being. But there is another side to this failure. If I did respond to and write about another matter and thought I got it right, I would have equally failed to write in blood; I would, through a kind of vampirism, have effaced the difference that moved my blood to write; I would have wrapped the other up in my terms as if my body, its meaning, and the matter that touches me and opens me to writing are finished. I may open my mouth and speak with confidence about the matter at hand, only to find I have swallowed it up, quenched my thirst, but failed to remain moved by the difference. Generosity that claims to achieve justice, once and for all, is impossible because, insofar as the response provoked by the other's alterity opens me beyond myself it is not yet finished, and, conversely, insofar as the response is finished by passing final judgment, this effects a violence toward, and closure to, the other.

That it is impossible to write in blood about another matter and get it right is not, however, a reason to say nothing or to write anything at all about the matter that moves what matters to us. While it is not easy or indeed impossible to understand the blood of another or one's own blood for that matter, without vampirism, it is this impossibility that inspires the attempt. The awareness of this impossibility, of the danger of effecting violence and injustice in every response, inspires a passionate politics that would work through generosity for a justice that is yet to arrive. For the blood of another, and the words it writes (whether privileged, autocratic, and dogmatic or disadvantaged, democratic, and open) only lives if, to paraphrase Nietzsche again, it is reanimated by my response that it provokes: "it is only *our* blood that constrains them to speak to *us*" (1986, 242). And we honor the expressions of other bodies "less by that barren timidity that allows every word . . . to remain in tact than by energetic endeavors to aid them continually to new life" (ibid., alternative translation).

What is called for by the impossibility of doing justice in response to another is a corporeal generosity that gives new life to its being-touched. There are two ways of effecting such a politics that have been explored in different ways in this book. The first is to admit one's failure to get it right, but rather than doing nothing, to write in blood against the discourses that obviously fail to do so, against those discourses that totalize and normalize bodies, that hide their own morality (the way that they are written in blood) behind claims to objectivity and detachment, and that deny their failure to capture and finish off the other matter that moves them. This would be to write in blood against those discourses that, as a result of these denials, would, through corporeal instantiations of cultural conventions, shore up privileged ways of being, including one's own, thereby reducing sexed or cultural identity to isolated, corporeal units, singled out for exchange, usury, judgment, correction, condemnation, or ridicule. The second way in which the generosity of intercorporeality would work for justice is if the privileged were to give new life to their being-touched, by allowing the contestations of that privilege to move them, without controlling what shape that new life might have. This kind of response has been asked of a number of privileged groups through the pages of this book (men, philosophers, clinicians, lawmakers, judges, members of parliament), but this call by the other to give over one's self-possession is a call to all of us (including those reading and writing this book). For while we may claim lack of privilege in some contexts (a woman in a male-dominated profession, to refer to one example explored in this book), we do enjoy privilege in other situations (a professional white woman in relation to most indigenous Australians, to recall another example explored earlier).

Whether responding to discourses that prolong cultural conventions that totalize and normalize bodies to the disadvantage of some, or responding to others that contest one's privilege, the generosity that writes in blood does so in similar-sounding words to those bodies that they address and that open them to discourse, but in a way that reanimates the trace of the difference that would otherwise be denied. Such blood writing not only *demonstrates* that the generosity of intercorporeality defies the conceptual borders that claim body integrity and singular identity and that perpetuate injustice accordingly, it also *performs* that defiance. Against a moralizing that fails its body by finishing itself through the vampirism of others, corporeal generosity effects an ethico-politics that would not. While necessarily harboring a touch of vampirism, this writing is also a blood donation that would touch and reanimate its being-touched, with its own blood and its morality for sure, but with a light touch that would feel the difference of the matter at hand without the certainty of knowing what that difference is, and so with a touch that keeps open those borders between the inside and outside, culture and nature, and self and other that cultural conventions would close. Corporeal generosity is a writing in blood that says this body carries a trace of the other, so this body and its cultural expression are not finished, and neither you nor I have the final word.

And that is why I love this blood writing so much. It animates and touches me rather than finishing me or others off. The provocations, contestations, and disturbances to my self-possession that have inspired a conceptualization of corporeal generosity, and so the writing of this book, are too numerous to repeat here. Nor is it possible to say exactly to what extent I have given new life to my being-touched by the blood writing of others, and to what extent I have failed and left myself and things intact. It is possible to say, however, that I think politics needs the writing in blood of corporeal generosity to reanimate and open us, as corporeal instantiations of our social imaginaries, to different ways of being. It is also possible to say by concluding that insofar as the writing of this book works through corporeal generosity for a justice that is not yet here, it does so through the gifts of others. Without being touched by their writing in blood, I would not, in the end, have heard Nietzsche say, "I love most what is written in blood," I would not have taken it so literally and, from the beginning, this book would not have happened.

NOTES

INTRODUCTION

1. "One Nation" is a political party led by Pauline Hanson that campaigns on a platform that opposes welfare, Asian immigration, taxation, and most forms of government intervention into social and economic affairs. In the federal elections of 1998, three years after the party was established, it won 10 percent of the vote overall in Australia and over 30 percent of the vote in the state of Queensland. The party has not sustained this level of success due to a lack of substantial policy and internal divisions. However, that it has commanded the level of popular support it has reflects a level of division in Australian society and a move toward the right in Australian politics.

2. Schrift has provided an informative discussion of various twentieth-century accounts of gift and gift giving that, while postdating my interest in the topic, and especially in Derrida's account, I have now found useful in organizing my thoughts.

CHAPTER ONE

1. Nietzsche makes a similar comment about the derivative nature of pleasure and pain in *Beyond Good and Evil* (1973, 135–36).

2. For a discussion of the problem of the actor in Nietzsche's philosophy, see Paul Patton (1991b).

3. Besides the cosmological and psychological doctrines of eternal recurrence, Wood discusses a third possible interpretation, the "ontological," which I have found useful.

4. Nietzsche makes a further connection between interpretation and will to power as a form giving force in *On the Genealogy of Morals* (1969, 79).

5. Nietzsche makes similar observations on the disjunction between self-interpretation and interpretation by another in *Beyond Good and Evil* (1973, 97, 142).

6. For Nietzsche's understanding of the different ways a man can possess a woman and what these say about the man's self-image, see *Beyond Good and Evil* (1973, 98–99).

7. For another discussion of Nietzsche's use of the metaphor of pregnancy, see Paul Patton (1991a, 49–52).

8. I discuss Nietzsche's opposition to feminism of equality in more detail elsewhere (Diprose 1989).

9. Nietzsche's claim that women put on something when they take off everything has often been interpreted as faking orgasm—woman's constitution of her own self-presence when appearing to guarantee man's. Or, as Gayatri Spivak suggests: "Women, 'acting out' their pleasure in the orgasmic moment, can cite themselves in their very self-presence" (1984, 22). I take issue with Spivak, only in her claim that it is self-presence (rather than undecidable difference) that is being cited in woman's dissimulation.

CHAPTER TWO

1. The idea that the self owns property in her or his person, including her or his body and the products of its labor, is usually attributed to John Locke, *Two Treatise of Government* Book II, Section 27 (1967, 288). While John Stuart Mill takes issue with Locke's contract model of social relations, he does assume Locke's concept of a person in his definition of liberty: "Over himself, over his own body and mind, the individual is sovereign" (1975, 15). For a critique of this model of a person assumed in contract theory, see Carole Pateman (1988).

2. See Locke, *Two Treatise of Government,* Book II, Sections 36 & 54 (1967, 292–93, 304) and Mill, "On Liberty," (1975, 16–18).

3. See Russell Scott, *The Body As Property* (1981, 192–96) for a discussion of the practical and legal problems surrounding the selling of blood in the United States.

4. I use the term *surrogate* in its conventional sense to mean a woman who agrees to gestate a fetus and relinquish the child to another after birth. I am aware that the term itself carries and determines certain problematic assumptions about motherhood. These are discussed in the literature and subject to my own criticisms in the remainder of the chapter. I retain the term for the sake of convenience only.

5. It has been suggested to me that this commodification may have been avoided if Whitehead had been judged to be the owner of her genetic material when she entered the contract. Even this determination would reduce her body to a storage facility, an incubator holding another body for future alienation. All that would change in this alternative judgment is the designated owner of the body property.

6. I single out this particular analysis from the wealth of literature on the topic for its systematic presentation of the most commonly held objections to surrogacy.

7. See, for example, Dodds and Jones (1989, 9) and Dr. Diana Kirby's submission to the National Bioethics Consultative Committee's (NBCC) *Surrogacy Report 1* (1990): 17).

8. A notable exception is Carol Pateman, whose critique of the surrogacy contract in *The Sexual Contract* is raised in the context of a thoroughgoing critique of contract theory in general. Also Dodds and Jones, to whose critique of surrogacy I have been referring, later modify their arguments against surrogacy to include a wider critique of contract and the idea of the body as property (1991). However, despite the broader application of their criticisms to other contracts, I still take issue with these theorists insofar as they locate the source of injustice of the surrogacy contract in the control it is said to secure over women's bodies.

9. This is only a small part of Pateman's critique of surrogacy, but the idea that the fetus is part of the pregnant self (or at least that there is an intimate link between the two) is shared by other opponents of surrogacy (e.g., Dodds and Jones 1989, 6; Overall 1987, ch. 6).

10. While to many this determination may be better for women than the reverse, it tends to trivialize and hide rape, and/or it leads to the ludicrous situation exemplified by a manual on sexual conduct at Antioch College, Ohio which suggests, according to the *New York Times* (reproduced in *The Australian*, October 6, 1993, p. 26), that "verbal consent should be obtained with every new level of physical and/or sexual contact or conduct in any given interaction, regardless of who initiates it" and that "the request for consent must be specific to each act."

11. I have already suggested that the male body accrues value through legal determinations that deem it the origin of procreative property, but there is also the question of sperm donation which, because men cannot give birth, is the most appropriate practice for comparison with surrogacy on the question of what sexed body property attracts value. While in Australia commercial trade in sperm is against the law, at least officially, the private sale of sperm (for cash or kind) is widely practiced without fear of the legal and moral condemnation that the practice of surrogacy attracts.

12. Merleau-Ponty's account of the intercorporeal basis of identity will be elaborated on in more detail in the next two chapters.

13. Moira Gatens (1995) contrasts feminism based on an ethics of "care" to feminism based on an ethics of "justice," arguing that both by themselves are not only inadequate for dealing with the injustices faced by women but serve to entrench the dualisms (public/private, culture/nature) that they seek to redress. "Justice" feminism, for example, in seeking special legal protection for women from men, tends to entrench the view of women as the weaker sex.

14. This is not Derrida's position in *Given Time* (1992). While he suggests that the question of the gift is prior to the law or the circle of exchange between self-present subjects (24) and "sets the circle going" (30), he also takes care to point out that "the overrunning of the circle by the gift, if there is any, does not lead to a simple, ineffable exteriority that would be transcendent and without relation" (30).

CHAPTER THREE

1. While male to female transvestism is transgressive, female to male transvestism, within limits, hardly raises an eyebrow, for reasons I do not have the space to properly explore. One suggestion for this might be that as maleness is the implicit signifier for the proper body in our culture, dressing like a man is merely reinforcing that norm rather than transgressing it.

2. I am referring here to a video clip of Madonna performing. "Like a Virgin" on the controversial *Blond Ambition Tour* of 1990.

3. Zita refers to this sign in her critique of the "postmodernist" claims of the malleability of body-identity. I will return to her critique shortly.

4. See Butler (1990, 93–110) for a detailed analysis of Foucault's discussion of this case.

5. For a more detailed discussion of the tension between Foucault's work on disciplinary power in *Discipline and Punish* and his "aesthetics of self" in his later work, see Diprose (1994, ch. 2).

CHAPTER FOUR

1. For critiques of radical feminism along these lines see, for example, Ferguson (1984) and Sawicki (1988).

2. As discussed in the Introduction, understanding generosity as a giving that enhances the self through the other goes beyond the English meaning of "generosity," defined as nobility, magnanimity, or liberal giving. There is also a precedent for this extended meaning in Descartes' philosophy. For example, in *The Passions of the Soul*, he defines generosity as a virtue based on the knowledge that nothing truly belongs to me and on the will to do what I judge to be best, a virtue that is the cause of rightful self-esteem and that prevents feeling contempt for others (Descartes 1985, 384). I am grateful to Genevieve Lloyd for directing me to this passage.

3. Thomas Martin's paper, "Sartre, Sadism, and Female Beauty Ideals" (1996), by using Sartre's model of sadism to argue against the objectification of women through beauty ideals, has alerted me to a possible connection between Sartre's discussion of love and desire and a radical feminist position. Whilst I depart from Martin on the question of how useful Sartre's ontology might be for resolving the issue of the objectification of women, I am grateful for the way our discussions have renewed my interest in Sartre's work in the area of love and sexuality.

4. See, for example, Margery Collins and Christine Pierce (1980).

5. For a more detailed analysis of Sartre's model of sadism, see Martin (1996). While Martin does not make this point, Sartre's condemnation of sadism, like his model of desire, relies on the problematic distinction between the body-in-situation (which in his analysis of sadism he calls the "graceful body") and the body as flesh (or the "obscene body").

6. My view that this is a positive move in Beauvoir's radical revision of Sartre's existentialism is not shared by many commentators. Jo-Ann Pilardi, for example, in an informative analysis of Beauvoir's account of female eroticism, evidences this passage as an example of how Beauvoir remains entrenched in the stereotypical view of female sexuality as a passive mindlessness that pervades the self (Pilardi 1989, 26). While Pilardi, in her reading of this passage, seems to equate "abolishing singularity" with passivity, I go on to argue that this abolition of singularity (and of the mind/body distinction) is neither essentially passive nor peculiar to women but is a feature of the ambiguity of existence. Beauvoir's point is that it is this ambiguity that is often denied by men at women's expense. Debra Bergoffen (1995, 1997), in her exceptional account of Beauvoir's philosophy of the erotic, makes this equation between the ambiguity of existence and becoming flesh. Also see Sonia Kruks (1990) for a positive interpretation of this point.

7. Beauvoir bases this claim on the argument that the ambiguity of existence not only rests on the claim that "between the past which no longer is and the future which is not yet, this moment when he [*sic*] exists is nothing" but also on the claim that as "an object for others, he is nothing more than an individual in the collectivity on which he depends" (Beauvoir 1994, 7). She also uses the figure of the "adventurer" to illustrate how independence is a ruse that denies one's dependence on others (58–63). For more detailed comparisons of Beauvoir's and Sartre's models of freedom, see Sonia Kruks (1991) and Monika Langer (1994).

8. For detailed analyses of Beauvoir's ambivalence toward the body, see Catriona Mackenzie (1986) and Moira Gatens (1991, ch. 3).

9. For critical accounts of Beauvoir's appropriation of Hegel's philosophy in her revision of Sartre's existentialism, see Genevieve Lloyd (1993) and Tina Chanter (1995, ch. 2).

10. Moi argues, with reference to Beauvoir's discussions of female sexuality, that Beauvoir's departure from Sartre on the structure of alienation of one's freedom in the other is due to her "elaboration on Lacan's notion of the alienation of the ego in the other in the mirror stage" (Moi 1992, 102). While there is little doubt that Lacan's model of the mirror stage does influence Beauvoir's understanding of female eroticism, this is more along the lines of Merleau-Ponty's elaboration of the model (which I go on to outline) and the understanding of the self-other, mind-body relations belonging to the phenomenological tradition. Hence, Beauvoir's understanding of erotic generosity carries traces of Merleau-Ponty's focus on body intentionality and the ambiguity (of being both mind and body, subject and object) that this involves. I therefore depart from Moi's claim that "by giving her own theory a slightly more Lacanian twist on this point [about alienation, Beauvoir] would have managed, at least in my view, to produce a better account of the relationship between the biological and the psychological" (111). I do, however, agree with Moi, that one problem underlying the difficulties in Beauvoir's account of female sexuality is her emphasis on unity with the other (or on recuperation of one's alienated image, as Moi puts it, p. 105).

11. Merleau-Ponty deals specifically with sexuality and the erotic encounter in the chapter "The Body in Its Sexual Being" in *Phenomenology of Perception* (1962). But, as he argues there, the structure of the erotic encounter is no different to that of personal existence in general, which he accounts for in the rest of the book.

12. For Merleau-Ponty's version of the body in situation for-itself-for-others, see *Phenomenology of Perception*, part 1, chapter 3 in particular. For a more detailed reading of this as well as Merleau-Ponty's model of intersubjectivity and freedom than I have the space to provide here, see Diprose (1994, ch. 6).

13. For his account of the genesis of the lived body with reference to Lacan's model of the "mirror stage" see Merleau-Ponty (1964a).

14. That for Merleau-Ponty the generosity of corporeal intersubjectivity does not involve unity with the other, nor therefore the elimination of difference, is central to the claim that generosity effects a transformation of existence that is open to difference. This reading of Merleau-Ponty's ontology is contrary to Levinas' critique of him. I take issue with Levinas' critique in chapter 9.

15. Beauvoir is inconsistent on this point. As I have argued above, for her, "genuine love," for example, involves consciousness transcending the body, while erotic generosity does not. However, Beauvoir implies elsewhere that the structure of the two is the same by claiming that sexuality "can be said to pervade life throughout" (Beauvoir 1972, 77). Merleau-Ponty explicitly and consistently holds the latter view, along with the view that living one's body involves self-transformation rather than objectification. He claims, for example, that in the case of " 'sight,' 'motility,' 'sexuality' . . . the body is not an object. . . . Whether it is a question of another's body or my own, I have no means of knowing the human body other than living it, which means taking up on my own account the drama which is being played out in it, and losing myself in it" (Merleau-Ponty 1962, 198).

16. In fact, Merleau-Ponty claims, in direct opposition to Sartre and to aspects of Beauvoir's account, that, while I am always embodied rather than consciousness transcending a body, I can never be reduced to a thing. For example, "Even if I become absorbed in the experience of my body and in the solitude of sensations, I do not succeed in abolishing all reference of my life to a world" (1962, 165).

17. Given this suggestion, I am departing from Judith Butler's claim that Merleau-Ponty bases his model of heterosexuality on a master/slave, domination/submission dynamic (Butler 1989, 91, 95–97). While it is true that Merleau-Ponty, in his chapter "The Body in Its Sexual Being," does pass through the master/slave model of sexuality, he revises it (as he does the psychoanalytic model) in favor of his own notion of ambiguity (of being autonomous *and* dependent rather than master *or* slave) (Merleau-Ponty 1962, 167). Merleau-Ponty also consistently and explicitly refutes the assumptions upon which the master/slave model depends: that the other is an object for consciousness and/or absolutely other (see, e.g., 1964a, 103; 1962, 346–65). Despite my departures from Butler, her paper is worth noting for the way it takes this aspect of Merleau-Ponty's philosophy seriously. For another, more recent account of Merleau-Ponty's model of intercorporeality that also takes his views on sexuality seriously, see Grosz (1994, ch. 4).

18. Judith Butler suggests, for example, that to the extent that Merleau-Ponty does refer to sexual difference in this chapter, he tends to betray a heterosexual bias and, within this, an assumption that women are objects rather than subjects of desire (Butler 1989, 92–94). While I agree with Butler on this point, I take issue in chapter 5 with other aspects of her analysis of Merleau-Ponty's model of sexuality.

19. Iris Marion Young argues, for example, with reference to Merleau-Ponty's ontology, that the social objectification of women manifests in a restricted body comportment in, for example, the way in which women throw (Young 1990). But as Young herself admits, it would be wrong to generalize about the relation between gender identity and comportment as such restrictions would vary with differences in race and class. I would also suggest that, as alterity is maintained within the synchronic relation to the other, and as social backgrounds vary in other ways besides race and class, women's body comportments would be more multifarious and open to change than Young's analysis implies.

CHAPTER FIVE

1. While my reading of Merleau-Ponty on affectivity and sociality centers on the chapter in *Phenomenology of Perception* entitled "The Body in Its Sexual Being," I will also be referring to aspects of his later work on perception and art, particularly "Eye and Mind" (1964b). I draw on Merleau-Ponty's aesthetics for two reasons: it is where the question of affectivity arises most obviously in Merleau-Ponty's later work and, while he does not deal explicitly with sexuality in his later work, the structure of affective perception there is slightly different in a way that needs to be taken into account. One difference is that in the *Phenomenology of Perception*, Merleau-Ponty tends to lean toward the idea that the body-subject structures its world (through perception), whereas in the later work perception is more obviously a two-way process of carnal intertwining and metamorphosis. My aim is to augment the earlier account of the body in its sexual being with what I think is a more developed understanding of perception in the later work. There is enough consistency of thought between the two bodies of

work to allow the connection. Finally, it should be noted that Butler does engage with Merleau-Ponty's chapter "The Body in Its Sexual Being" in a paper entitled "Sexual Ideology and Phenomenological Description: A Feminist Critique of Merleau-Ponty's *Phenomenology of Perception*" (Butler 1989). While this paper may have been a more obvious choice for a comparison between the two thinkers, it is not representative of Butler's work on the body and social power, and it contains, I think, some problems in its reading of Merleau-Ponty, which I address briefly in note 4.

2. Homosexuality is melancholic, according to Butler, not because it involves the disavowal of a possibility (heterosexuality) foreclosed through social prohibition, but insofar as it involves a disavowal of "a constitutive relationship to heterosexuality . . . [that] is to some degree an identification *with* a rejected heterosexuality" (Butler 1997, 148–49).

3. Indeed, Kelly Oliver, in a detailed and an informative critique of Butler's use of the idea of foreclosure, argues that Butler's account of the formation of melancholic identity leaves her without an adequate explanation of how performativity (reiteration and resignification) could be transformative (Oliver 1999).

4. It is instructive, for a comparison between Merleau-Ponty's model of affectivity and the Freudian model that Butler holds, that Butler seems to misunderstand Merleau-Ponty on this point. In a critical assessment of Merleau-Ponty's account of "the body in its sexual being," Butler criticizes him for his "masculinist" and heterosexual bias (Butler 1989). This bias is particularly evident, according to Butler, in Merleau-Ponty's use of the case of Schneider, whose deficient "sexual inertia" rests in part, for Merleau-Ponty, on his inability to find anonymous women attractive (Butler 1989, 92–94). On the basis of these sort of comments, as well as Butler's claim that Merleau-Ponty holds that sexuality is primordially "natural" and only secondarily social (90–91), Butler concludes that Merleau-Ponty's "normal" masculine desiring subject is a "disembodied voyeur" (faced with an essentially unchanging female body) (93). This is a curious interpretation that relies on ignoring Merleau-Ponty's central thesis in *Phenomenology of Perception,* about the intersubjective (and therefore essentially social) structure of perception (and hence erotic perception). First, Butler's claim that sexuality, for Merleau-Ponty, is primordially natural rests on incorrectly equating Merleau-Ponty's model of perception (which, as I will describe in more detail shortly, is prepersonal or intersubjective and prereflexive or based in body motility) with the presocial. Second, Butler's claim that Merleau-Ponty's model of normal sexuality is based on a masculine, disembodied voyeur implies that what Merleau-Ponty thinks is wrong with Schneider is that he cannot sexually objectify an anonymous woman. However, the reverse is the case. What he thinks is wrong with Schneider is he can *only* objectify others and the world if faced with an unfamiliar situation. This means that the intersubjective, social, affective, and therefore erotic structure of perception has been reduced in Schneider so that he finds everything and everyone equally meaningless and unaffective. What Merleau-Ponty considers "normal" to erotic perception and personal existence in general is being a body immersed in an ambiguous social situation of the other's body and the world. Erotic perception, and perception in general, is not, for Merleau-Ponty, based on object-cathexis by a natural or an individualized body, and this, arguably, marks his most obvious departure from more psychoanalytic accounts. Merleau-Ponty may privilege vision within his account of body intentionality, as Cathryn Vasseleu argues (1998), but this is not in the order of objectification by a disembodied voyeur. None of this denies Butler's more general claim, however, that Merleau-Ponty's account carries heterosexual and masculinist biases.

5. I begin my interpretation of Merleau-Ponty's account of affectivity and sexuality with his discussion of erotic perception in "The Body in Its Sexual Being" from the *Phenomenology of Perception*. As I will be dipping into the chapter rather than giving an exposition of it and as he engages directly with the psychoanalytic model of sexuality in this chapter, it is worth offering a brief overview of the chapter here as I understand it. Merleau-Ponty begins the chapter (pp. 154–57) by setting up a commonly held conception of affectivity that he refutes, using the case of Schneider (a person suffering from deficiencies in perception that Merleau-Ponty has interpreted more fully in an earlier chapter, "The Spatiality of One's Own Body and Motility"). In this refutation he offers a sketch of his own view of erotic perception, claims some common ground with psychoanalysis, and establishes the frame for further discussion of erotic perception in terms of the role of the body in expression of meaning. He sets up the discussion in these terms in order to (1) continue to refute the common view that affectivity is the conscious representation (expression) of natural bodily stimuli, and (2) challenge the psychoanalytic view that sexuality is the bodily expression of a repressed memory or an unconscious representation. The critique of the psychoanalytic model dominates the next part of the discussion (pp. 160–64) and is conducted through a case of hysteria (loss of voice) arising in a girl who has lost her love object through her mother's prohibition. In the process of refuting the psychoanalytic interpretation of this case, Merleau-Ponty begins to build his own view of the role of the body in expression and hence his own model of the relation between erotic perception and social meaning. His own view (that the body expresses existence as it realizes it through the intersubjective world) becomes the focus of discussion from p. 164 to the end of the chapter. Here he not only distances himself further from the psychoanalytic model of sexuality but also passes through and modifies the Hegelian master/slave model of desire (p. 167) or, rather, Sartre's use of the Hegelian model in his discussions of sexual desire. It may not be obvious that Merleau-Ponty is criticizing Sartre's model of desire in this brief reference: true to the phenomenological method, Merleau-Ponty does not always signal explicitly or immediately the ways in which he departs from the positions he sets up. For a detailed discussion of how Merleau-Ponty and Beauvoir depart from Sartre's view of sexual desire, see chapter 4.

6. While I have begun my account of Merleau-Ponty's view on sexuality and affectivity with reference to the chapter "The Body in Its Sexual Being" from the *Phenomenology of Perception,* I am making reference here to his later work on perception and art. See note 2 for a justification of this move.

7. As I also discussed in chapter 3, Merleau-Ponty provides a developmental account of how this "open circuit" or intertwining between the body and its perceived world is established in terms of the development of a body image and postural schema with reference to the mirror image of the other (1964a). With regard to perception, he argues that perception of others (and the world in general) requires this development of a system of "indistinction" or confusion between my body as I live it, my body as others perceive it, and the other's body (135). While the confusion is reduced as the child takes up a subject position in language, it remains in operation as the basis of perception. Hence, perception is always prereflexive inhabiting the space of other bodies, and vice versa, without either a division or synthesis between the two. See also Diprose (1994, 119–22) and Weiss (1999, ch. 1) for more detailed accounts of this development of the body image through the mirror of the other's body.

While there are similarities between Merleau-Ponty's account of the formation of the body image and Schilder's and Lacan's, Merleau-Ponty, unlike the psychoanalytic interpretation, does not view the "mirror-stage" as involving identification with and internalization of an ideal body image as the basis of an ideal ego alienated in the other. Nor, therefore, does Merleau-Ponty hold the psychoanalytic view that the mirror phase sets the stage for a sexuality based on cathexis of the object to complete one's ego ideal. For Merleau-Ponty, the mirror phase establishes confusion between one's body image and the other's as the basis of affectivity and perception, not internalization of the other's body image as the deceptive basis of the self and desire. There is a second point at which Merleau-Ponty departs from the psychoanalytic interpretation. While for Merleau-Ponty the system of indistinction established between bodies is reduced as the child becomes a subject of language, this does not involve repression of attachment to the body of the first (m)other, as it does in the psychoanalytic account. For Merleau-Ponty, the body image and its intertwinings form the atmosphere of perception rather than unconscious content. For a detailed comparison between Merleau-Ponty's interpretation of the "mirror phase" and the psychoanalytic accounts, see Weiss (1999, ch. 1).

8. The paradox of expression is another way to put the structure of sensibility that I have just described: that the body expresses, gives meaning to, a world through the other, a significant world it did not create yet would not exist as significant without that expression. That this is a labor of desire is because expression takes place outside the "self" through the bodies of others and is affective. I will return to the point about the expression of meaning shortly.

9. "I perceive the other as a piece of behaviour, for example, I perceive the grief or anger of the other in his conduct, in his face or his hands, without recourse to any 'inner' experience of suffering or anger, and because grief and anger are variations of belonging to the world, undivided between body and consciousness and equally applicable to the other's conduct. . . . But then, the behaviour of another, and even his words, are not that other. . . . For him these situations are lived through, for me they are displayed. . . . Paul suffers because he has lost his wife . . . I suffer because Paul is grieved . . . and our situations cannot be superimposed on each other" (Merleau-Ponty 1962, 356).

10. The extent to which Merleau-Ponty allows for difference in his account of perception is debatable. I argued in chapter 4 that alterity is a condition of and is maintained in perception and will argue further toward this point in chapter 9. For other discussions of this point, see Dillon (1988, 41–46) and Vasseleu (1998, 32–36). For a discussion of how Merleau-Ponty's model of perception can account for disturbances in the case of a clash of different "sexualities," see the account of the clinical encounter in the following chapter.

11. I am grateful to Karen Williams for directing me to this passage.

12. See, for example, Merleau-Ponty's analysis of the corporeal effects of losing a "love-object" through prohibition in *Phenomenology of Perception* (1962, 160–71).

CHAPTER SIX

1. For critiques of the medical model of the body and discussion of the implications of these critiques for medical ethics, see the various papers in *Troubled Bodies: Critical Perspectives on Postmodernism, Medical Ethics, and the Body* (Komesaroff 1995).

2. The definition of sexuality I elaborate here might be broader than expected. A dictionary definition, for example, would confine itself to sex and/or gender and/ or sexual intercourse. But already such a definition locates and limits sexuality in a way that does not reflect the variety, richness, and ambiguity of the pleasures that inhabit people's lives. (Indeed, the dictionary definition could be accused of the same reductionism leveled at medical discourse.) Such a definition also presupposes an individualist ontology that is under attack in this book. The definition of sexuality I offer here is based on a different ontology, already explored in some detail in chapters 5 and 6. This ontology better captures the nature of both sexuality and the clinical encounter, and I will justify it further later in this chapter. For the moment, I am concerned with including, within a definition of sexuality, three terms: the pleasures of one's own body, the other, and the social discourses within which these are embedded.

3. For early discussions of this issue see, for example, Watney (1987) and Diprose and Vasseleu (1991).

4. Or, as Foucault puts it later in *The History of Sexuality, Volume 1,*

the notion of "sex" made it possible to group together, in an artificial unity, anatomical elements, biological functions, conducts, sensations, and pleasures, and it enabled one to make use of this fictitious unity as a causal principle, an omnipresent meaning, a secret to be discovered everywhere . . . sex is the most speculative, most ideal, and most internal element in the deployment of sexuality organized by power in its grip on bodies and their materiality, their forces, their energies, sensations, and pleasures. (Foucault 1980a, 154–55)

5. For a number of such critiques see, for example, papers in *Body/Politics: Women and the Discourses of Science* (Jacobus et al. 1990) and in *Vital Signs* (Shildrick and Price 1998).

6. These two examples and the two I use to illustrate the second kind of problem are based on reports by friends of their experiences, although I have changed the names of those involved. While common, at least among people I know, these are the sort of stories rarely documented in sociological or medical studies, presumably because the kind of discomfort that their telling generates means that they are usually reserved for private conversations between friends. I am therefore grateful that I am privy to these stories and have permission to use them here.

CHAPTER SEVEN

1. One of the more infamous of these dismissals is a recent book by Alan Sokal and Jean Bricmont, *Impostures Intellectuelles* (Paris: Odile Jacob, 1997), in which Sokal and Bricmont criticize a range of French theorists (including Deleuze and Kristeva) for distorting and misusing scientific concepts, and for what they take to be their opaque style and fraudulent scholarship.

2. Jean Curthoys, quoted here, explicitly condemns what she calls "deconstructive" feminism for seeking rather than opposing power and for promoting "intellectual confusion" through its irrational methodology. This is one of the main themes of her book. Her condemnation of academic feminism for transgressing the concepts of the

natural sciences is less obvious, emerging more from the choices she makes in the feminist work she targets (much of which is critically engaged with the natural sciences) rather than from any explicit sustained defense of science from feminist criticism. Still, at times in the book, the link that Curthoys makes between feminist criticism of scientific concepts and failure "to meet the tests of genuine reason" is too strong to be considered coincidental. For example, in criticizing a paper of mine on the operation of difference in genetic theory (Diprose 1991), I am charged with promoting intellectual confusion by failing to realize that science is an "autonomous enterprise" that "constitutes its objects internally" and, as such, should only be subject to "intellectually relevant considerations" rather than "external social/ethical considerations" (Curthoys 1997, 89–90).

3. While this formulation of the plane of immanence tends to imply that images of thought will determine conclusively what concepts emerge and when, the plane is as unstable and open to transformation as the concepts that emerge in it.

4. Nietzsche also claims a connection between the type of concept and the mode of existence of the philosopher who creates it by suggesting, for example, that philosophers who hold the ascetic ideal "see in it an optimum condition for the highest and boldest spirituality and smiles—he does not deny 'existence,' he rather affirms *his* existence and *only* his [. . .] he is not far from harboring the impious wish: *pereat mundus, fiat philosophia, fiat philosophus,* **fiam**! [*let the world perish, but let there be philosophy, the philosopher,* **me**!]" (1969, 108).

5. According to Curthoys, this concept of the human is confirmed to its discoverer by the observation that the exercise of power, which does not respect the need for recognition, leads to "distortions" in human behavior (Curthoys 1997, 49).

6. Norman Wirzba's discussion of philosophical autonomy and its alternative companion, heteronomy, is an informative and a detailed account of Levinas' idea of teaching. In it he makes the observation that the link between maieutics and anamnesis in Plato's thought differentiates the Socratic notion of autonomy from the modern idea of self-legislation. "In the Socratic view the turn inward does not stop with the self. The self is, as it were, opened to the *eidé*. . . . In modern philosophy this turn beyond the self gets cut off" (Wirzba 1995, n. 4, 143).

7. There is an "inequality" in the relation, so that I am obligated to the other, and the relation is not reversible. For an account of how this "inequality" allows for justice through a "third party," see Chanter (1995, 190–96).

8. See, for example, Irigaray (1988), Ainley (1988b), Chanter (1995, ch. 5, 2001a, and 2001b), Vasseleu (1998, part 3) and Ziarek (2001a).

9. There is at least one other consideration that allows this, Levinas' idea of the "third party," described as that which opens the ethical relation to the whole of humanity (1969, 213; 1981, 160–61). While I am obligated to welcome (and so remain open to) the other who contests me, the other is in relation to a third party to whom she or he is responsible and who treats me, alongside the other I face, as someone to be welcomed. By rendering the one who is contested as also one who is welcomed, the third party not only tempers the "inequality" of the relation to the other without either rendering the relation reversible or allaying responsibility, it also works against classifying the alterity that contests and the alterity that welcomes in terms of any class of human existence, including sex.

10. Therefore, claiming that the disturbance of complacency effected by the other's alterity inspires creative thinking and the production of concepts does not

contradict Levinas' insistence that this exposedness to the other is not "consciousness of" or thematization, at least not primordially. For an interesting discussion of how Levinas' model of the ethical relation involves a response to alterity that dethematizes rather than objectifies, see Sullivan (2001).

11. Or, as Levinas puts it, "language accomplishes the primordial putting in common" (1969, 173). I add the qualification that this putting in common signals only a *possibility* of a common world to avoid the conclusion that language overcomes alterity and achieves absolute cultural commensurability. For Levinas, alterity, and hence the disturbance that founds responsibility, expression, thinking, and communication, is irreducible. He elaborates on the relation between alterity and cultural commensurability more thoroughly in "Meaning and Sense" (1987b). I will take up this issue more centrally in the following two chapters.

12. I will take up this issue of Levinas' apparent subordination of ontology and politics to ethics more directly in the following two chapters.

CHAPTER EIGHT

1. Confidential submission 318 to the National Inquiry into the Separation of Aboriginal and Torres Strait Islander Children from Their Families. The inquiry was convened by Michael Lavarch, attorney general of Australia, in August 1995, in response to requests by indigenous agencies and communities. Sir Ronald Wilson, president of the Human Rights and Equal Opportunity Commission (HREOC), and Mick Dodson, Aboriginal and Torres Strait Islander Social Justice Commissioner, took primary responsibility for conducting the hearings of the National Inquiry. The Report of the Inquiry, entitled *Bringing Them Home,* was published by the HREOC and submitted to the Australian government in April 1997.

2. "Protecting children from neglect and abuse" was often used as a reason to justify the removal of indigenous children from their families, and the National Inquiry includes such cases in its terms of reference if removal of children was by compulsion (HREOC 1997, 10). However, such justification was secondary to the policies of assimilation that were the driving force behind the large-scale forcible removal of children from indigenous communities during this period.

3. The actual figures have been difficult to estimate. A national survey in 1989 found that 47 percent of Aboriginal respondents of all ages had been separated from both parents some time in childhood (compared to 7 percent for nonindigenous people) (HREOC 1997, 37). But as this figure includes separation due to hospitalization and juvenile detention as well as removal, the National Inquiry settled for a figure of between one in three and one in ten to indicate the extent of forcible removal (ibid.). That the removal of children was *forced* under assimilation policies is the main criterion in estimating this figure. The HREOC report defines "forcible removal" as the removal of children by compulsion (authorized or illegal coercion), duress (involving threats or moral pressure) or undue influence (improper pressure) (HREOC 1997, 5–10).

4. See the HREOC report on the way children, by absorbing the values of a culture, are necessary for the continuity of that culture (pp. 218–19).

5. *Walking Together,* pamphlet published by the Council for Aboriginal Reconciliation (CAR n.d., 2). The CAR was established by federal legislation on September 2,

1991, comprising twenty-five members, twelve of whom are Aboriginal, two Torres Strait Islanders, and eleven representatives from the wider Australian community.

6. In 1989, Theo van Boven conducted a study concerning reparation for victims of violations of human rights on behalf of the United Nations Sub-Commission on Prevention of Discrimination and Protection of Minorities. His report, published in 1996, is entitled *Basic Principles and Guidelines on the Right to Reparation for Victims of Gross Violations of Human Rights and Humanitarian Law* (HREOC 1997, 280).

7. Perrin and Veitch (1998), for example, point to the difficulty in achieving reconciliation based on the idea of recovering a past that is irrecoverable and on telling a truth that is unspeakable. They conclude that the best that can be hoped for is the *promise* of reconciliation, by which I presume they mean that reconciliation is an ongoing process rather than a final settling of a debt.

8. For another discussion of race relations in Australia that argues similarly for expressions of alterity rather than reconciliation based on commonness and agreement, see Linnell Secomb (2000).

9. See Reynolds (1987) for a detailed discussion of the effect of the principle of *terra nullius* on the history of indigenous land rights in Australia, and see Nettheim (1998) and Patton (1997) for discussions of the impact of the Mabo judgment on both the principle of *terra nullius* and the future of cultural difference.

10. In "On Truth and Lies in a Nonmoral Sense," to which I have been referring so far in this discussion, Nietzsche holds to a distinction between the "immediately perceived world" and the world constructed by universalizing these impressions under concepts (see, e.g., 1979, 84). This distinction between perception and meaning allows him to claim that meaning, and hence one's world, can be changed by holding more to one's first impressions (89). However, he discards this distinction the more critical he becomes of Kant in his later work.

11. Levinas discusses the connection between colonization and the Platonic model of meaning and perception in "Meaning and Sense" (1987b). For a useful commentary of this discussion, see Bernasconi (1991).

12. Nietzsche mentions this kind of lying in passing in, for example, "On the Uses and Disadvantages of History for Life" (1983, 118–19).

13. Plato discusses "medicinal lying" in the *Republic* (382a–e, 459d–460c) and what is called the "noble lie" in the *Republic* (414b–415c). For a recent detailed discussion of the role Plato gives lying in the *Republic*, see David Simpson (1996).

14. *Bringing Them Home* documents some of the effects that policies of forcible removal have had on the families and communities from which the children were taken (HREOC 1997, 212–20). These include individual grief, the sense of shame families members felt for "letting welfare get their children," a loss of confidence in their own parenting abilities, and a gradual self-denial of Aboriginality among community members, either through shame or to prevent their children from being taken.

15. I have borrowed the term *vertical history* from Johnson (1993), who uses it in an account of Merleau-Ponty's understanding of temporality and forgetting.

16. While I have found Johnson's elaboration of Merleau-Ponty's account of forgetting enormously helpful, I do not, as the following analysis suggests, agree with his conclusion that forgetting allows "me to forget my past which is to forget myself and stand outside myself and see, really see" (Johnson 1993, 205). For Merleau-Ponty, as I go on to argue, forgetting involves the past adhering to the body through habit.

One cannot be released from this past, but it can be transformed through an open relation to the other. Any trauma resulting from this "forgotten" past can also be similarly transformed through the other. This has been discussed, with reference to Merleau-Ponty, in some detail in chapter 5. For an account consistent with Merleau-Ponty's model of intercorporeality of how a cross-cultural encounter can be traumatic, in the sense of effecting an ontological closure to the other, see Biddle (2002).

17. Australian Prime Minister John Howard has consistently insisted on taking a more "positive" attitude to the past than that highlighted in *Bringing Them Home*, focusing on aspects of his own heritage and the efforts of his own ancestors in contributing to the prosperity of Australian culture. Celebrating the contribution of Australians to the First and Second World Wars and to the defense of Australia in the Vietnam War has been a dominant theme in this "positive" historical rhetoric in the years since *Bringing Them Home* was published.

18. Durie (1999) provides a comprehensive and an informative comparison between Husserl's and Levinas' approaches to temporality that I have found useful in formulating my reading of Levinas' account of memory.

19. These are the words of former Labor Prime Minister Paul Keating. The current conservative government, under the leadership of John Howard, has recently (August 1999) passed legislation expressing the government's regret for the suffering caused by forcible removal policies, but this regret denies responsibility of the present government.

20. For other detailed discussions of the "third party" and justice regarding the ethical relation see, for example, Bernasconi (1999), Chanter (1995, ch. 5), Thomas (1999), and Ziarek (2001b).

CHAPTER NINE

1. Derrida discusses the way Schmitt's concept of the political, for example, is based on knowing the difference between the enemy and the friend and points to the impossibility of determining the difference (Derrida 1997, ch. 5). Penelope Deutscher explores this impossibility, in interesting ways, with immigration policies and the plight of political refugees seeking asylum (2001).

2. I have compressed here a complex and at times contradictory thesis in Merleau-Ponty's work about the relation between the imaginary and the real, the cultural-historical and the "natural." For a detailed analysis of this aspect of Merleau-Ponty's philosophy, which pays particular attention to his various understanding of "imaginary" in *The Visible and the Invisible,* see Castoriadis (1997).

3. Levinas engages directly with Merleau-Ponty's philosophy of meaning, perception, and intersubjectivity in a number of places, for example, in "Meaning and Sense" (1987b), which I considered in chapter 8, in "The Philosophical Determination of the Idea of Culture" in *Entre Nous* (1998), and in "On Intersubjectivity: Notes on Merleau-Ponty" (1994), which will be my focus here. I am grateful to Ewa Ziarek (2001b), whose own work on Levinas and the political, drawing in particular on Levinas' later work, has prompted my reconsideration of the issue here, in relation to Merleau-Ponty.

4. Simon Critchley provides a convincing argument toward this claim (1992, 219–36).

5. This alternative way of reading Merleau-Ponty's model of intercorporeality is not restricted to the paper "Dialogue and the Perception of the Other" (1973). The same idea pervades all of his work (although arguably is more apparent in his later work) and informs my analyses in chapters 4 to 6.

6. John Caputo makes a similar point about deconstruction in his excellent discussion of "The Messianic: Waiting for the Future" (Caputo 1997, ch. 6). There he says, after noting that justice is never here, that " 'undecidability' and *différance* do not imply decision and delay. On the contrary, they serve to underlie and expose postponement, to make the retardation of justice look bad, to make salient the urgency of decision. For deconstruction, if there is such a thing, is a passion, an impassioning, an impatience, for justice" (180).

CONCLUSION

1. The conference was the Australian Women's Studies Association Annual Conference held at Macquarie University, Sydney, January 31–February 2, 2001.

2. The nodal point around which this connection congealed was "blood" and everything it may signify to me. Among the provocations that led me to this way of concluding, besides Rosengarten's work on blood and Keane's on other body matter, included: a conference paper by Jacqueline Scott, "Nietzsche and Mixed Race" (2000), which takes literally what Nietzsche says about mixed blood being necessary for a healthy culture; a conference paper by Erika Kerruish, "Moving Words: Nietzsche on Language and Affectivity" (2000), which contains a quote from Nietzsche about our blood being necessary to animate the words of others; and a comment from someone in discussion of the latter, who responded to my interest in the quote with "but surely there is no need to take Nietzsche's comments on blood literally."

3. Keane and Rosengarten (2001) propose these two opposite ways of understanding the relation between social concepts and the body, although not exactly in the way I have set it out here.

BIBLIOGRAPHY

Ainley, Alison. 1988a. " 'Ideal Selfishness': Nietzsche's Metaphor of Maternity." Pp. 116–30 in *Exceedingly Nietzsche: Aspects of Contemporary Nietzsche-Interpretation*, ed. David Farrel Krell and David Wood. London: Routledge.

———. 1988b. "Amorous Discourses: 'The Phenomenology of Eros.' " Pp. 70–82 in *The Provocation of Levinas: Rethinking the Other*, ed. Robert Bernasconi and David Wood. London and New York: Routledge.

Aristotle. 1975. *The Nicomachean Ethics*. Trans. Hippocrates Apostle. Dordrecht: Reidel.

Beauvoir, Simone de. 1972. *The Second Sex*. Trans. H. M. Parshley. Harmondsworth: Penguin.

———. 1994. *The Ethics of Ambiguity*. Trans. Bernard Frechtman. New York: Citadel Press.

Bergoffen, Debra B. 1995. "Out from Under: Beauvoir's Philosophy of the Erotic." Pp. 179–92 in *Feminist Interpretations of Simone de Beauvoir*, ed. Margaret A Simons. University Park: Pennsylvania State University Press.

———. 1997. *The Philosophy of Simone de Beauvoir: Gendered Phenomenologies, Erotic Generosities*. Albany: State University of New York Press.

Bernasconi, Robert. 1991. "One-Way Traffic: The Ontology of Decolonization and Its Ethics." Pp. 67–80 in *Ontology and Alterity in Merleau-Ponty*, ed. G. Johnson and M. Smith. Evanston: Northwestern University Press.

———. 1997. "What Goes Around Comes Around: Derrida and Levinas on the Economy of the Gift and the Gift of Genealogy." Pp. 256–73 in *The Logic of the Gift: Toward an Ethic of Generosity*, ed. Alan D. Schrift. New York: Routledge.

———. 1999. "The Third Party. Levinas on the Intersection of the Ethical and the Political." *Journal of the British Society for Phenomenology* 30 (1): 76–87.

Biddle, Jennifer. Forthcoming 2002. "Bruises That Won't Heal: On Loss, Lies, and License." *Mortality* 7: 1–18.

Bourdieu, Pierre. 1997. "Marginalia—Some Additional Notes on the Gift." Pp. 231–41 in *The Logic of the Gift: Toward an Ethic of Generosity*, ed. Alan D. Schrift. New York: Routledge.

Butler, Judith. 1989. "Sexual Ideology and Phenomenological Description: A Feminist Critique of Merleau-Ponty's *Phenomenology of Perception*." Pp. 85–100 in *The Thinking Muse: Feminism and Modern French Philosophy*, ed. Jeffner Allen and Iris Marion Young. Bloomington: Indiana University Press.

————. 1990. *Gender Trouble: Feminism and the Subversion of Identity*. New York: Routledge.

————. 1997. *The Psychic Life of Power: Theories in Subjection*. Stanford, Calif.: Stanford University Press.

Caputo, John. 1997. *Deconstruction in a Nutshell*. New York: Fordham University Press.

Castoriadis, Cornelius. 1997. "Merleau-Ponty and the Weight of the Ontological Tradition." Pp. 273–310 in *World in Fragments: Writings on Politics, Society, Psychoanalysis, and the Imagination*, trans. David Ames Curtis. Stanford:, Calif.: Stanford University Press.

Chanter, Tina. 1995. *Ethics of Eros: Irigaray's Rewriting of the Philosophers*. London and New York: Routledge.

————. 2001a. *Time, Death, and the Feminine: Levinas with Heidegger*. Stanford, Calif.: Stanford University Press.

————, ed. 2001b. *Feminist Interpretations of Emmanuel Levinas*. University Park: Pennsylvania State University Press.

Cixous, Hélène. 1981. "Castration or Decapitation?" Trans. Annette Khun. *Signs* 7 (1): 41–55.

Collins, Margery, and Christine Pierce. 1980. "Holes and Slime: Sexism in Sartre's Psychoanalysis." Pp. 112–27 in *Women and Philosophy: Toward a Theory of Liberation*, ed. Carol Gould and Marx Wartofsky. New York: Perigee Books.

Cornell, Drucilla. 1991. *Beyond Accommodation: Ethical Feminism, Deconstruction, and the Law*. New York: Routledge.

Council for Aboriginal Reconciliation (CAR). n.d. *Walking Together*. Pamphlet. Canberra: Commonwealth of Australia.

Critchley, Simon. 1992. *The Ethics of Deconstruction: Derrida and Levinas*. Oxford: Blackwell.

Curthoys, Jean. 1997. *Feminist Amnesia: The Wake of Women's Liberation*. London: Routledge.

Deleuze, Gilles, and Félix Guattari. 1994. *What Is Philosophy?* Trans. G. Burchell and H. Tomlinson. London: Verso.

Derrida, Jacques. 1979. *Spurs: Nietzsche's Styles*. Trans. Barbara Harlow. Chicago: University of Chicago Press.

————. 1981. *Positions*. Trans. Alan Bass. Chicago: University of Chicago Press.

————. 1982. "Différance." *Margins of Philosophy*. Trans. Alan Bass. Chicago: University of Chicago Press.

————. 1990. "Force of Law: The 'Mystical Foundations of Authority.'" *Cardozo Law Review* 11: 919–1045.

————. 1992. *Given Time*. Trans. Peggy Kamuf. Chicago: University of Chicago Press.

————. 1997. *Politics of Friendship*. Trans. George Collins. London: Verso.

————. 1999. *Adieu to Emmanuel Levinas*. Trans. Pascale-Anne Brault and Michael Naas. Stanford, Calif.: Stanford University Press.

Descartes, René. 1985. "The Passions of the Soul." Pp. 325–404 in *The Philosophical Writings of Descartes*. Volume I. Cambridge: Cambridge University Press.

Deutscher, Penelope. 2001. "Already Weeping the Other's Absence: Immigration, Colonialism, Deconstruction." *Studies in Practical Philosophy* 3(1): 4–19.

Dillon, Martin C. 1988. "Desire: Language and Body." Pp. 34–48 in *Postmodernism and Continental Philosophy*, ed. Hugh Silverman and Donn Welton. Albany: State University of New York Press.

Diprose, Rosalyn. 1989. "Nietzsche, Ethics, and Sexual Difference." *Radical Philosophy* 52:27–33. Reprinted in 1995. Ed. Peter R. Sedgwick. *Nietzsche: A Critical Reader*. Oxford: Blackwell.

———. 1991. "A 'Genethics' Which Makes Sense." Pp. 65–78 in *Cartographies: Poststructuralism and the Mapping of Bodies and Spaces*, ed. Rosalyn Diprose and Robyn Ferrell. Sydney: Allen & Unwin.

———. 1994. *The Bodies of Women: Ethics, Embodiment, and Sexual Difference*. London: Routledge.

Diprose, Rosalyn, and Cathryn Vasseleu. 1991. "Animation-AIDS in Science/Fiction." Pp. 145–60 in *The Illusion of Life*, ed. A. Cholodenko. Sydney: Power Publications.

Dodds, Susan, and Karen Jones. 1989. "Surrogacy and Autonomy." *Bioethics* 3 (1):00–00.

———. 1991. "Surrogacy and the Body As Property." Pp. 119–34 in *Cross Currents: Philosophy in the Nineties*, ed. Stephen Darling. Adelaide: Flinders University Press.

Durie, Robin. 1999. "Speaking of Time . . . Husserl and Levinas on the Saying of Time." *Journal of the British Society for Phenomenology* 30 (1):35–58.

Ferguson, Ann. 1984. "Sex War: The Debate between Radical and Libertarian Feminists." *Signs* 10 (1):106–12.

Ferrell, Robyn. 1998. " 'Untitled.' " In *the Wake of Terra Nullius*. Ed. Colin Perrin. Special issue of *Law Text Culture* 4 (1):308–19.

Foucault, Michel. 1979. *Discipline and Punish: The Birth of the Prison*. Trans. Alan Sheridan. Harmondsworth: Penguin.

———. 1980a. *The History of Sexuality, Volume I: An Introduction*. Trans. R. Hurley. New York: Vintage Books.

———. 1980b. "Introduction." Pp. vii–xvii in *Herculine Barbin: Being the Recently Discovered Memoirs of a Nineteenth Century French Hermaphrodite*, trans. Richard McDougall. New York: Pantheon Books.

———. 1984. "On the Genealogy of Ethics." Pp. 340–72 in *The Foucault Reader*, ed. Paul Rabinow. Harmondsworth: Penguin.

Freud, Sigmund. 1957. "Mourning and Melancholia." Pp. 237–58 in *The Standard Edition of the Complete Psychological Works of Sigmund Freud*, vol. 14, ed. and trans. James Strachey. London: Hogarth.

———. 1961. "The Ego and the Id." Pp. 1–66 in *The Standard Edition of the Complete Psychological Works of Sigmund Freud*, vol. 19, ed. and trans. James Strachey. London: Hogarth.

Gatens, Moira. 1991. *Feminism and Philosophy: Perspectives on Difference and Equality*. Cambridge: Polity Press.

———. 1995. "Between the Sexes: Care or Justice?" Pp. 42–57 in *Introducing Applied Ethics*, ed. Brenda Almond. Oxford: Blackwell.

———. 1996. *Imaginary Bodies: Ethics, Power, and Corporeality*. London and New York: Routledge.

———. 1997. "Are We Responsible for the Past?" Plenary Address, Annual Conference of the International Association of Philosophy and Literature, Mobile, Alabama, May.

Grosz, Elizabeth. 1994. *Volatile Bodies: Toward a Corporeal Feminism*. Sydney: Allen & Unwin; Bloomington: Indiana University Press.

Human Rights and Equal Opportuntiy Commission (HREOC). 1997. *Bringing Them Home*. Report of the National Inquiry into the Separation of Aboriginal and Torres Strait Islander Children from Their Families. Canberra: Commonwealth of Australia.

Hunt, Lester. 1975. "Generosity." *American Philosophical Quarterly* 12 (3):235–45.

Irigaray, Luce. 1981. "And One Does Not Stir without the Other." *Signs* 7 (1): 60–67.

————. 1985. "This Sex which Is Not One." Pp. 23–33 in *This Sex Which is Not One*, trans. C. Porter. Ithaca, N.Y.: Cornell University Press.

————. 1988. "The Fecundity of the Caress." Pp. 231–56 in *Face to Face with Levinas*, ed. Richard A. Cohen. Albany: State University of New York Press.

Jacobus, M., E. Fox Keller, and S. Shuttleworth, eds. 1990. *Body/Politics: Women and the Discourses of Science*. New York and London: Routledge.

Jeffreys, Sheila. 1990. "Sexology and Antifeminism." And "Eroticizing Women's Subordination." Pp. 14–27, 132–35 in *The Sexual Liberals and the Attack on Feminism*, ed. Dorchen Leidholdt and Janice G. Raymond. New York: Pergamon Press.

Johnson, Galen A. 1993. "Generosity and Forgetting in the History of Being: Merleau-Ponty and Nietzsche." Pp. 196–212 in *Questioning Foundations: Truth/Subjectivity/Culture*, ed. Hugh J. Silverman. New York: Routledge.

Kaite, Berkeley. 1987. "The Pornographic Body Double: Transgression Is the Law." Pp. 150–68 in *Body Invaders: Panic Sex in America*, ed. Arthur Kroker and Marilouise Kroker. New York: St. Martin's Press.

Keane, Helen. 1999. "Adventures of the Addicted Brain." *Australian Feminist Studies* 14 (29): 63–76.

Keane, Helen, and Marsha Rosengarten. 2001. "The Biology of Sexed Subjects." Plenary address delivered to the Australian Women's Studies Association Annual Conference, Macquarie University, Sydney, January 31.

Kerruish, Erika. 1997. "Derrida and 'I': Dealing with Nietzsche's Women." Unpublished paper, School of Philosophy, University of New South Wales.

————. 2000. "Moving Words: Nietzsche on Language and Affectivity." Conference paper read to the Australian Society for Continental Philosophy Annual Conference, University of New South Wales, November 23.

Komesaroff, Paul, ed. 1995. *Troubled Bodies: Critical Perspectives on Postmodernism, Medical Ethics, and the Body*. Durham: Duke University Press; Melbourne: Melbourne University Press.

Kruks, Sonia. 1990. *Situation and Human Existence: Freedom, Subjectivity, and Society*. London: Unwin Hyman.

————. 1991. "Simone de Beauvoir: Teaching Sartre about Freedom." Pp. 285–300 in *Sartre Alive*, ed. R. Aronson and A. ver de Hoven. Detroit: Wayne State University Press.

Langer, Monika. 1994. "A Philosophical Retrieval of Simone de Beauvoir's *Pour une Morale de L'ambiguité.*' " *Philosophy Today* 36:181–90.

Le Doeuff, Michèlle. 1991. *Hipparchia's Choice: An Essay Concerning Women, Philosophy, Etc.* Trans. T. Selous. Oxford: Blackwell.

Leidholdt, Dorchen, and Janice G. Raymond, eds. 1990. *The Sexual Liberals and the Attack on Feminism*. New York: Pergamon Press.

Levinas, Emmanuel. 1969. *Totality and Infinity: An Essay on Exteriority*. Trans. Alphonso Lingis. Pittsburgh: Duquesne University Press.

———— 1981. *Otherwise Than Being or Beyond Essence*. Trans. Alphonso Lingis. The Hague: Martinus Nijhoff.

————. 1986. "Dialogue with Emmanuel Levinas." Pp. 13–34 in *Face to Face with Levinas*, ed. Richard A. Cohen. Albany: State University of New York Press.

———— 1987a. "Philosophy and the Idea of Infinity." Pp. 47–60 in *Emmanuel Levinas: Collected Philosophical Papers*, trans. Alphonso Lingis. Dordrecht: Martinus Nijhoff.

———— 1987b. "Meaning and Sense." Pp. 75–108 in *Emmanuel Levinas: Collected Philosophical Papers,* trans. Alphonso Lingis. Dordrecht: Martinus Nijhoff.

———— 1994. "On Intersubjectivity: Notes on Merleau-Ponty." Pp. 96–103 in *Outside the Subject,* trans. Michael B. Smith. Stanford, Calif.: Stanford University Press.

————. 1998. *Entre Nous: On Thinking-of-the-Other.* Trans. Michael B. Smith and Barbara Harshav. New York: Columbia University Press.

Lingis, Alphonso. 1994. *The Community of Those Who Have Nothing in Common.* Bloomington: Indiana University Press.

Lloyd, Genevieve. 1993. *The Man of Reason: "Male" and "Female" in Western Philosophy.* 2d ed. London: Routledge.

Locke, John. 1967. *Two Treatise of Government* (1690). 2d ed. Introduction by P. Laslett. Cambridge: Cambridge University Press.

Machan, Tibor R. 1990. "Politics and Generosity." *Journal of Applied Philosophy* 7 (1):61–73.

Mackenzie, Catriona. 1986. "Simone de Beauvoir: Philosophy, and/or the Female Body." Pp. 144–56 in *Feminist Challenges: Social and Political Theory,* ed. Carole Pateman and Elizabeth Gross. Sydney: Allen & Unwin.

Mackinnon, Catharine A. 1990. "Liberalism and the Death of Feminism." Pp. 3–13 in *The Sexual Liberals and the Attack on Feminism,* ed. Dorchen Leidholdt and Janice G. Raymond. New York: Pergamon Press.

Martin, Thomas. 1996. "Sartre, Sadism, and Female Beauty Ideals." *Australian Feminist Studies* 11 (24):243–52.

Mauss, Marcel. 1967. *The Gift: Forms and Functions of Exchange in Archaic Societies.* Trans. Ian Cunnison. New York: Norton Library.

Merleau-Ponty, Maurice. 1962. *Phenomenology of Perception.* Trans. Colin Smith. London: Routledge & Kegan Paul.

————. 1964a. "The Child's Relations with Others." Pp. 96–155 in *The Primacy of Perception,* ed. James M. Edie, trans. William Cobb. Evanston: Northwestern University Press.

————. 1964b. "Eye and Mind." Pp. 159–90 in *The Primacy of Perception,* ed. James M. Edie, trans. Carleton Dallery. Evanston: Northwestern University Press.

————. 1964c. "Indirect Language and the Voices of Silence." Pp. 39–83 in *Signs,* trans. Richard McCleary. Evanston: Northwestern University Press.

————. 1964d. "The Philosopher and His Shadow." Pp. 159–81 in *Signs,* trans. Richard McCleary. Evanston: Northwestern University Press.

————. 1968. *The Visible and the Invisible.* Trans. Alphonso Lingis. Evanston: Northwestern University Press.

————. 1973. "Dialogue and the Perception of the Other." Pp. 131–46 in *The Prose of the World,* trans. John O'Neill. Evanston: Northwestern University Press.

Mill, John Stuart. 1975. "On Liberty" (1859), in *J. S. Mill: Three Essays.* Oxford: Oxford University Press.

Moi, Toril. 1992. "Ambiguity and Alienation in *The Second Sex.*" *boundary 2* 19 (12):96–112.

Nadeau, Chantal. 1995. "Girls on a Wired Screen: Cavani Cinema and Lesbian Sadomasochism." Pp. 211–30 in *Sexy Bodies,* ed. Elizabeth Grosz and Elspeth Probyn. New York: Routledge.

National Bioethics Consultative Committee (NBCC). 1990. *Surrogacy Report 1.* Canberra: Commonwealth of Australia.

Nettheim, Garth. 1998. "Native Title, Fictions, and 'Convenient Falsehoods.'" *In the Wake of Terra Nullius.* Ed. Colin Perrin. Special issue of *Law Text Culture* 4 (1):70–80

Nietzsche, Friedrich. 1967. *The Will to Power.* Ed. Walter Kaufmann. Trans. Walter Kaufmann and R. J. Hollingdale. New York: Random House.

———. 1968. *Twilight of the Idols and the Anti-Christ.* Trans. R. J. Hollingdale. Harmondsworth: Penguin.

———. 1969. *On the Genealogy of Morals and Ecce Homo.* Trans. Walter Kaufmann. New York: Random House.

———. 1973. *Beyond Good and Evil.* Trans. R. J. Hollingdale. Harmondsworth: Penguin.

———. 1974. *The Gay Science.* Trans. Walter Kaufmann. New York: Random House.

———. 1978. *Thus Spoke Zarathustra: A Book for All and None.* Trans. Walter Kaufmann. Harmondsworth: Penguin.

———. 1979. "On Truth and Lies in a Nonmoral Sense." Pp. 79–91 in *Philosophy and Truth: Selections from Nietzsche's Notebooks of the Early 1970s,* trans. and ed. D. Breazeale. Atlantic Highlands, N.J.: Humanities Press.

———. 1983. *Untimely Meditations.* Trans. R. J. Hollingdale. Cambridge: Cambridge University Press.

———. 1984. *Human, All Too Human: A Book for Free Spirits.* Trans. Marion Faber, with Stephen Lehmann. Lincoln: University of Nebraska Press.

———. 1986. "Assorted Opinions and Maxims." Pp. 215–99 in *Human, All Too Human,* volume 2, part 1, trans. R. J. Hollingdale. Cambridge: Cambridge University Press.

Nussbaum, Martha. 1994. "Pity and Mercy: Nietzsche's Stoicism." Pp. 139–67 in *Nietzsche, Genealogy, Morality,* ed. Richard Schacht. Berkeley: University of California Press.

Oliver, Kelly. 1999. "What Is Transformative about the Performative? From Repetition to Working-Through." *Studies in Practical Philosophy* 1 (2):144–66.

Overall, Christine. 1987. *Ethics and Human Reproduction.* Winchester, Mass.: Allen & Unwin.

Pateman, Carole. 1988. *The Sexual Contract.* Cambridge: Polity Press.

Patton, Paul. 1991a. "Nietzsche and the Body of the Philosopher." Pp. 43–54 in *Cartographies: Poststructuralism and the Mapping of Bodies and Spaces,* ed. Rosalyn Diprose and Robyn Ferrell. Sydney: Allen & Unwin.

———. 1991b. "Postmodern Subjectivity: The Problem of the Actor (Zarathustra and Butler)." *Postmodern Critical Theorizing.* Ed. A. Yeatman. Special issue of *Social Analysis* 30: 32–41.

———, ed. 1993. *Nietzsche, Feminism, and Political Theory.* London: Routledge.

———. 1996. "Concept and Event." *Man and World* 29:315–26.

———. 1997. "Justice and Difference: The Mabo Case." Pp. 83–98 in *Transformations in Australian Society,* ed. Paul Patton and Diane Austin-Broos. Sydney: Research Institute for Humanities and Social Sciences, University of Sydney.

Peperzak, Adriaan. 1993. *To the Other: An Introduction to the Philosophy of Emmanuel Levinas.* West Lafayette, Ind.: Purdue University Press.

Perrin, Colin, and Scott Veitch. 1998. "The Promise of Reconciliation." *In the Wake of Terra Nullius.* Ed. Colin Perrin. Special issue of *Law Text Culture* 4 (1):232–40.

Pilardi, Jo-Ann. 1989. "Female Eroticism in the Works of Simone de Beauvoir." Pp. 18–34 in *The Thinking Muse: Feminism and Modern French Philosophy,* ed. Jeffner Allen and Iris Marion Young. Bloomington: Indiana University Press.

Plato. 1955. *The Republic*. Trans. H.D.P. Lee. Harmondsworth: Penguin.

Reynolds, Henry. 1987. *The Law of the Land*. Harmondsworth: Penguin.

———. 1998. *This Whispering in Our Hearts*. Sydney: Allen & Unwin.

Rosengarten, Marsha. 2001. "A Pig's Tale: Porcine Viruses and Species Boundaries." Pp. 168–82 in *Contagion: Historical and Cultural Studies*, ed. Alison Bashford and Claire Hooker. London and New York: Routledge.

Sacks, Oliver. 1991. *Awakenings*. Rev. ed. London: Picador.

Sandford, Stella. 1998. "Writing As a Man: Levinas and the Phenomenology of Eros." *Radical Philosophy* 87:6–17.

Sartre, Jean-Paul. 1989 (1958). *Being and Nothingness: An Essay on Phenomenological Ontology*. Trans. Hazel E. Barnes, with introduction by Mary Warnock. London and New York: Routledge.

Sawicki, Jana. 1988. "Identity Politics and Sexual Freedom." Pp. 177–92 in *Foucault and Feminism*, ed. Irene Diamond and Lee Quinby. Boston: Northwestern University Press.

Schrift, Alan D. 1994. "On the Gift-Giving Virtue: Nietzsche's Unacknowledged Feminine Economy." *International Studies in Philosophy* 26 (3):33–44.

———. 1997. "Introduction: Why Gift?" Pp. 1–22 in *The Logic of the Gift: Toward an Ethic of Generosity*, ed. Alan D. Schrift. New York: Routledge.

Scott, Jacqueline. 2000. "Nietzsche and Mixed Race." Conference paper read to the Thirty-Ninth Annual Meeting of the Society for Phenomenology and Existential Philosophy, Pennsylvania State University, October 7.

Scott, Russell. 1981. *The Body As Property*. London: Allen Lane.

Secomb, Linnell. 2000. "Fractured Community." *Hypatia* 15 (2):133–50.

Shildrick, Margrit, and Janet Price, eds. 1998. *Vital Signs: Feminist Reconfigurations of the Bio/logical Body*. Edinburgh: Edinburgh University Press.

Simpson, David. 1996. "Administrative Lies and the Philosopher-Kings." *Philosophical Inquiry* 18:45–65.

Spivak, Gayatri Chakravorty. 1984. "Love Me, Love My Ombre, Elle." *Diacritics* 14 (4):19–36.

Stock, Wendy. 1990. "Towards a Feminist Praxis of Sexuality." Pp. 148–56 in *The Sexual Liberals and the Attack on Feminism*, ed. Dorchen Leidholdt and Janice G. Raymond. New York: Pergamon Press.

Sullivan, Nikki. 2001. *Tattooed Bodies: Subjectivity, Textuality, Ethics, and Pleasure*. Westport, Conn.: Praeger.

Thomas, Elizabeth. 1999. *Emmanuel Levinas: Ethics, Justice, and the Human Beyond Being*. Ph.D. thesis, Department of Philosophy, University of Sydney.

Vasseleu, Cathryn. 1998. *Textures of Light: Vision and Touch in Irigaray, Levinas, and Merleau-Ponty*. London and New York: Routledge.

Watney, Simon. 1987. "The Spectacle of AIDS." *October* 43:71–86.

Weiss, Gail. 1999. *Body Images: Embodiment As Intercorporeality*. New York and London: Routledge.

Winterson, Jeanette. 1989. *Sexing the Cherry*. London: Vintage.

Wirzba, Norman. 1995. "From Maieutics to Metanoia: Levinas's Understanding of the Philosophical Task." *Man and World* 28:129–44.

Wood, David. 1988. "Nietzsche's Transvaluation of Time." Pp. 31–62 in *Exceedingly Nietzsche: Aspects of Contemporary Nietzsche-Interpretation*, ed. David Farrel Krell and David Wood. London: Routledge.

Young, Iris Marion. 1990. "Throwing Like a Girl," in *Throwing Like a Girl and Other Essays in Feminist Philosophy and Social Theory.* Bloomington: Indiana University Press.

Ziarek, Ewa. 2001a. "The Ethical Passions of Emmanuel Levinas." Pp. 78–95 in *Feminist Interpretations of Emmanuel Levinas,* ed. Tina Chanter.

———. 2001b. *Ethics of Dissensus: Postmodernity, Sexual Difference, and the Politics of Radical Democracy.* Stanford, Calif.: Stanford University Press.

Zita, Jacquelyn N. 1992. "Male Lesbians and the Postmodernist Body." Hypatia 7 (4):107–27.

INDEX

action at a distance, 38–9
aesthetics of self, 40–43, 66–67
affectivity: in the clinical encounter, 114, 116–20; and generosity, 12, 14, 75, 95, 102–7, 127, 191; individualistic models of, 96–97, 100–1; of intercorporeality, 95, 100–2; Merleau-Ponty on, 100–6, 118–19; and self-transformation, 75, 90, 102–5; and social power, 95–100; and thinking, 125, 127, 132–33, 143
Ainley, Alison, 41, 207n. 8
Aristotle, 2–4
alterity: and cultural diversity, 161–63; and generosity, 13–14, 191–93; in Levinas, 13–14, 136–41, 146, 161–66, 172; in Merleau-Ponty, 90, 103, 118–19, 182–85; and thinking, 136–41; and transformation of social imaginaries, 184–88; witness to, 162–63, 165–66
ambiguity of existence/identity, 65–66, 68; Beauvoir's idea of, 78, 87–88, 200n. 7; Merleau-Ponty's idea of, 102–3, 116–18, 175–77
apology, 148, 159, 165–66
autonomy: as control over one's body, 46–47, 78; critiques of, 49–50, 54, 87–88; democratic concept, 35–36; Levinas' conception of, 135–41
autonomous thinking, 126, 133–36

Beauvoir, Simone de, 15, 139; on ambiguity of existence, 78, 87–88, 200n. 7; on becoming flesh, 86, 88; on domination and submission, 87, 92, 93; erotic generosity, conception of, 78, 86–87, 201n. 10; on freedom, 84–88; on love, 84–85; Merleau-Ponty, relation to, 89, 201n. 15; Sartre, critique of, 84, 86–87; on women's sexuality, 84–89, 200n. 16
Being and Nothingness (Sartre), 78–83
Bergoffen, Debra, 86
Bernasconi, Robert, 3–4, 166, 170, 209n. 11, 210n. 20
Biddle, Jennifer, 210n. 16
blood: sale of, 47, 52; writing in, 190–94
body: discipline of, 21–23, 66, 96, 151, 167; as flesh, 81–82, 86, 88; imaginary, 170–73; and meaning, relation between, 67, 103–5, 133, 151, 171, 173–75, 182–83, 191–93; as property, 46–47, 49–50; in situation, 80–81, 86, 89; sexed, 37, 43–45, 53–54, 56, 63–64, 67, 79; as work of art, 21, 24, 66
body-identity, performance of, 61–72
Bourdieu, Pierre, 9
Bringing Them Home (HREOC), 146–48, 154, 159, 208nn. 1–4, 209n. 14
Butler, Judith, 11, 15, 61; Foucault, use and critique of, 66, 97, 99, 101, 199n. 4; Freud, use of, 97, 99, 101; on

221